THE FLYING SAUCER CONSPIRACY

By the Same Author:

M-Day

Flying with Lindbergh

The Flying Saucers Are Real

Flying Saucers from Outer Space

The Flying Saucer

Conspiracy

Major Donald E. Keyhoe

U. S. Marine Corps, Retired

FIELDCREST PUBLISHING CO., INC.

210 5TH AVENUE, NEW YORK, N. Y.

For Tom Gill

Foreword

Since 1953, when I wrote *Flying Saucers from Outer Space* sightings of the so-called Unidentified Flying Objects have multiplied. In practically every country this increased saucer surveillance has been confirmed by pilots, radarmen, or trained ground observers. From the details of these world-wide reports it is evident that the saucers have moved into a new phase of operations—one that may change the lives of every one on this globe.

Here in the United States, the official investigation has been greatly intensified. Scores of prominent scientists and engineers are now working behind the scenes, helping to evaluate the facts.

Most of the public is unaware of these developments, for since December, 1953, the Air Force has refused to release any official reports of flying-saucer encounters.

In revealing this censorship, I am not attacking the Air Force as a whole. Most of the officers and officials I have encountered are simply obeying orders. Nor do I attribute unpatriotic motives to the "silence group" members who originate these orders. Undoubtedly they are actuated by a high motive—the need, as they see it, to protect the public from possible hysteria.

Nevertheless I believe that this censorship is dangerous. The thousands of UFO reports by veteran observers prove beyond question that the saucers are machines from outer space. The Air Force's insistence that it has no answer only heightens the possibility of hysteria.

If the public is not informed of all the facts, fear of the unknown may prevail. That can lead to the most dangerous kind of panic.

In *The Flying Saucer Conspiracy* I have covered, as far as possible, the important developments of the past two years. I have received help from more than 300 sources: pilots, scientists, radar experts, airport tower operators, flying-saucer investigators, and many others, both here and abroad. In particular, I should like to thank the following either for new information on UFO's or valuable opinions on this subject:

Air Chief Marshal Lord Dowding, of England; Professor Hermann Oberth, world authority on space-travel plans; Admiral Delmar Fahrney, USN, Retired, former head of Navy guided-missile development; Admiral Calvin Bolster, USN, Retired, formerly Chief of Naval Research; Captain Edward J. Ruppelt, USAF Reserve, former chief of Project Blue Book, UFO investigating agency; Frank Edwards, noted radio and television news commentator; Robert J. Stirling, Chief of the Washington Bureau, United Press radio; Douglas Larsen, N.E.A. feature writer; Larry Cates, Washington representative of the Air Line Pilots Association; John Du Barry, formerly associate editor of *True* magazine; Miss Isabel Davis, researcher for Civilian Saucer Intelligence, New York, N. Y.; Ted Bloecher, president of Civilian Saucer Intelligence, New York, N. Y.; Mrs. Coral Lorenzen, director of APRO; Leonard H. Stringfield, director of CRIFO.

I wish also to thank Captain Robert White, USAF spokesman on flying saucers, for his courteous discussions, and Lieutenant Colonel Joseph Bloomer, of the Air Force Directorate of Intelligence, who helped to correct a false report on *Flying Saucers from Outer Space*.

For editorial advice and assistance in preparing *The Flying Saucer Conspiracy*, I am deeply indebted to Robert Lescher, whose cooperation during the final revision was invaluable.

Finally, I wish to thank the readers of *Flying Saucers from Outer Space* and *The Flying Saucers Are Real* for their thousands of helpful letters. Though it has been impossible to answer each one personally, I greatly appreciate the interest shown and the many confirmed UFO reports.

Donald E. Keyhoe
Major, U. S. Marine Corps, Retired

October 4, MCMLV

Contents

THE FLYING SAUCER CONSPIRACY

1 Blackout

For several years the censorship of flying-saucer reports has been increasingly tightened. In the United States this top-level blackout is backed by two strict orders.

I learned of the first order, a Joint-Chiefs-of-Staff document, in the fall of '53. Known as JANAP 146 (Joint-Army-Navy-Air Publication), this order sets up a top-priority radio system for the most urgent Intelligence reports. Pilots are directed to report Unidentified Flying Objects (UFO's) immediately from all parts of the world, using this emergency system—and to keep these sightings *secret*.

Under Section III any pilot who reveals an official UFO report can be imprisoned for one to ten years and fined up to 10,000 dollars. (*Title 18, U. S. Code, 793.*)

Three months later, in December, 1953, I discovered the second order, which carries court-martial penalties. For several days I had been checking on a strange story from Kimross Air Force Base, near Sault Sainte Marie, Michigan. The facts had been hurriedly covered up, after a brief Air Force admission. . . .

It was the evening of November 23, and wintry darkness had settled over Michigan. At an isolated radar station Air Defense operators were watching their scope in a routine guard against possible enemy attack.

Suddenly the "blip" of an unknown machine appeared on

13

the glass screen. The Ground Control Intercept officer took a quick look. The "unknown" was flying over the Soo Locks— and no aircraft was scheduled near that important target. Whatever it was, it had to be identified swiftly.

In less than two minutes an F-89 from Kimross Field was streaking toward the locks. At the jet's controls was Lieutenant Felix Moncla, Jr., a veteran at 26. Behind him was Lieutenant R. R. Wilson, 22-year-old Oklahoman, acting as radar observer. Guided by Ground Control, Moncla climbed steeply toward the "unknown."

Back at GCI, the controller watched the jet's blip on his glowing radarscope. As it moved toward the UFO's blip, the strange craft changed course. The controller called Moncla, gave him the new bearing. From the scope he saw that the F-89 was now over Sault Sainte Marie, though to the crew the city's lights would be only a blur, quickly lost behind.

The UFO, flying as fast as a jet airliner, was heading toward Lake Superior. At over 500 miles per hour the F-89 raced after it, out across Whitefish Bay.

Nine more minutes ticked by in the tense quiet of the GCI radar room. Gradually the F-89 cut down the gap. By now, the controller knew, Wilson should have spotted their quarry on the fighter's short-range radar. Watching the chase, he cut in his microphone and called the flight's code name.

"Target should soon be visual. Still bearing——"

He broke off, staring at the scope.

The two blips had suddenly merged into one.

Whether the strange machine had abruptly slowed or Moncla unaccountably had put on full power, no one in the room could tell.

But one thing seemed grimly certain: the two machines were locked together, as if in a smashing collision.

For a moment longer the huge, ominous blip remained on the glass. Then it quickly went off the scope.

Marking the position, the controller flashed word to Search and Rescue. Moncla and Wilson might have bailed out in time. Both had life jackets and self-inflating rafts; even in the icy water they might survive for a little while.

The mystery craft and the F-89 had come together far offshore, about 100 miles from Sault Sainte Marie and 70 miles from Keweenaw Point. As quickly as possible, search planes with flares were roaring over Lake Superior. After a fruitless night search, boats joined the hunt as American and Canadian flyers crisscrossed a hundred-mile area.

But no trace was ever found of the missing men, the F-89 —or the unknown machine.

My first word on this mystery came from an old friend in Detroit, a former Army Air Corps navigator I'd met in earlier days, when I was aide to Colonel Charles A. Lindbergh. The night the jet vanished, he called me at my home near Alexandria, Virginia.

"This may be just a wild story," he said, "but there's a rumor out at Selfridge Field that an F-89 from Kimross was hit by a flying saucer. All I know is that the plane's missing. You think there could be any truth in the UFO angle?"

"It's possible," I answered, "but most of those 'saucer collision' stories turn out to be ordinary crashes."

"Well, I hope this is too. I'd hate to think that the saucers are hostile."

"Even if it did happen, it could have been an accident. But thanks for the tip. I'll check with the Pentagon."

Next morning I called the Air Force Press Desk and got First Lieutenant (now Captain) Robert C. White. A 34-year-old bomber pilot, White was serving as a PIO (Public Information Officer). He admitted the F-89 was missing and gave me the names of the crew.

"It's obvious," he added, "they had engine trouble and crashed in the lake."

"Why were they out there?" I asked.

"Intercept mission—checking on an unknown."

"Did they identify it?"

"I'm not sure. Let me call you later."

"I'm about to take off for Des Moines," I said. "I'll phone when I get back."

Before driving to Washington Airport, I called radio commentator Frank Edwards—we had exchanged flying-saucer reports since 1949. Frank whistled at the Kimross tip.

"If it's true, this thing's getting serious! Kimross probably won't talk, but I'll give it a try. Right now I'm waiting for a Wisconsin call on that Truax crash."

"What was that?"

"A jet from Truax Air Force Base crashed near there yesterday, at Madison. Several witnesses said a saucer flew near the plane, just before it dived into a swamp. It may be just bunk, but I'm checking on it."

"How soon can you phone Kimross?" I asked.

"I'll try to rush it. Call me before you take off."

Thirty minutes later I phoned from the airport.

"Don," Frank exclaimed, "your Detroit man had it dead right! Truax Field just made an official statement on the Kimross jet."

"Admitting the collision?" I said incredulously.

"Listen to this: 'The plane was followed by radar until it merged with an object 70 miles off Keweenaw Point in upper Michigan.' That's the statement they gave the Associated Press."

"That's amazing! You sure Truax really said it?"

"Absolutely. I made a fast check. It's already on the AP wire at Sault Sainte Marie."

"You said Truax——"

"Here's what happened. An AP man at Sault Sainte Marie queried Kimross. They told him to clear with the OPI for the area, at Truax. He did—and got that official answer."

"It's incredible—their releasing it. I knew some PIO's were against the blackout, but to let this out——"

"It certainly raised the devil at the Pentagon," said Frank. "I just called there. At first they said it was some silly rumor, but when I told them Truax gave it to the AP, they hit the ceiling. I'll bet they're burning up the wires right now."

"Can they make the AP kill it?"

"I don't know. But they can say it was a mistake and ask them to run a correction. To avoid that the AP will yank it, if there's time."

In a few hours I had a hint that Frank was right. At Chicago, where I changed planes, there was no sign of the AP story. Later I learned it had appeared in the early edition of the Chicago *Tribune,* headed "Jet, Two Aboard, Vanishes Over Lake Superior." It was deleted from all other editions.

Because of a late Des Moines landing I missed Frank's broadcast, and during my Iowa trip I heard no more on the mystery. The night I returned, I called the Mutual station in Washington, but Frank had left for New York after his ten o'clock program.

Next morning, after trying to reach White, I went in to the Civil Aeronautics Board to see Arthur Caperton, one of the CAB's senior crash investigators. A quick, decisive man, square-jawed and ruddy-faced, Caperton had been, like myself a Marine Corps pilot. Later he had become an airline captain, flying DC-6's before joining the Board.

In my case, an injury from a night crash at Guam had put me out of uniform until World War II, though I'd flown nonmilitary planes while writing on aviation. Meanwhile I'd drawn several good-luck assignments which gave me valuable contacts all over the country. As chief of information for Civil Aeronautics, I had made an air tour with Floyd Bennett, Admiral Byrd's pilot on the historic North Pole flight. The next year, by another lucky break, I flew as Colonel Lindbergh's aide on a 48-state tour, after his famous "Lone

Eagle" flight to Paris. Many of the pilots and aviation experts I met on these tours were later to give me important UFO reports.

Caperton and I had talked about the saucers before, and I knew that the Board and the Air Force often exchanged unusual crash reports.

"What do you know about a flying saucer hitting an F-89 on November 23?" I asked him.

Caperton stared. "An actual collision? It must be under wraps. I haven't heard a thing."

I told him what had happened.

"Good Lord!" said Caperton. "If Truax said that, it must be true. Those Ground Control operators are tops."

"The question is, was it accidental?"

"Accident or not, it's a real jolt." Caperton shook his head. "I think it's dangerous, ordering jet pilots to chase the saucers. Of course, they don't often get close—the UFO's run away from them."

That noon at the Press Club Caperton and I got a new slant on the Kimross case. It came from an airline pilot, Captain Ed Stone, a sober-faced six-footer with prematurely gray hair. (Since his company, like most lines, asks its pilots to avoid saucer publicity, I have changed his last name.) Stone said he had not heard of the F-89 disaster.

"But that must be what Frank Edwards was talking about the other night," he added. "He said two Canadian pilots denied being over the Soo Locks or seeing an F-89. I missed the first part, so it was Greek to me."

The Canadian angle was new, and as we were leaving I called the Pentagon from a Press Club booth. This time I caught White at his desk.

"The unknown in that case was a Canadian DC-3," he told me. "It was over the locks by mistake."

I started to repeat the Canadian pilots' denial, then changed my mind.

"Let me get this straight," I said. "Obviously the F-89 didn't collide with a Canadian airliner—there'd have been a big row in the papers. So what did it hit?"

"It didn't hit anything," White said emphatically.

"Then what happened to it?"

"Probably engine trouble, as I said before. They must have bailed out—or ditched—too fast to report."

"Wait a minute," I said. "Truax Field gave the AP an official statement that the F-89 'merged' with an object 70 miles off Keweenaw Point."

"That's not true!" White said quickly.

"The AP story was wrong?"

"Well . . . no. Truax made the statement. But the 'merging' part was a mistake. That second blip was from some object actually miles from the F-89."

"*Miles* from it? Then why in heaven's name did GCI say they merged?"

"They just read the scope wrong," said White.

It was an incredible answer, and I was sure he knew it. No GCI controller capable of such a colossal blunder would be tolerated for a minute by the Air Defense Command. These specially selected radar technicians must be able to guide jet fighters into close-range attacks on enemy bombers. This means making swift, precise measurement of distance between planes—in yards, not miles. Without this accurate measurement, interception at night and in bad weather would be impossible. Our country would be tragically helpless against massed enemy bombers. It was impossible to believe that expert technicians had misread the scope, and I was sure White was merely acting under orders.

"Does that clear up everything?" White asked, after a silence.

"No. I'd like to see the Air Force investigation report."

"I'm sorry, that will be classified."

"Well, did the F-89 actually intercept the DC-3, so that the Canadians had to identify themselves?"

"I'm not sure. That's a classified Air Defense report. But we're certain the DC-3 was over the locks."

"Then what was the *other* unknown—the object GCI said was 70 miles off Keweenaw Point?"

"Maybe another plane, we just don't know. But they did *not* merge."

When I relayed White's story, Caperton snorted.

"That's idiotic! Who are they trying to kid?"

"What would you have said?" Stone said somberly. "Unless the Pentagon admitted a UFO hit the jet, they had to explain away the radar report."

"But this phony answer," growled Caperton. "Why didn't they hang it on the Truax PIO?"

"It would look suspicious," I said. "Why would he make up that Ground Control report? And not many people know radar."

"Maybe so. But that cockeyed DC-3 story—" Caperton glanced at the clock. "I've got to run, but if you have time, check the intercept angles. You'll see what I mean."

Captain Stone had time before his next flight, so we worked out the intercept problem.

When the F-89 began the chase, the unknown machine had just passed over the Soo Locks, a few miles north. Guided by GCI, the F-89 hurtled after it at over 500 miles per hour. (Under Air Defense Command rules, maximum intercept speeds cannot be given.)

In average flights a DC-3 cruises at about 165 mph. But even at its maximum, about 215, the Canadian airliner would have been overtaken in three minutes, including time for the F-89 to slow down and avoid overshooting.

Under Air Defense orders, Moncla would have closed in quickly, to identify the unknown as a friendly aircraft or challenge it if it proved hostile. The jet's reduced speed and close approach would have been seen clearly on the GCI radarscope.

If the Canadian pilots failed to answer the jet's radio call, Moncla would have "buzzed" the airliner so that the crew could see the jet's lights. As a final resort he would have fired a warning burst with guns or rockets.

No airline captain in his right mind would fail to answer that warning. Unless he did respond, with proof that his flight was friendly, his airliner might be shot down.

After identifying the plane the F-89 crew would have relayed the information to Ground Control. Mission accomplished, they would then have turned back to Kimross Field.

Instead of all this, Moncla flew out over Lake Superior, more than 100 miles beyond the locks. During this time he was *pursuing* the unknown machine, guided and tracked by Ground Control.

To keep ahead of the F-89 this long, the mysterious craft had to fly at more than 450 mph. Since this is more than twice the top speed of a DC-3, the Canadian airliner could not possibly have been the unknown in this chase.

Even if the F-89 had intercepted the airliner (which ignores the pilots' denial) this still would not explain the 100-mile flight, the second unknown, and the merging—all officially admitted in the Truax statement.

"How did they expect to get away with that story?" Captain Stone said as we finished.

"They had to produce something to explain what the jet was chasing. And they knew not many people would stop to figure it out."

Stone gazed down at the flight diagram.

"It must have been a saucer—I don't see any other answer. A jet would explain the speed, but no planes of *any* kind were lost that night, except the F-89."

He paused.

"One thing, this certainly knocks down that crazy rumor

about the saucers being U. S. weapons. The Air Force wouldn't risk its pilots' lives like that—besides, why chase our own missiles?"

"That secret-weapon answer was exploded long ago," I told him. "Even if you toss out all the older reports, we know the saucers have been operating here for at least nine years. Our pilots sighted hundreds of them over Europe and the Pacific in '44—so did the Germans and the Japs. If we had such a super-weapon then, why didn't we use it to end the war? It would have saved a lot of lives. And the Reds wouldn't have dared start the Korean war."

Stone nodded. "Also, we wouldn't be afraid now of an H-bomb attack. With those terrific speeds and maneuvers, the saucers could knock down ordinary jet bombers without half trying. Besides that, why spend billions on ordinary planes and carriers and foreign bases if we have saucers with a world-wide range?"

"That goes for the Russians too," I said. "If they'd had flying saucers in '44, they'd have used them against Hitler, and by now they'd own the world. But the Soviet wasn't even producing jets in World War II. And right now they're working like mad on planes and missiles, just like us."

Stone stood up. "You're right," he said as we went to get our coats. "No nation on earth could have had the discs in '44."

"Not even now," I added. "Air Force radar has tracked mother ships and discs maneuvering at over 9000 miles an hour. Even our latest missiles can't approach that—and no missile on earth can stop dead, hover over a city, and then streak straight up into the ionosphere at thousands of miles an hour."

We went out to the elevators. Under his cap visor, Stone's face had an intent look.

"That could be the reason," he muttered. He glanced at me sidewise. "I mean why the Pentagon is so desperate about hushing it up. Maybe Moncla or Wilson gave Ground Control the answer to all this before the collision."

"They probably didn't have time——"

"I don't mean the very last instant. But put yourself in Moncla's place. You're closing in on the thing. The last few seconds you see something—maybe you suddenly know what's behind all this. Wouldn't you yell it into your throat-microphone?"

"I might if I weren't too scared to talk."

"Even then you'd almost instinctively yell something, and Ground Control would hear it. If we could only see that Air Force inquiry report! It could be the key to this whole saucer business."

When I saw Frank Edwards, a day or so later, he confirmed what Stone had said about the Canadian pilots.

"They denied the whole thing—they were pretty sore about it." Frank looked at me with no trace of his usual whimsical humor. "This Kimross thing must be something terrific, the way the Air Force has covered up. What do you think happened?"

"I can't figure it out. It's the most baffling saucer report I've ever heard . . . even stranger than the Mantell case."

(On January 7, 1948, Captain Thomas Mantell was killed while pursuing a huge flying saucer under Air Force orders. Just before his F-51 fighter disintegrated, the World War ace radioed the tower at Godman Field, Kentucky, that the saucer looked metallic and was tremendous in size.)

"Whatever they've found out," said Frank, "I think the public should be told. It can't be a much worse threat than the H-bomb. And this could have been an accident, as you've said."

"Well, I'm going to keep after it, though it won't be easy——"

"That reminds me," Frank broke in, "have you ever heard

of an order called AFR 200? I got a tip that someone at Truax may be in trouble because he broke that order."

"It's new to me," I answered, "but I'll try to get a line on it."

During my four-year investigation several fellow Marines, Annapolis classmates, and friends in the other services had given me UFO leads, when security was not involved. Checking with some of them, I soon found that AFR 200-2 was withheld from the public; but after two days' digging I had most of the key points. (These were confirmed later by an official copy. See Appendix, p. 312.)

Classed as "Restricted," AFR 200-2 was issued on August 26, 1953, by order of the Secretary of the Air Force, Harold E. Talbott.

Even though I knew some of the facts, this hidden order was a revelation in its apparent distrust of the American people.

Under Paragraph 9, ironically called "Release of Facts," it was provided that only *hoaxes, practical jokes, and erroneous UFO reports can be given to the press.*

All *genuine* UFO reports received by the Air Force must be kept from the public. These include thousands of verified sightings from military pilots, radarmen, guided-missile trackers, and other trained observers under government control.

Under AFR 200-2, all confirmed flying-saucer reports must be rushed to Intelligence by teletype or radio. When possible, all tangible evidence must be flown immediately to ATIC (Air Technical Intelligence Center) at Dayton. Such evidence includes:

1. *Parts of flying saucers—ac ·˙ or "suspected."*

2. Photos of radarscopes show. ˩ 'saucer" maneuvers and speeds.

3. Genuine pictures of flying saucers.

To conceal flying-saucer discoveries, AFR 200-2 confines actual UFO investigation to three super-secret groups:

The Directorate of Air Force Intelligence at the Pentagon; the 4602d Air Intelligence Service Squadron, which has special investigators at all Air Defense bases; the ATIC (Air Technical Intelligence Center) at Dayton, Ohio.

Even top-ranking Air Force officers are warned not to probe beyond the first stage—securing UFO reports for the three groups.

Because of JANAP 146 and AFR 200-2, hundreds of new, dramatic encounters have been kept under cover.

Some reports, of course, are bound to leak out, especially when saucers are sighted near cities. But even when local papers run front-page stories, the UFO censors often deny the reports or quickly explain them away. One such incident occurred in August of '54.

At 8:30 P.M., on August 28, 1954, a formation of 15 flying saucers approached Oklahoma City. Picked up by radar, the strange machines were spotted from Tinker Air Force Base.

Within seconds, by standing orders of the Air Defense Command, a flight of jets was dispatched.

Under AFR 200-2, emergency teletype messages were flashed to ADC Headquarters, to ATIC, and to the Pentagon.

At the same time, warning alerts were phoned to Will Rogers Airport, the Oklahoma State Police, and to GOC (Ground Observer Corps) posts in a radius of 200 miles.

Meanwhile, in precise triangular formation, the 15 saucers had raced over the edge of the city. The jets, guns set to fire, hurtled after them at full power. Abruptly the formation broke. Changing into a semicircle, the saucers speeded up and vanished into the west.

Immediately, additional alerts were flashed to western Air Filter Centers. When the Tinker Field pilots landed, after a fruitless chase, they were bombarded with questions by a team of Intelligence officers. Then the teletypes clattered again, with urgent follow-up reports.

But though the saucer chase had been seen by hundreds in the city, and the alert was confirmed by the State Police, Tinker Field officers refused to admit the sighting.

Time and again, in the past year, Air Defense fighters have streaked up into the night, trying to force down saucers hovering over our cities. Yet few of these incidents are officially admitted.

From abroad hundreds of reports indicate that this new surveillance covers the entire globe. In 1954 low-flying UFO's set off panic in several countries, among them France, Italy, Morocco, and Venezuela. On September 15, at Bihar, India, a flying saucer suddenly descended to a height of 500 feet and hovered over an Atomic Energy Commission mine. Eight hundred frightened Biharis fled into their homes, as a *sadhu* warned them the object was "something from Heaven." After its close-range observation of the mine, the disc-shaped machine disappeared in a swift, vertical climb.

Since the fall of '54, secret investigations have been made in 21 countries, including England, France, Italy, Brazil, Venezuela, and South Africa. After strange reports by hundreds of foreign airmen, several new, mysterious developments have been linked with the so-called UFO's. But in most countries strict government censorship hides these dramatic discoveries.

In Brazil one close encounter came perilously close to tragedy.

It was the night of November 21, 1954, and a Brazilian airliner, bound for Rio de Janeiro, was cruising along in the dark. Flying at 8000 feet, the plane was over the Paraiba River when a strange glow suddenly appeared ahead.

In a moment a weird formation took shape—19 round machines, each more than 100 feet in diameter. Glowing like hot metal, the mysterious craft approached at supersonic speed. Before the pilot could move his controls, the saucers were flashing past and beneath his wings.

As several machines streaked by the cabin, the 13 passengers stampeded. One woman, screaming, ran into the pilot's compartment. Another passenger, battling a crewman, tried to reach the main exit.

For two or three minutes the cabin was a madhouse. With the danger of a crash mounting, crewmen had to use force. But the frightened passengers were finally subdued, and the plane landed safely.

Swiftly the story spread through Rio de Janeiro. In less than an hour it was on the Brazilian press wires, being relayed to foreign countries.

Early the next day I had a call from Robert J. Stirling, United Press feature writer and Washington director of the UP's weekly radio roundup.

"Don, a terrific saucer report just came in." He read me the report.

"That was close!" I said. "No wonder Brazil's asking for help."

"What do you mean?"

"The Brazilian Air Force is badly worried—they admit that flying saucers have been maneuvering over their bases. The government wants all countries to pool their secret UFO information so that Brazil will know what it's up against."

"Well, why don't they?" inquired Stirling.

"I don't know, but everyone's apparently going it alone. The Swedish Defense Ministry ordered a new secret inquiry October 1, the French two days later, and Yugoslavia on October 27. They all admit making serious investigations, but then the lid goes down."

"This is maddening," said Stirling. "One day an Air Chief Marshal in the Royal Air Force says they're space ships. Next day the Pentagon says there's no evidence the saucers even exist. Then come all the pilots' reports, like this one, and the hush-hush investigations. What's back of all the secrecy—bad news?"

"Maybe it's only *fear* of bad news. They still may not have the full answer. It could be something we've never thought of—and no real danger to us."

"Then you've changed your mind about those accidents?"

"Not exactly. But I have a feeling I've missed something that might be a key. It's like a painting—you stand too close and you don't really see the picture. I'm going to put all the developments since '47 on a big chart and see if I can spot a pattern. If I get it, I'll let you know."

But it was not until months later that I learned the full story behind the official silence.

2 The First Clue

        Back in September, 1953, I had learned that the Air
Force was hiding a new flying-saucer discovery. This was less
than a month before *Flying Saucers from Outer Space*, which
included official Air Force saucer reports, was scheduled to
be published.

Meanwhile, *This Week* magazine had assigned me to interview Admiral Arthur W. Radford, Chairman of the Joint
Chiefs of Staff, for an article on national defense. Years before, Radford and I had trained together at Pensacola. In
World War II, I had served with him at Washington, and I
knew his general policies.

I was planning the first interview early one evening, when
a strange call from Art Caperton drove it out of my mind:

"Have you heard any queer saucer report—something that
might scare a pilot out of his wits?"

"No," I said. "An attack, or a near-collision?"

"Neither one, apparently. I'll give you what I have; it's
not under JANAP 146."

"You mean there's a Joint Chief's order on UFO's?" I said
quickly. This was my first knowledge of the order.

There was a silence. Then Caperton said tersely:

"Forget that. I thought you knew." After a moment he
went on. "This was an interceptor pilot, probably Air Force
—I'm not sure. I think he was on special patrol during a

saucer alert. When he landed, he was hysterical. Whatever happened, it's upset Air Force and Navy Intelligence."

"That's all you know?"

"Except that it was in August. If I get any more I'll tell you—unless it's under security."

Puzzled, I put down the phone. It sounded like a flimsy rumor. But Caperton was a careful, hard-headed investigator, expert at appraising sources. He wouldn't pass on such a story unless he believed it to be true.

I took a quick look at the verified August reports. There were three which might possibly fit.

On the night of August 9, at Moscow, Idaho, three Sabrejets had chased a large flying saucer, described by GOC observers as a glowing disc 200 feet in diameter. As the ground observers watched through binoculars, the jet pilots circled in warily. But the disc abruptly speeded up and left the fighters behind.

More than one interceptor pilot, recalling Mantell's death, had told me of the tension in flying-saucer chases. But unless something unusual had occurred, that night over Idaho, there seemed no reason for hysteria. And it looked like a routine pursuit.

The second case occurred ten nights later. A small round object, flaming like red-hot iron, had plunged from the sky into East New Haven, Connecticut, flashing past cars and pedestrians. It had pierced a metal billboard at Middleton Avenue and Front Street. After crashing through the heavy-gauge steel, the mysterious object had angled sharply upward, streaked over the trees, then vanished.

Its upward course, and the strange copper deposits it left on the billboard, showed that it was no ordinary fireball. If it were a missile, or something that had fallen from a saucer, Intelligence would have had good reason to be alarmed. But no pilot had been involved, unless some UFO encounter had been kept secret.

In the third case which had happened earlier, a giant ship had been sighted over California four nights in a row. On July 29, the huge saucer had raced past Moro Rock in Sequoia-Kings National Park, its brilliant yellow glow lighting a nearby canyon.

According to press reports, Park Superintendent E. T. Scoyen saw an enormous UFO zoom into the sky. Its diameter, he estimated, was at least 1000 feet.

On the next three nights other park officials saw the huge machine—or a similar one—as it streaked over the area. Simultaneous reports from Visalia and other California cities confirmed Scoyen's estimate: to have been visible so far, the saucer must have been gigantic.

By Air Defense orders, fighters were placed on patrol the last two nights. On August 1, though the Air Force refused to admit it, interceptors were reported diving toward the low-flying, giant saucer. If the huge ship had suddenly climbed, with a jet flying overhead, I knew such a close escape could have terrified the pilot.

But Caperton had seemed sure it was not a near-collision.

Afterward, I remembered his slip about JANAP 146. The term "JANAP" meant "Joint-Army-Navy-Air-Publication" —a Joint-Chiefs-of-Staff document. But I hadn't heard of No. 146. For several days I tried to find the answer. Like AFR 200-2, it was a restricted order. Finally I learned what it covered.

Under the subhead "CIRVIS" (Communication Instructions for Reporting Vital Intelligence Sightings), JANAP 146 orders pilots to radio their emergency reports from any part of the world. By the security clause, however, *anyone* who makes a CIRVIS report—or learns what one contains—is forbidden even to reveal its existence.

Backed by the threat of fines and imprisonment, this order applies to military, naval, and airline pilots making CIRVIS reports on UFO's. In addition, it muzzles all members of the

Defense Department, the CAA, the Civil Aeronautics Board, and any other agency involved with CIRVIS reports. Even a private citizen could be prosecuted for disclosing a saucer sighting, if in some way he learned the details from a CIRVIS message. (See Appendix, p. 301.)

It was my first official proof of the blackout on UFO reports. By a coincidence it came on the day before my appointment with Admiral Radford. On my way to the Pentagon, next morning, I was tempted to ask him about the flying saucers. From JANAP 146 it was plain that the Chiefs of Staff were seriously concerned. And Radford knew, from personal experience, that the saucers were real; in 1952 two UFO's had buzzed his plane on a flight between Guam and Hawaii.

But I was not on active duty, and to ask Radford about the saucers would have meant presuming upon our personal friendship. Even if I had asked, he would not have broken security—I knew him too well to expect that.

After we discussed the article on national defense, Radford told me to prepare a first draft.

"Some writers," he said, "give the impression the United States is almost helpless, and that's ridiculous. Others talk as if Russia were no threat at all, implying that the Soviet is just pretending to have the A-bomb. I'll sign only an honest article, showing the true dangers and our defenses—within security limits."

As I left the anteroom with Colonel C. E. Hutchin, the admiral's press aide, an officer with a mass of campaign ribbons came down the hall. I recognized him as a captain I had known for years.

Colonel Hutchin was leading me to his office, just across from Radford's.

"Before Admiral Radford signs this," he said, "every word must be checked by all the armed forces and the National Security Council. And since the President also is going to make a statement on the subject, it may have to be checked with the White House."

The captain had stopped. He came over to me as Hutchin went into his office.

"Can you call me when you're through here?" he said abruptly.

"I'll be out in a minute," I told him, puzzled at his tone.

When I came back, he got me to one side.

"I should have known you'd be in on it," he said in an undertone.

I looked at him blankly.

"I never believed it," he went on. "You know that. But after what happened at Pearl Harbor last month . . ." He shook his head solemnly. "You certainly turned out to be a prophet."

Then it hit me. He was talking about flying saucers. I waited with an electric feeling. It must have been something big to change him from a skeptic.

Two Army officers went by. The captain waited until they had passed then turned back quickly.

"Is it a fact that one of the big ones is orbiting us?" he asked.

"*Orbiting?* You mean a space base?"

He stared at me.

"If it's true, I should think Admiral Radford would know. Didn't he tell you?"

"We weren't talking about the UFO's," I said.

A stunned look came into his face.

"But that colonel said——"

"He meant a defense article I'm doing for Radford's by-line."

"Good God, I thought they'd decided to reveal—" he broke off. "Forget what I said. It was all just a crazy rumor."

"Wait. This thing at Pearl! What happened?"

He shook his head wordlessly and hurried on down the

corridor. For a minute I stood there, weighing what he had said. The Pearl Harbor mystery, whatever it was, must have been dramatic. And if a space base were really circling the earth, it was tremendously important.

There might be nothing to the satellite report even though the captain had seemed convinced. Yet it could easily be true. To swing one of the large mother ships into an orbit would be no problem. We ourselves had already worked out the calculations. In a few years we hoped to have small experimental satellites, a foot or two in diameter, circling the earth under electronic control. (This was planned long before the announcement made by the White House in July of 1955.) In ten to 20 years we might have true space bases, from which rocket ships would take off for the moon and the solar-system planets.

In Russia and other countries plans for the first tiny artificial "moons" also were under way. But all of these ideas were still in the planning stage, with launching and propulsion problems still to be licked.

With such small satellites as these still only on the drawing boards, the discovery of a full-sized space base could have but one explanation. The unknown race which controlled the flying saucers was stepping up its reconnaissance of the earth.

If it were true, our government would be doing everything possible to locate and identify the space base.

But it was not until six months later that word of the armed forces' satellite search leaked out in New Mexico. Because of this leak, the Pentagon hastily admitted the "sky-sweep" project. The search was headed by Dr. Clyde Tombaugh, discoverer of the planet Pluto. (Oddly enough, Dr. Tombaugh was the only famous astronomer who had ever admitted sighting a saucer. In 1951, with other witnesses, he had reported seeing a strange oval-shaped craft—

"some unknown kind of ship"—flying faster than any jet aircraft.)

To prevent public alarm the unknown satellites were called "moonlets"—which were explained as strange natural objects supposed to be circling the earth.

The fears of what this unidentified satellite might be were carefully kept hidden. To the UFO censors the discovery of the space base was far more ominous than most of the flying-disc reports. Most of the saucers were considered to be harmless. But the American people had been warned, officially, of a satellite's destructive power.

One of the first warnings came in 1948, when Defense Secretary James Forrestal announced the Earth Satellite Vehicle Program. The Pentagon then also confirmed a Nazi scheme for a deadly "sky platform." Revealed in Germany after World War II, the plan was based on designs by Professor Hermann Oberth, a world authority on space-travel plans.*

In 1929 Oberth had designed a space base to orbit the earth every four hours, circling 600 miles out. By means of an enormous concave mirror, assembled from sections of metallic sodium and controlled from the space base, the sun's rays could be sharply focused on the earth or spread out by adjusting the mirror sections.

In friendly hands, Oberth said, it could control the weather, melting certain ice fields and evaporating water in other areas. By broadly reflecting the sun's rays during our normal night hours, it could even provide artificial daylight.

But as a weapon, Oberth warned, the giant sun mirror would be diabolical. By concentrating its force, whole cities could be burned to ashes. Water in reservoirs could be

---

* Professor Oberth, Rumanian-born, author of *The Rocket Into Interplanetary Space,* is now working in this country under contract with the United States government.

boiled off as steam, and forests and grain fields quickly reduced to cinders.

It was the memory of this grim warning that now worried the UFO censors.

Because of their secrecy, the American people had not been prepared for an admission about our space visitors.

Months before, fearing just such a crisis, some Intelligence officers and PIO's had tried to reveal this outer-space observation, emphasizing the lack of hostility. For in their six years' systematic observation of the earth, the space beings had given no evidence of deliberate attack—Mantell's death and the other incidents could have been accidental.

But the silence group had never revealed these facts.

If the space-base story broke now, it might be too late to reassure the public. In itself, the satellite's appearance was no proof of danger—it might even be the first step of another planet race toward a peaceful contact with our world. But the press would remember Oberth's warning and the Pentagon's confirmation in 1948. What that could do was enough to make the censors shudder. Trapped by their own policy, they had no choice. The satellite discovery had to be kept hidden.

That day at the Pentagon I knew that if the report were true the censors would slam down the lid. But the captain I'd met in the hall had already heard the story, and after 25 years in Washington, I was sure there must have been other leaks. Even so, getting the truth would be a tough job. I knew a dozen men who probably had the answer, but only two who might be free to talk.

The first, a well-known aeronautical engineer, had helped me privately since '49. His technical opinions, under the name of Paul Redell, had appeared in my first book, *The Flying Saucers Are Real*. As an aircraft company representative, Redell had good contacts in the armed services and outside. More than once he'd surprised me with leads I'd later confirmed. If he'd heard of the satellite, he probably would tell me, unless he'd learned it from a strictly official source.

The second man was Admiral Delmer Fahrney, known in the Navy as "the father of guided missiles." Fahrney and I were old friends; we had been in the same battalion at Annapolis. In 1950, after the Air Force denied that the saucers existed, Fahrney had quietly told me:

"There have been too many convincing reports, and if the flying saucers do exist they must be interplanetary. Certainly neither we nor the Russians have anything remotely like them."

After he retired, the Navy had called Fahrney back to write the official history of guided missiles. Even if he knew of the space base, the odds were he couldn't talk. He was probably committed to silence. But still it was worth a try.

I found a phone booth near the Mall entrance and called the Navy Department. Fahrney had left for a week end at his home in Pennsylvania. My call to Redell's office also drew a blank; Paul had flown to the Coast for a month at his company's plant.

With no other sources available, I tried to figure out what the appearance of this satellite meant.

It could not be operated by any nation on earth. Obviously it had to come from another world, perhaps from Mars or even a planet outside our solar system. There were several possible reasons for its appearance. Probably it had assumed this orbit to launch flying discs for a more intensive observation of our world.

Even without the slightest evidence of hostility, the discovery of this space base would seem ominous to many people. To the UFO censors, I knew, this might be sufficient cause for a complete blackout.

3 The Silence Group Strikes

My conjectures about the space base were interrupted by a new development. I was checking a translation
of Oberth's warning when I had a call from Donn Munson, a
Washington *Times-Herald* reporter.

"You're in trouble," he warned me. "The Pentagon is
raising the devil—they've just seen galley proofs of your new
book."

"Probably *Look* magazine brought them in—they're running some extracts in the next issue. I knew there'd be some
squawks from the silence group."

"*Squawks?* You're going to be slaughtered, from what I
hear."

"What can they do? All the Intelligence reports were
cleared."

"Do the top Intelligence people know that?"

"The Director himself—General Samford—okayed the release. And three top Directorate officers knew it." I gave him
their names: Colonel W. A. Adams, Colonel Wesley Smith,
and Major Dewey Fournet. "Besides that, I have an official
list of all the Intelligence reports ATIC cleared. It's in the
book."

"Do the others know it—the ones you call the silence
group?"

"No, they think I got just a few minor cases."

"Then you'd better be on your guard," said Munson.

Though I couldn't see how the silence group could hurt me, I hurriedly thought back, looking for a loophole.

The year before, in August, 1952, the censors temporarily lost control, after mass sightings in July had caused wide alarm. Under a new policy, set by General Samford, I was invited to the Pentagon and offered the most baffling UFO reports in Air Force Intelligence files—cases pointing clearly to the interplanetary answer. From August until late February, 1953, these Intelligence reports, ranging from "Secret" to "Restricted," were declassified specifically for my use. I did not know, at that time, that I was the only unofficial investigator to see these reports.

Besides General Samford and the Directorate officers, the release of this material to me was known by the Commander of ATIC and by Captain Edward J. Ruppelt, head of Project Bluebook, the agency coordinating all UFO reports.

At the Pentagon three Air Force PIO's also knew that ATIC cases had been cleared for me: Colonel James K. Dowling, Press Branch chief; Colonel Max Boyd, his assistant; and Lieutenant Colonel Richard Searles.

In addition, all the ATIC cases and official statements were listed in a signed clearance letter, by Albert M. Chop, the civilian press official assigned to handle flying-saucer information.

Near the end of this period a fierce battle had developed between the censor-fighters and the silence group. Unaware that I had the key cases, the dethroned censors struggled to regain control before the facts could leak out.

One of their opponents was Major Dewey Fournet, the Pentagon's ace UFO investigator. For weeks Fournet had urged General Samford to reveal all the evidence, including a secret film showing a flying-saucer formation near Tremonton, Utah. Under Fournet's plan, backed by Colonels Adams and Smith as well as by Chop, the secret Utah film would be shown to the press, with an official analysis proving that the UFO's could not be earth-made machines.

In December, as the fight neared a climax, Fournet's active duty period ended. But the other censor-fighters kept on. During February, 1953, they began a last battle to reveal the Utah film. When the smoke cleared, the press showing had been canceled, the silence group had gained control, and Chop had resigned in disgust.

But the UFO censors were still unaware that I had the crucial Intelligence reports.

For six months, believing these dramatic cases safe under lock and key, they followed their old policy of explaining away the saucers. And now they found that I had published the information in my book.

It was mid-September when the storm finally broke and I learned the full power and fury of the men behind the blackout.

It was *Look* magazine, as I'd guessed, that had set off the uproar.

Early one morning a staff man had arrived at the Pentagon with galley proofs of *Flying Saucers from Outer Space,* from which the editors of *Look* had selected nine Intelligence reports. The startled censors took a quick glance. There on the very first galley was one of the hidden reports. Hurriedly, they started to check the other cases. With a shock they recognized the most dangerous report of all.

Just before dawn on December 6, 1952, a B-29 bomber had encountered three saucer formations over the Gulf of Mexico. Approaching at fantastic speed, the strange, glowing machines were tracked by radar at 5240 mph. Amazed crewmen, watching from blister windows, saw several of the weird craft flash by, only blue-white streaks in the sky.

Meanwhile a giant machine had shown up on the bomber's three radarscopes. Converging on this huge mother ship, the last group of saucers was swiftly taken aboard. Instantly the enormous craft began to accelerate. Before it went off the scopes, its speed was computed at more than 9000 mph.

When the B-29 landed, its radar equipment was found to be in perfect condition. Detailed statements by the pilot, radar officer, and crew members confirmed every astonishing detail.

For weeks the case had been analyzed by ATIC officers and prominent scientists under secret Air Force contract. In clearing this astounding Intelligence report, ATIC had not only given me the crew's statements but had summed up the secret analysis:

"All possibilities were checked for known aerial phenomena, with negative results." The identity of the strange machines, ATIC said, was unknown.

When word of this break reached the National Security Council—the top defense policy group—there was immediate consternation. With a strange satellite reported circling the earth, it was the worst possible time for this mother-ship story to appear.

In their haste to act quickly the UFO censors had missed my official clearance letter. Acting under top-level orders, an Air Force colonel rushed a call to Captain Edward Ruppelt, who had charge of all UFO records. Unknown to the colonel, Ruppelt had asked for inactive duty, and by sheer coincidence he had orders detaching him that very day.

"Find out how Keyhoe got those reports!" the colonel snapped. "If we can prove a security violation——"

"Not a chance, Colonel," said Ruppelt. "They were all officially cleared."

There was a hurried conference at the other end.

"We're sending out these galleys by special plane," said the colonel. "Go through them with a fine-tooth comb. Find every possible flaw!"

"No, sir, I can't do it," said Ruppelt.

"Captain, this is an order!" roared the colonel.

Ruppelt's exact answer, unfortunately, still remains undisclosed. But months later he told me: "Even if I'd wanted to, I couldn't have torn down those cases. You had them just as we cleared them."

After this new jolt the UFO censors carefully went through the galleys, hoping to find some way to prevent the book's publication. As they read the massed evidence, their dismay increased. In case after case ATIC had bluntly admitted the saucers could not be man-made. These admissions were revealed in my book.

The following are typical of the cases I reported:

On December 4, 1952, at Laredo, Texas, an Air Force F-51 fighter had almost been hit head-on by a weird, blue-lighted machine. The frightened pilot had cut off his lights and streaked for the ground.

A month later, over Santa Ana, California, B-29 pilots had encountered a V-formation of glowing blue saucers, flying at supersonic speed.

Near Dayton, in broad daylight, Air Force Sabrejets had chased and photographed a round, mysterious craft.

And at March Field other jets had vainly tried to reach a strange ship, as it circled above 50,000 feet in a *"controlled orbit."*

There were other convincing Intelligence reports: Jet chases at Goose Bay Air Force Base in Labrador; over Japan; Germany; Port Huron, Michigan; and Washington, D.C., as well as over other cities and bases throughout the world.

Linked together, the 41 cases which had been cleared for me made a powerful chain of evidence. But there was one besides the Gulf of Mexico case that made the censors break out in a cold sweat. It involved the secret flying-saucer film taken in northern Utah.

At Tremonton, Utah, shortly before noon on July 12, 1952, Navy Warrant Officer Delbert C. Newhouse had sighted a formation of 14 round, bright-glowing objects moving swiftly overhead. After shooting 40 feet of color film, he had asked the Navy to relay the pictures to the Air Force. For three months, at Dayton, the film was analyzed, frame by frame, in the Photo-Reconnaissance Laboratory. Copies were also confidentially analyzed by private laboratories, and later, for three months, by the Navy Photo-Interpretation Center.

After ruling out all natural phenomena and man-made objects, the secret Air Force-Navy analysis admitted that the objects could not be identified. But from the terrific speeds and maneuvers one thing was clear: the strange machines were from outer space.

Besides these key cases, three other revelations which I had made added to the censors' headaches:

1. In 1952, Colonel W. C. Odell, U. S. Air Force Intelligence, had prepared an article strongly implying that the saucers contained beings from a dying planet—creatures in search of a new home. He had immediately been forbidden to use his Air Force title in connection with the article.

2. In an official statement to me, the Air Force had retracted its "temperature inversion" or mirage answer for the mysterious Washington sightings which had occurred in 1952. It was made obvious that this explanation had been used to prevent public alarm. In other cases ATIC again had wrecked this favorite alibi of the silence group—Dr. Donald Menzel's natural phenomenon-mirage answer.

3. The final blow was an Air Force letter to my publishers, Henry Holt and Company. Signed by Chop, as the Air Force spokesman on UFO's, this letter confirmed the ATIC clearances. Chop had added a conclusion shared by many Air Force officers:

"If the apparently controlled maneuvers reported by many competent observers is correct, then the only remaining explanation is the interplanetary answer."

With so many cases proving controlled maneuvers by the

saucers, this was practically an official admission that the saucers were known to be space ships.

When the shaken censors finished the galley proofs, they were faced with a fateful decision. They had to discredit the book or admit the truth to a totally unprepared public.

Searching for a weapon, they found a loophole I had overlooked.

No one else had the hidden Intelligence reports. They had been given to me during the period of confusion.

Here is how the confusion arose: In July, 1952, General Samford told newsmen there was no reason for UFO reports to be withheld. Several correspondents then asked to see the Intelligence records. But no order had yet come through, and their requests were denied.

A few days later I made the same request and was turned down. But within two hours I was called back to the Pentagon and told that under a new policy set by General Samford, any Intelligence reports I specified could be released to me. During the next eight months I was guided by the censor-fighters to the most vital UFO reports.

Apparently this policy reversal was not discovered by any of the press. Having been refused the information, none of them asked for it again.

By the time they learned of the reversal, through my book, the policy had again been changed, with only minor reports —easily explained—then being given out. Within a few weeks all the releases were stopped.

When it was first discovered that I alone had these cases, it seemed to some censors a quick way out. They could label my reports as false.

But the pitfalls were soon apparent. If they denied that my reports were authentic, they would also have to label the official clearance list as false. Too many Press Branch and Intelligence officers would balk at that. Even if the men on active duty were silenced, Captain Ruppelt would back

Chop. So would Major Fournet; he and Chop, working together, had become close friends.

But there might be another way . . .

That night I had a long-distance call from Chop, who was living in California, working with Douglas Aircraft.

"Don," he said tautly, "you know I never slipped you any secret UFO reports!"

"*Slipped* them to me?" I exclaimed. "What are you talking about?"

"The Air Force has been phoning me all day. It's that *Look* article. They say you claim I gave you Intelligence reports out of secret Air Force files, and they made me sign a statement denying you'd seen any secret reports."

"Al, that's a trick! I made it plain all those cases were officially cleared. They'll use that statement to make it seem I never received any Intelligence reports."

"Well, I'll straighten that out," Chop said grimly. "I'll fire them an air-mail letter tonight, putting the whole thing on record."

Before he hung up, he told me the calls had come from Colonel James Dowling and Lieutenant Colonel Hugh Day. I was astonished, for I was sure these men knew the reports had been given to me.

Some time back Colonel Dowling and I had discussed Lindbergh's World War II combat service, when the Air Force was planning to give Lindbergh a medal. Dowling had not mentioned the saucers, though he knew I was getting the Intelligence reports; but I had been told that he, and Day as well, were opposed to the silence policy. Either something serious had happened to change their opinions, or they were both under top-level pressure.

Though it was late, I phoned one of the censor-fighters, an Intelligence officer who'd helped me in '52. He knew the situation.

"They pulled a fast one on Chop," he said. "And they're

up to something on that *Look* deal—I couldn't find out what."

"But General Samford knows the true story——"

"They might muzzle him—this goes pretty high. If I were you, I'd get hold of Ruppelt. He'll back you; he had guts enough to tell them off about knifing your book."

Next day I tried to locate Ruppelt, but failed.

My only official proof then was the signed clearance list. And I knew if the silence group dared, they would ruthlessly sacrifice Chop.

For two days I tried to find out what was going on behind the scenes. When I did hear, the news gave me a cold chill. For ATIC had been told to "recheck" the reports for possible changes before they were given to *Look*.

The possibility of changing the evidence and conclusions had come up after one UFO censor flatly denied the first two reports he saw. One was on the near-collision case at Laredo, Texas. Though the object was officially declared to be a UFO, he now insisted it was a plane. The second case, a vitally important encounter, described a sighting by a veteran Air Force officer, Colonel D. J. Blakeslee, Commander of a Fighter Escort Wing in Japan. (In *Flying Saucers from Outer Space*, through an Air Force error, he was called Colonel Curtis Low.)

On December 29, 1952, a peculiar type of "saucer" with rotating lights had been sighted by Colonel Blakeslee, by an F-94 fighter pilot, and by the crew of a B-26 bomber.

When Colonel Blakeslee, flying an F-84 jet, tried to close in, the mysterious machine raced off, vanishing in five seconds. After he landed, the wing commander told Intelligence officers the saucer had three fixed shafts of white light. One section of the UFO, he said, was revolving steadily, alternating from red to green to white at regular intervals.

In an unusual comment the Intelligence officer who interrogated Colonel Blakeslee stated how profoundly he had been impressed by the wing commander's account.

"The pilot reporting," he said, "has held responsible command assignments for some time. The accuracy of his statements was consistent despite repetitive interrogation. His sequence of times, locations, and descriptions did not vary at any time. He is stable and thoroughly reliable. There were no activities of a meteorological nature or any inversion which could account for these sightings . . . This is a graphic description of an object falling definitely into the family of UFO."

When *Look* asked about this case, an angry UFO censor at the Pentagon brushed the report aside—in spite of the previous confirmation and the extraordinary tribute paid to Blakeslee's skill and experience. Ridiculing the "rotating-lights" description, he insisted that the wing commander had been confused by the planet Jupiter.

But the *Look* researcher had quietly asked to see the ATIC report at Dayton—not only on Blakeslee but on all the cases. To avoid suspicion the silence group had to agree—but before he reached Dayton, ATIC was told to recheck for any new conclusions, including the Jupiter answer.

When I heard of the order, I realized for the first time the silence group's cold determination. This impressive UFO report by a veteran wing commander would carry too much weight. Rather than let it stand, the UFO censors would try to brand him a fool, unable to recognize a twinkling star in the sky.

A few hours after this ominous news, I had a call from Frank Edwards. I told him what I had heard about the orders to ATIC.

"That's bad," he said. "You can see what they're up to. *Look's* due out the same day as your book——"

"I know. The Air Force will say, '*Look* has the true story

as confirmed by us.' It'll be murder. My only hope is that *Look* won't fall for the switch."

"Why don't you jump the gun—blast the silence group first?"

"How?"

"You can go on my program tonight. I'll give you five minutes, enough to blow it wide open."

"I'll have to check with my publishers. They've got a press conference set for next Thursday——"

"Why don't you come over here now? We can work out a broadcast. Then if they okay it, you'll be ready."

When I met Frank at the Mutual station, he told me he had just learned something new.

"They're making *Look* run a long Air Force statement before the article—the usual line about mirages, balloons, meteors, and so on—saying there's no evidence the saucers exist. Also, they're insisting on official Air Force inserts sprinkled through your story, to keep sniping at it."

"Maybe you're right about jumping the gun," I said. "I'll call New York."

"Wait a minute. I'd forgotten this is Friday. If you cut loose tonight, the silence crowd will have two days to smear you before I could get you on the air again. Unless they release something today—and it's not likely at this late hour—it may be smarter to wait until Monday. Then if they go ahead with this smear campaign, you can answer them the next day."

"That sounds better," I agreed.

"I'll give it a buildup tonight. And if I have time, I'll use two or three recent sightings. You knew there'd been a jump in reports?"

"Yes, but I haven't had time to check them."

Frank showed me the reports he'd selected, all verified sightings. On September 7, two Navy pilots flying Corsair fighters had been paced by a saucer north of Dayton. Illuminated by a brilliant white light, the UFO streaked under the planes, then zoomed up and disappeared.

That same day, at Tangmere Airport, Sussex, England, a large saucer hovered briefly over the field. Seen by scores of Royal Air Force pilots and ground men, the machine suddenly accelerated, vanishing over the English Channel.

At Modesto, California, on September 9, two former Air Force navigators sighted another huge saucer. Its dazzling glow, they reported, was brighter than 50 airplane landing lights. As it swept over Walker Lake, the UFO's weird glare shone down through the clouds, frightening dozens who saw it.

Four nights later, at Chiloquin, Oregon, two flying saucers were sighted by most of the population. Appearing silently, from opposite directions, the strange machines stopped for several minutes and hovered over the town. Through binoculars, Police Chief Lewis Jones and Glenn Kircher, a radar expert, saw that each saucer had red, green, and white rotating lights, with a brilliant glow from the under sides.

"Here's one that just came in." Frank picked up a report from his desk. "Last Monday an airline pilot named Leon Hood spotted a big saucer 15 miles south of Waseca, Minnesota. He told reporters it was making about 900 miles an hour."

"How could he tell?"

"It was flying near some clouds that were at 35,000 feet. Knowing its distance above him, he could figure its approximate size and speed." Frank gave me an ironic look through his glasses. "An airline pilot's judgment should mean something, but I suppose the Pentagon hush-hush people will say it was an hallucination."

We started to work on the Monday broadcast. Halfway through, I stopped.

"Frank, you don't think I've been wrong, trying to break this story?"

"No. Somebody's got to do the job. As it is, we're not prepared for anything—even a peaceful contact."

"All this pressure to keep it secret worries me. And yet General Samford and ATIC let those cases out——"

"It's my guess," said Frank, "they still don't know the whole answer. It could turn out okay, but in case it's bad news the silence group would rather let people go on living in a fool's paradise."

"Well, I'd rather have the truth . . . I think most people would."

Driving home after planning the broadcast, I felt a little less worried, knowing I could tell my story on a coast-to-coast network. A special air-mail from Chop, with copies of two letters to Lieutenant Colonel Hugh Day, also helped ease the tension. Writing to Day on September 17 and 21, Chop had made four points crystal clear:

1. All 41 Intelligence reports, *originally classified,* had been declassified specifically for me by ATIC.

2. I had received official ATIC statements that the UFO's were not secret U. S. weapons, and that despite Menzel's theories and other explanations, hundreds of sightings, by the most competent witnesses, were unsolved.

3. His statement to Henry Holt and Company was *not* merely his own opinion; a number of Air Force officers believed, on the basis of controlled maneuvers, that the UFO's were interplanetary.

4. With the approval of Air Force Intelligence, he had revealed to me the existence of the secret Utah film analysis and cancellation of the planned public showing.

But my relief at receiving the letter died a quick death, for that night I learned the final details of the censors' plan of attack. The letters to Colonel Day had changed nothing; the silence group simply would not use them. By Monday they would have a final proof or an advance copy of *Look*. With the changed cases as evidence, an Air Force statement would be released, blasting my book. To make it a front-page story, they would try to use a high-ranking Air Force spokesman—either General Sory Smith, Director of Information, or Secretary Talbott himself.

Deliberately misquoting Chop, the Air Force would even deny that UFO reports had ever been classified. All the official statements given me, including those teletyped by ATIC to the Pentagon, would be labeled as merely Chop's personal opinions.

With perfect timing, this story would be released for the Thursday morning papers—only hours before I would meet newsmen at the Press Club. It was a master stroke. With the Air Force's story in *Look,* most reporters would be convinced that I had distorted the facts. And once branded, I might never be able to clear myself.

By Monday morning I began to realize how a condemned man feels. I was counting the hours to the broadcast when Donn Munson called. Twice before, he had started to break the story—by a mistake his advance copy had no release date. But this time I couldn't stop him.

"This thing's getting hot," he said. "I'm going to break it today."

With a promise to help write the story, I got him to wait until noon. Then I phoned Frank Edwards.

"Go ahead!" he said instantly. "It won't hurt the broadcast. But ask him to hold off until you get copies to the wire services."

At three-thirty the *Times-Herald* story came out, covering the Gulf of Mexico case and the battle to reveal the secret Utah pictures. By this time it was also on the press wires. Knowing the Pentagon teletypes would immediately pick it up, I braced myself for the Air Force blast. With their attack already prepared, I was sure they'd hit back within minutes. But at five o'clock, when I talked with Frank, the Air Force still had not answered.

"I just checked," he told me. "All they'd say was that their statement wasn't ready. Something must've gone wrong."

A few hours later I learned what had happened.

That morning, when an advance copy of *Look* arrived, the censors were dumfounded. Except for Colonel Blakeslee's encounter and the Laredo case, not a single report had been changed.

From all indications, someone at ATIC must have confirmed all my key cases. By doing so ATIC had completely offset the silence group's sniping inserts in *Look*.

Even the two changes the censors made would appear ridiculous when compared with my full reports.

In the Laredo case the UFO was now labeled as "possibly" an unidentified plane. But Intelligence had previously ruled out such uncertainty because of the round shape, supersonic speed, and eerie blue glow of the machines. Suddenly reversing the original conclusion now, despite the weeks of careful investigation, showed this to be merely a clumsy cover-up trick.

In the Blakeslee case the reversal was even more obvious. The angry Pentagon censor had failed to note that the saucer with the "rotating lights" had been tracked by Air Force radar. Since the radar set's range was about 100 miles, and Jupiter was millions of miles away, this explanation was either a plain lie—or a new height in stupidity.

Furious over this "double cross" by ATIC at Dayton, the silence group searched for a way to repair the damage. They were still at it when Munson's story showed up on the Pentagon press wires.

For two hours the censors tried to write a new answer to my claims. What they feared most was the mother-ship report. But how could they deny it, with *Look* ready to back it up? Or, if denial was impossible, how could they distract attention from this amazing incident?

At last a solution was found. From my handling of the Tremonton, Utah, case, it seemed obvious that I had no written official proof of the secret film analysis. But though it seemed safe to deny it, no ranking officer would allow his name to be used.

Finally an unnamed "spokesman," ignoring the Gulf case entirely, focused an attack on my Utah picture claims. Denying the film was ever secretly analyzed, he insisted it had been returned to Warrant Officer Newhouse with the implication it was of no importance. All the Air Force opinions quoted in my book, he added, were Chop's personal ideas. There was not a hint that any Intelligence reports had ever been cleared for me.

It was a meek retort compared with what they had planned. But behind the scenes I was savagely denounced to the Pentagon press corps.

"They say you're lying about the Utah pictures," one newsman told me at the Press Club conference. "Also, one top PIO—I won't say who—is passing around an extract from a statement he claims Chop made. It says you never got any classified Intelligence reports."

I showed him Chop's letter, with the main points Chop had relayed to Colonel Day.

"They certainly didn't let me see this stuff," he said. "Why didn't you ask Day to come in here and explain it?"

"I did. He was invited along with General Sory Smith, Colonel Dowling, and some others. They haven't shown up."

Considering the backstage attacks, I was given surprisingly fair treatment by most of the press. This was partly due to Douglas Larsen of NEA, Clay Blair of *Life,* and others who had worked on the saucer story and knew of Air Force secrecy.

Again, General Sory Smith's office sharply denied my story

of the Utah pictures. I knew I had to strike back. If this went unchallenged, many Americans might believe the whole book a hoax.

I knew that the original film was never returned to Newhouse. Over a score of copies had been made for the Air Force, for the Navy, and for private laboratories to study. What Newhouse received was a blurred copy of his own film, deliberately given him to offset any charge of secrecy.

When the film was sent to him, Newhouse was not told one word about the analysis conclusions. Instead, he was led to believe the film was worthless.

Though I couldn't prove this, I did have an ace in the hole.

Early in '53, when Intelligence planned to reveal the Utah film, a long press statement was prepared. After the silence group killed the plan, an officer who had fought them met me privately and gave me a copy of the canceled press release.

"This officially has been killed," he said. "But it has *not* been classified, so I'm letting you have it. It covers the main points of the secret analysis. Maybe somebody in the Navy will confirm it for you. Don't use it publicly unless you have to—it will set off an unholy row."

Describing how Newhouse had taken the pictures, this Air Force press release stated:

"The pictures were studied for months by the Air Force Photo-Reconnaissance Laboratory at Dayton, and later by the Navy Photo-Interpretation Center at Washington."

Both laboratories, the Air Force statement went on, came to these conclusions:

1. The average speed of the unknown objects was somewhere between 653 and 980 mph.

2. All the objects appeared round, of the same size, and they gave off a bluish-white glow of very high intensity.

3. The objects seemed to be maneuvering in a circular or elliptical pattern within the group, at very high speeds.

4. Because of these high speeds, the objects obviously could not be balloons or birds.

5. They were not any type of known aircraft.

6. The sighting could not be explained by any conventional answer. . . .

On the strength of this hidden release, on October 1, 1953, I sent the following telegram to Air Force Secretary Talbott and General Sory.Smith, with copies to the press wire services:

"On Sept. 29, the Air Force publicly implied that I misrepresented the Air Force analysis of the Utah flying-saucer pictures. If this is true, then as a Marine Corps officer I should be subjected to disciplinary action . . ."

After listing the main points of the analysis, I concluded:

"If my claims are incorrect, I suggest you ask that I be court-martialed for making false statements about the Air Force analysis."

When this challenge reached General Smith he was seriously perturbed; apparently misled as to the facts, he had believed I could not possibly refute the Air Force denial.

What could the Air Force say now? Did I have the entire analysis to back me up? I could get into serious trouble if I gave it to the papers—it was still classified "Secret." But I might risk it to prove I was telling the truth.

There was only one safe answer. Tartly, General Smith told the press:

"The Air Force has no comment."

Even though this answer was not a complete vindication, I felt relieved when I heard of it. Had it not been for Chop, the other Air Force censor-fighters—and Ruppelt's refusal to attack the book—I would probably have been crucified.

Much later, on April 11, 1954, Ruppelt gave me a signed statement confirming what I had said. Though it came too late to help me through this crisis, it did verify my statements that I had seen the declassified Intelligence reports.

"The procedure," he wrote, "was that I would receive a request for the data either from OPI [Office of Public Information] or the Director of Intelligence, by wire or telephone. It would go back by wire or telephone, cleared by my superiors. In many instances, I was informed that the data were for you.

"I have read your book, *Flying Saucers from Outer Space*, and to the best of my knowledge the sightings you credit to the Air Force and the conclusions on each are those I sent to you through the OPI/DD. [Defense Department.]"

Giving me full permission to quote him, Captain Ruppelt listed three other points:

1. After the secret Utah film analysis, he had wired a press release to the Pentagon, for use at the planned public showing.

2. The letter from Chop to Henry Holt and Company was "correct in all respects."

3. Menzel's theories were rejected by ATIC, except for a few cases already explained. "This was communicated to you," Ruppelt said, "through the Office of Public Information, again cleared by my superiors."

If I'd had this letter in September of '53, it would have helped me to fight the UFO censors.

As it was, without any such evidence, I felt lucky to have withstood the attack.

4 Unknown Worlds

In the first week of October, 1953, I took off from Washington Airport for a series of TV and radio appearances in New York.

The Convair airliner climbed up over the Mall, passing the Washington Monument, and banked to pick up its course. As the lights of the capital swept below, I thought of the satellite supposed to be circling the earth.

Perhaps even now it was over the Western Hemisphere... the unknown beings aboard looking down at this country.

With a big enough ship the space beings could use powerful telescopes to watch the cities on earth.

If the satellite circled from north to south, the unknown watchers would see the earth rotate like a colossal desk globe. Even with the naked eye they could see the continents, oceans, and mountains as the earth revolved below.

What would we look like from 500 miles out?

At this hour, early evening, they would see the glow of great cities—Boston, New York, Washington, and Miami. From 500 miles up, the space men could see far to the West —past Pittsburgh and Cleveland to Chicago and the Midwest.

With an orbiting mother ship to receive them, space creatures in smaller discs could plan closer visits, then return to the space base, knowing its exact position. This would explain why so many saucers suddenly climbed straight up after reconnaissance missions over our cities and bases.

If desirable, the space base might even leave its orbit temporarily to enter our atmosphere, slowing down to take its "saucers" aboard, as in the case over the Gulf of Mexico. Or perhaps the smaller discs had television-type scanners which relayed pictures of the earth to the satellite. As a pilot, I knew what the UFO beings could see at this lower altitude.

Obviously the appearance of the satellite base meant a change from intermittent observations. The unknown beings were moving into a new phase of their operations. It could be part of a plan for mass landings.

I was still puzzling over the possible motives for such close observations when the Convair landed at La Guardia Airport.

On the following day I began my week of interviews with Mary Margaret McBride, Emily Kimbrough, Bill Leonard, Barbara Welles, George Hamilton Combs, Tex and Jinx, Alma Dettinger, and Bob Considine, among others.

Within a short time I was convinced of one thing—a larger number of thoughtful people accepted the interplanetary answer than the Air Force dreamed. One of these believers, a radio executive, privately told me that his doubts had been ended by Dr. Harlow Shapley, the former director of Harvard Observatory.

"But I thought Dr. Shapley refused to admit the saucers were real," I said.

"He doesn't mention the UFO's—this is something from a new book he's written, due in December. He worked for two years with other astronomers and scientists on the effects of climatic change—and what is required for life to evolve on a planet."

"Then he admits there may be other worlds?"

"Here's exactly what he says." The radio executive watched my face. " 'There must be at least one hundred million inhabited planets.' "

"One hundred million! That's amazing. Coming from a man with Shapley's reputation, it will be a jolt to the Air Force."

"And it'll be a wallop to all the people who think the earth is the only inhabited world. He also said—and this will really bruise a lot of egos—that the inhabitants of many of those other worlds will be far superior to us in every way."

Later that night, in my room at the Commodore, I stood looking absently out over the city.

It was a haunting thought, to realize there were millions of inhabited planets—unknown worlds—scattered through the metagalaxy. Most of them we would never know, nor our descendants, even when they learned to travel far into outer space. Nor would many of those unknown worlds come to know us—or that we existed—though even by now they might have learned to travel at almost the speed of light.

More than one space-travel planner today believed that such fantastic speed in empty space eventually would be realized. The technical problems were appalling now, but so had been the problem of flight itself just fifty years ago. Even at such speeds no earthling could hope to traverse more than a small part of the metagalaxy. It would take four billion years to cross a universe so vast, even at the speed of light. Perhaps it would take even longer; since 1951 astronomers had twice doubled their estimates of its size.

On many of those far distant worlds there would be great civilizations, developed far beyond our own. In strange, perhaps beautiful worlds, beings forever beyond our reach had probably reached near-perfection, ending disease, poverty, and the primitive struggle for existence. There would be some whose knowledge and attainments were beyond our wildest dreams.

Most of these, for a reason known only to the Creator, we would never meet.

But out of those millions of worlds, some were bound to be within our reach when man finally freed himself from the earth.

From one or more of these nearer star systems—if not from our own—had come the strange machines we called the flying saucers.

But their mission, their purpose, was as much a mystery as ever. . . .

That thought came back to me, two weeks later, when Frank Edwards and I met in New York for the "Author Meets the Critics" program.

On the morning of the program Frank's office phoned him a dramatic story just confirmed by the Civil Aeronautics Authority.

At midnight the passengers and crew of a DC-6 airliner had had a narrow escape over Conowingo Dam, Maryland. Flying south toward Washington, an American Airlines plane, piloted by Captain J. L. Kidd, was cruising at 8000 feet when a brilliant light appeared ahead.

The unknown machine was coming swiftly toward them on a collision course. Instantly Captain Kidd shoved the controls forward. As the DC-6 dived, the mysterious craft streaked overhead and vanished.

The unexpected dive threw two or three passengers into the aisle. Captain Kidd radioed to Washington Airport for ambulances and doctors. Fortunately no one was seriously injured.

From the description given by Captain Kidd and the co-pilot, the unknown craft had been a huge machine, as large as the DC-6. Immediately the CAA made a check of every scheduled airliner and other cruising aircraft within 100 miles of Conowingo Dam. But not one had been near the DC-6.

A day or so after this I asked Charles E. Planck, chief of

the CAA press section, what Captain Kidd had radioed the Washington Airport tower.

"I don't have the exact words," said Planck. "But he yelled that he'd almost been hit by this plane and——"

"Wait a second, Charley. Kidd said it was a *plane?*"

"Well, no—he said, 'somebody almost hit me,' if I remember correctly."

"Did he get a good look?"

Planck shook his head.

"He had to dive too fast. But he and the copilot saw aircraft lights."

"The first news flash said Kidd called it a 'brilliant white light'—when did he change it?"

Planck looked at me uncomfortably. "Look, Don, I'm not the one to talk about this. The Civil Aeronautics investigators have taken over."

"But the CAA did say they searched the area, didn't they?"

"Yes. Air Traffic Control checked immediately. They couldn't find any aircraft near enough to explain it."

"How many other near-collision cases do you know of like this?" I cut in.

"There was one in '51, near Longmeadow, Massachusetts. Something almost hit a United Airlines DC-4. But I think the report said it was an 'unidentified aircraft.' "

"If they couldn't identify it, how do they know it was an aircraft?"

Planck threw up his hands.

"All I know is that they saw red, green, and white lights. What else could it be?"

"Okay, Charley," I said. "Just one more thing. May I see the CAA reports on saucers—the ones you get from the towers and radar controllers?"

"No, I'm sorry. There's an order against it."

"Meaning JANAP 146?"

"I don't know what you're talking about," Planck answered. As I started to leave, he added, "About this Cono-wingo affair—what good does it do to frighten people? What if some unknown plane did stray off-course? Our air transport safety record is the highest in the world——"

"I'm not trying to scare people, Charley. And I *don't* think it was an airplane."

It was remotely possible, I knew, that some unscheduled plane could have been involved. But Captain Kidd and the copilot both had insisted the unknown machine was as big as a multi-engined airliner. And with every airliner's flight plan on record, the Civil Aeronautics Authority would have identified the culprit quickly.

Red, green, and white lights, Planck had said.

Rotating red, green, and white lights, Colonel Blakeslee's report to Intelligence had read.

Red, green, and white lights, with a brilliant white light underneath, the Colquin, Oregon, reports had said.

It didn't add up to proof. But many a man had been jailed on flimsier circumstantial evidence.

Going through the mail after I got home, I remembered what Planck had said about frightening the public. Judging from most of my readers' letters, the close approaches I'd reported had raised no great alarm. People were interested, not frightened, and they wanted to know more about the situation.

Even the reported incidents, like the Mantell case, were apparently considered accidents by the majority of readers. Very few people showed any fear at the idea of space visitors.

Out of scores of letters containing UFO reports, there were several which I knew, from previously verified accounts, to be true.

On October 9 there had been four sightings. At Rock Island, Illinois, two detectives had sighted a huge, gleaming saucer streaking across the sky, traveling many times faster than the speed of a jet. In the Netherlands observers had seen three UFO's flying in triangular formation. Like many other saucers, all three glowed a bright orange-red, the color of hot metal. About four hours later that same night one of the blue-white UFO's had raced over the North Sea. As witnesses watched, it climbed almost straight up, at terrific speed, then dwindled to a speck and vanished. Finally, near midnight, another blue-white saucer was sighted by an astronomer at South Gate, California.

There were many other reports, which sounded equally authentic. But since they lacked proof, I marked them "Unconfirmed."

I had almost finished the reports when I was startled by an air-mail letter from Honolulu. It was signed by a well-known businessman, a licensed pilot with Navy connections, and contained the following statements:

"On August 6, between 5 P.M. and midnight, at least 75 lighted objects, some hovering, some moving swiftly, were observed in the Hawaiian area, especially near Barbers Point [Naval Air Station, Pearl Harbor]. Many of these UFO's were seen by the control tower, others by pilots. The objects appeared as blips on the radar scopes. At about 9 P.M. a Navy pilot on patrol picked up the blip of a UFO approaching head on at an alarming rate of speed. Seconds later, a glowing object made three close passes at his plane. The pilot landed immediately at Barbers Point.

"After this report, the Captain and Executive Officer were summoned, emergency patrols were ordered after midnight. At 11 minutes past two, the pilot of a TV-1 jet sighted a strange, glowing object streaking up from directly behind. When approximately 100 feet astern, the UFO shot to starboard and paced the TV-1 for four seconds. It then accelerated swiftly to an estimated speed of 1000 mph—and disappeared.

"According to ground crew and officer, the pilot was very

pale and frightened when he landed. He kept saying, 'I actually saw *him* . . .' "

I read the letter again carefully.

Barbers Point and August 6—this tied in with the information given me by Caperton and the captain I'd seen at the Pentagon. There might be one simple explanation; all could have heard the same unfounded rumor. But Caperton and the captain were not easily misled. And this letter had the ring of an official report.

But what, exactly, had the Navy pilot seen? What kind of being—or creature? It sounded like one of the "monster" stories beginning to circulate, yet there *could* be another explanation.

I had always been wary of the space-man-monster tales. Two had popped up in 1952 with frightening details. In one case, after a saucer was supposed to have landed on a West Virginia hilltop, witnesses claimed to have seen a gruesome creature nine feet tall. The witnesses appeared to be sincere; they seemed to believe they had actually seen the monster.

Several investigators who checked at the scene also believed it was possible. But I had always kept it on my "doubtful" list.

In the second case, another night encounter, a West Palm Beach scoutmaster claimed to have seen a saucer hovering just over his head. A fearful creature, he said, had appeared in the control section, releasing a paralyzing ray.

Captain Edward Ruppelt, after investigating this personally, had advised me through Albert Chop to ignore the story.

"Ed will give the reasons sometime," Chop told me. "I'm positive there's nothing to it."

But this Pearl Harbor story did not appear to be a hoax.

Next day I met Frank Edwards and told him the Pearl Harbor story. He didn't laugh it off, as I'd half expected him to do.

"With those three sources it sounds on the level," he said. "It's certainly possible. After all, planets with different sizes and different atmospheres couldn't evolve people just like us, could they?"

"That's a tough question, Frank. In the first place, some people think it's blasphemy even to suggest there is intelligent life on another planet."

"Yes, and even if they accepted the idea, many would balk at the 'strange creature' angle."

"Well, many of us were brought up to believe that man was made in God's image. It's hard to reconcile that with——"

"But even here on earth," said Frank, "look at the difference in people and races. It's partly a matter of climate. And if different climates can have such an effect on the inhabitants of *this* world, think what the different atmospheres and higher or lower gravity might make of the creatures on other planets."

"I'm not arguing against it," I answered. "It's just that I still brush off the usual monster stories. But we may yet have to brace ourselves to meet some queer-looking creatures."

After this Frank said he had something important to tell me.

"Remember you read a report on the Bob Considine show about the Utah film analysis?"

"Yes, it was the canceled Air Force press release."

"Well, the Air Force is anxious to know what the actual document was. In one close-up they could tell it was a photostat, but that was all. A few days ago one of the newsmen at the Pentagon asked me if I knew what it was. Since he and General Sory Smith are close buddies, I told him it was so secret you wouldn't even show it to me."

"Now they'll be sure I have a copy of the secret analysis."

"Well, you've got them worried. I also found out they're swamped with mail from people who read your book. Most of them want the truth on the Utah pictures. The Air Force is trying to figure how to answer without admitting anything."

After thinking over Frank's warning, I made an appointment with Admiral Calvin Bolster, Director of the Office of Naval Research. Like Fahrney, Bolster was an Annapolis classmate of mine. We had discussed the saucers before, though tight ONR security kept him from even hinting at any secret conclusions.

When I asked him about the Utah pictures, I expected at best a guarded reply. To my surprise he fully confirmed the official analysis.

"I can tell you," he said, "because the analysis will soon be acknowledged in an article by Captain Walter Karig, Special Information Deputy to the Secretary of the Navy."

"That's a surprise to me," I said. "The Air Force will scream its head off."

"It surprised me too," said Bolster. "But Karig has top-level clearance."

"Since that's been cleared, I wonder if there's any chance of your confirming a report I've heard." Then I gave Bolster the Barbers Point story. He listened with no change of expression.

"Even if the Navy had such a report," he answered, "only the Air Force could release it. But I'll let you talk with our Air Force liaison man, Lieutenant Commander Frank Thomas."

Before I left, I told the admiral I'd heard he was secretly briefed on the UFO's by an Air Force Intelligence officer. He admitted it was true.

"Maybe I shouldn't even ask this, Cal," I said, "but do you —does anyone—know the final answer?"

He slowly shook his head.

"No, I only wish we did."

Frank Thomas, a friendly young officer with a Texan drawl, told me he had seen the Utah pictures a dozen times. Without showing him the canceled press release, I went over the main points it disclosed.

He looked at me curiously.

"I won't ask where you got them, but those are the conclusions in the Navy Photo-Interpretation analysis."

It was not long after this when I finally saw Paul Redell, the aeronautical engineer. We made a date for dinner, and I met him at his hotel.

Redell looked the same as when we'd first met, six years before, a short, wiry man, quick-moving, with a sharply alert face. Though he was past 50, his black hair showed no sign of gray. I waited until we had ordered dinner before asking about the satellite.

"Who told you?" he demanded.

Without revealing the man's name, I gave him my source.

"Well, he got it straight," said Redell. "That is, they've spotted a satellite between 400 and 600 miles out. But you can't write about it yet. Even though I didn't learn it through classified channels, I got it confidentially."

"How big is it?"

"Big enough for a mother ship. They don't know exactly—they're having a hard time trying to track it. Ordinary telescopes won't pick it up. It's moving too fast, and besides that it apparently is a light-absorbing color."

"How'd they first discover it?"

"It was an accident. An experimental long-range radar caught it the first time. It seems to be circling at about 18,000 miles an hour, in an orbit near the equator."

"What's the Defense Department doing about it?"

"What can they do but try to track it? They're working on a search plan with some top astronomers. At first some of the Pentagon brass—men who don't know missile problems—were scared the Russians had beat us to it."

"That's impossible. I've talked with Dr. C. C. Furnas, at Cornell Aeronautical Laboratory, and Rear Admiral Sides——"

"I know him," said Redell. "He's in charge of Navy guided missile work."

"Well, they both said we were years from even the first tiny satellite. We don't even have detailed plans for a space base, and the Reds aren't any further along."

A little later, up in Redell's room, I asked if he'd heard of the Pearl Harbor story.

"No. But it could be true. Why should we think man is the only intelligent creature?"

He went over to the window and peered up into the night. Above the glow from F Street's light, the stars and a crescent moon were faintly visible. Redell turned back and gave me an odd look.

"Do you know about the moon study?" he said abruptly.

"No—what do you mean?"

"Some of the biggest astronomers are making secret observations of the moon for the Pentagon. Palomar is in on it, and so is the Naval Observatory."

"I knew there'd been some strange lights reported in certain craters——"

"I'm talking about actual changes," Redell interrupted.

"Changes?"

"Building—construction!" said Redell.

I stared at him. "They've actually found a saucer base on the moon?"

Redell gave me an impatient glance.

"Confound it, you yourself suggested it in your book—you and that Canadian scientist, W. B. Smith."

He filled his pipe, eyed me over the bowl as he flicked his lighter.

"Go through all the recent astronomers' journals. Look for

reports by Dr. H. P. Wilkins *—he's English, one of the world's most respected experts on the moon. Also look for one by J. J. O'Neill, science editor of the *Herald Tribune*. You won't find *all* the dope . . . after O'Neill and Wilkins let it out, they were put under pressure to stop talking. But you'll find enough."

"But what did they see? You said building——"

"Look it up and decide for yourself. I'll tell you this: it makes the satellite thing look pretty small. If Wilkins and the others are right, the moon may hand us the biggest surprise of all."

* Not to be confused with Harold T. Wilkins, English author of a flying-saucer book.

5 Enigma on the Moon

Driving home after I left Redell, I went over what he had said. Even though I had considered a moon base as a possibility, I found myself resisting the idea.

Yet even we were planning, working hard, to build a base on the moon. The advantages from a military viewpoint would be overwhelming. Willi Ley, an authority on space-operation plans, had summed it up in an article called "Invasion Base on the Moon."

After a technical discussion Ley stated that the moon's terrain, scarred with countless craters, had thousands of excellent sites for offensive bases. The aggressor who sets up the first interplanetary outpost on the moon, he said, can dominate not only our world but our entire solar system.

Like other space-travel experts, Ley had suggested an underground base, to escape the terrific heat of daylight and bitter cold of night.

Other experts had agreed with Ley that missiles could be launched from the moon and guided toward any point on earth. Because of the thin atmosphere, telescopes could clearly show the earth's details far better than we—with our dense atmosphere—could see the moon's.

Because of the moon's lower gravity—one sixth that of the earth—space ships could easily take off for other planets or for a reconnaissance of the earth. It would be an ideal base, and both we and the Russians hoped to be on the moon within 20 years, perhaps even sooner.

In spite of these factors it was not easy to admit that the moon might already be occupied by an unknown race.

Then I realized why the thought was disturbing. Like most people, I'd grown up with a friendly, safe feeling about the moon. It had always seemed our special property, placed in the sky for our convenience. The suggestion that it was now occupied by living creatures from another world was still hard to accept.

However, it might not be true. As cagey as Redell was, he could have been taken in. More than once I myself had started to follow some dramatic lead, only to find it had no foundation.

But Redell was on more solid ground, as I learned later . . .

On the night of July 29, 1953, John J. O'Neill, science editor of the *Herald Tribune,* settled himself at his telescope for an evening's observation of the moon. It was 6:30 U.T., and the moon, on its northerly course, was approaching the equator when O'Neill made an amazing discovery.

Stretching above the Mare Crisium crater was a gigantic bridge!

For a moment O'Neill refused to believe his senses. It might be an optical illusion. With utmost care he rechecked his telescope. He was using a 90X eyepiece. The "seeing"— an astronomer's term for visual conditions—was excellent.

He took another look.

The bridge was still there. Stretching in a straight line from pediment to pediment, it was more than 12 miles long.

The thing seemed impossible. In all the years he had watched the moon, there had been no bridge—nothing at all —above the Mare Crisium.

But there it was.

Fascinated, O'Neill watched the mysterious bridge for an hour and a half. Twice he changed eyepieces, to 125X and

250X. Both times, under the higher magnification, the huge structure appeared sharply in outline, an unbelievable engineering marvel apparently erected in weeks, perhaps in days.

Knowing the furor it would cause among astronomers, a man with less courage would have kept silent. As it was, not even O'Neill dared to tell the whole story. In his report to the Association of Lunar and Planetary Observers, he called his discovery a "gigantic natural bridge." But the sudden appearance of such a structure by an act of nature was absolutely impossible, as many privately admitted.

As O'Neill expected, he was quickly attacked by some astronomers. But most critics were abruptly silenced. For in August, 1953, one month after O'Neill's discovery, the existence of the bridge was fully confirmed by the great British astronomer, Dr. H. P. Wilkins. The following month it was also reported by another English lunar authority, Patrick Moore, a leading member of the British Astronomical Association.

The courage shown by O'Neill, Wilkins, and Moore soon led several astronomers to speak out on other moon mysteries —especially the strange lights so frequently seen in some craters.

On September 16, 1953, a peculiar, bright flash was seen on the moon by Rudolph M. Lippert, a member of the Lunar Section of the British Astronomical Association. Through his eight-inch Cassegrain reflector, with 90X power, the mysterious light glowed a yellowish orange, as bright as a first-magnitude star. Like the previous reports of strange lights, this was quickly explained away by more skeptical astronomers, who claimed it was a meteor hitting the moon.

But there was no way to brush off the Mare Crisium bridge discovery.

In public Dr. Wilkins, like O'Neill, had called it a strange "natural bridge." But his private comments had astonished members of the Royal Astronomical Association and the British Interplanetary Society.

It was not long before word of his comments reached the Pentagon. There the silence group learned with alarm that Wilkins was planning to make public his opinion of the bridge.

There was no way for the Pentagon censors to muzzle a British subject. All they could do was to pray the censors in London would somehow keep him from talking.

As I puzzled over the question of a moon base, I vaguely remembered some of the earlier recorded observations of the moon.

Within a short time, after I had talked with astronomers and searched astronomy records, a startling picture began to emerge.

For almost 200 years astronomers had watched mysterious activities on the moon.

Early in the nineteenth century Sir John Herschel, one of England's great astronomers, reported seeing strange, bright lights when the moon was darkened by an eclipse. Some of the lights, he said, seemed to be moving "above the moon."

Later, startling geometrical patterns resembling city streets were seen by the astronomer Gruithuisen.

In 1869 a sudden eruption of mystery lights, in regular patterns, caused a three-year investigation by the Royal Astronomical Society of Great Britain. Most of these puzzling lights were seen in the Mare Crisium area, where the gigantic bridge was later discovered. Watched by dozens of astronomers, the lights appeared in circular groups, triangular formations, and straight lines, their intensity varying as if by intelligent control.

Though the Royal Astronomical Society would not admit it publicly, some of its members believed this was an attempt by an unknown race on the moon to signal the earth. Until

1871 careful records were made every night, in the hope of deciphering the messages. Then, after nearly 2000 observations, the strange lights ceased to appear. If they were signals, their meaning was still a riddle.

Beside the puzzling lights, several mysterious dark objects had been sighted moving over the moon's surface. In 1912 Dr. F. B. Harris picked up a huge black object with his telescope. Estimated to be at least 50 miles across, it was clearly visible as it traversed the shining face of the moon.

Since 1915 straight and curving walls had suddenly appeared in several craters, among them Archimedes and Aristarchus.

On March 30, 1950, Dr. H. P. Wilkins, using a 15¼-inch reflector, picked up a weird glow in the Aristarchus-Herodotus region. Oval-shaped and strangely brilliant, it apparently came from some type of glowing machine hovering near the crater floor.

Three months later an almost identical light was sighted at the same spot by an experienced American astronomer, James C. Bartlett, Jr.

Most recent of all were the mystifying white "domes"—strange round formations, which appeared abruptly in many of the moon's craters.

All the evidence suggested not only the existence of a moon base, but that operations by an intelligent race had already begun. If so, who could the creatures be? Were they from other planets or did they originate on the moon?

The possibilities were numerous.

Surface creatures may have inhabited the moon long before its atmosphere thinned. If this were so, they might have adapted to changing conditions by creating a synthetic "atmosphere" underground.

But it was more likely that any moon race—if one actually existed—had always lived underground, protected there from the constant meteor bombardment. In that case the moon creatures might merely be animals with a low intelligence.

But this would not account for the strange geometric light formations or the many other mysteries that had occurred on the moon during the last 200 years.

If these strange reports were correct, an intelligent race must have been on the moon for nearly two centuries.

A highly advanced race could have achieved space travel before we had even steamships. In the moon's thin atmosphere they might have trained telescopes on the earth and seen our cities grow. Their space ships might have circled our globe periodically, checking on our progress.

That would explain scores of old sighting reports, going back to the eighteenth century.

Such a race might not have understood what they saw. To them we could have seemed merely strange animals, or creatures too primitive to attract their interest.

But as our planes and rockets appeared, and our A-bombs exploded, their picture of us would have changed. Perhaps the historic radio message which the U. S. Signal Corps bounced off the moon—"What hath God wrought?"—had been mistaken as a signal to them.

If this were true, and a highly intelligent race inhabited the moon, the danger from us would be obvious. The moon would be the first target for our space ships and exploration rockets. From the A- and H-bomb explosions seen on our globe, and the almost constant wars they had watched, they could easily have supposed one thing: We planned to take over the moon.

Ironically, they wouldn't have been far wrong, for we and the Soviet had announced plans to use the moon as a base.

But it was only one of a dozen possible answers.

The moon could have been inhabited long ago, then abandoned as conditions changed. Its creatures could have reached Mars and established a civilization there, to return "home" only at frequent intervals. Perhaps *they* used the moon as a space base for travel to other planets.

Or there may never have been a moon race at all. The lunar sphere could have been occupied by outsiders—from Mars, for example, or from a planet beyond our solar system. Gradually a base could have been built up, most of it underground to avoid meteor falls. The intermittent use of the moon as a space base would explain the strange lights of the past two centuries, as well as the mysterious radial cracks or lines which might be caused by intense heat from "blast-offs."

This unknown race might have regarded with increasing interest our own world. They too may have feared our explorations.

There was one other possible answer.

The creatures on the moon might be a *combination* of several races from other planets. We might never know until we reached the moon—unless one of their space ships landed on earth.

Could the moon race have been enslaved and forced to build the space base for outsiders? Perhaps so. It was even possible that a strong moon race, perhaps with unknown weapons, could have overwhelmed the space visitors and now might be in control.

As to which was the right answer, I could only speculate. But the evidence of *some* intelligent race on the moon seemed undeniable. . . .

Fortunately for the silence group, very few besides astronomers knew of the moon bridge. But if Wilkins revealed his startling opinion, the press might look into all the historic reports.

As the weeks passed, with no word from London, the Pentagon censors began to breathe easier.

Then the news broke. On December 23 in a British radio

broadcast, Dr. Wilkins disclosed the dramatic story. He was interviewed at his telescope by BBC radio commentator Bernard Forbes, after this opening statement: *

"Since the beginning of this century, astronomers have been observing features on the surface of the moon which have not been noticed before. During the last few years many dome-like swellings have been seen through powerful modern telescopes, and only a few months ago astronomers detected what is perhaps the most curious feature of all. It looks like a gigantic bridge, and the Director of the British Astronomical Association, Dr. H. P. Wilkins, when interviewed, discussed this new discovery.

"*Dr. Wilkins:* . . . If you look through the eyepiece [of the telescope], you will see one of the most interesting regions on the moon . . . called the Mare Crisium. It's that comparatively small, dark oval marking.

"*Forbes:* Yes, I can see it now.

"*Dr. Wilkins:* I've mentioned this gap in the mountain barrier . . . but there now exists what looks like a bridge across this gap.

"*Forbes:* That's most extraordinary.

"*Dr. Wilkins:* Now this is a real bridge. Its span is about 20 miles from one side to the other, and it's probably at least 5000 feet or so from the surface beneath.

"*Forbes:* It must be a most gigantic arch if it's 5000 feet high.

"*Dr. Wilkins:* It certainly is.

"*Forbes:* How wide is it?

"*Dr. Wilkins:* The width is about a mile and a half to two miles. It tapers—narrows, rather—in the center.

"*Forbes:* Are you quite certain that you haven't mistaken it for some other object?

"*Dr. Wilkins:* Oh, no, there's no mistake at all. It's been

* This is a verbatim transcription from the BBC tape recording, secured for me by Isabel L. Davis, of Civilian Saucer Intelligence, N.Y.C.

confirmed by other observers. It looks artificial. It's almost incredible that such a thing could have been formed in the first instance, or if it *was* formed, could have lasted during the ages in which the moon has been in existence. You would have expected it either to be disintegrated by temperature variations or by meteor impact.

"*Forbes:* And when you say it looks artificial, what do you mean exactly by that?

"*Dr. Wilkins:* Well, it looks almost like an engineering job.

"*Forbes:* (Exclamation of astonishment.)

"*Dr. Wilkins:* Yes, it is most extraordinary.

"*Forbes:* And is it more or less regular in outline?

"*Dr. Wilkins:* Absolutely regular in outline. That makes it all the more remarkable.

"*Forbes:* And does it cast a shadow?

"*Dr. Wilkins:* Yes, it casts a shadow under a low sun and you can see the sunlight streaming in beneath it."

Next day a brief cable report on Wilkins' historic broadcast appeared in U. S. papers. Significantly, the mysterious structure was called a "natural" bridge, though Wilkins had not used this word once in his broadcast.

But even with this reprieve, the message shook the Pentagon censors. For Dr. Wilkins or some other famous astronomer still could deny the possibility of any natural bridge.

At any time this would have been bad news. But it came just as the silence group was facing a new crisis. Starting in late October, increased saucer sightings, combined with blows from all sides, had driven the UFO censors into a tight corner. . . .

After the Conowingo incident several UFO reports had increased the pressure on the Air Force.

On the afternoon of October 24 a round, silvery, metallic machine streaked above the Massachusetts coast at a speed between 900 and 1200 mph.

That night, in Iowa, state highway police sighted a huge disc, glowing blue-white, near the town of Cascade.

From England, too, the reports came in. Several dramatic sightings had upset the Air Ministry.

On October 18 two British airline pilots, Captain Peter Fletcher and First Officer R. L. Lemon, saw a strange craft flying over the English Channel. It had the appearance of two saucers with their rims together.

In his official report to the Air Ministry, Captain Fletcher said, "We have no doubt whatsoever the object was solid . . . that it was constructed of metal. . . ."

On November 3 there had been an even more startling encounter. Two RAF pilots, Flying Officers T. S. Johnson and C. H. Smythe, had sighted a UFO from their Vampire jet. Moving at tremendous speed, the saucer also was tracked on radar by the 256th Heavy Anti-Aircraft Regiment.

On November 12 the Canadian government revealed it had set up a flying-saucer observatory near Ottawa.

"Defense research scientists," the Ottawa release said, "have never pooh-poohed the flying saucers."

Dr. O. M. Solandt, Chairman of the Defense Research Board, told the press that the government had given orders to ship captains, meteorologists, and other special observers to report UFO's at once.

The wide publicity given the story in this country increased suspicion that the Air Force was covering something up. This infuriated the silence group, but they did not dare to criticize the Canadian government.

Seven days later the British War Office confirmed the saucer encounter and radar report of November 3 and released statements from radarmen and the two RAF pilots.

"Apparently," Frank Edwards remarked on his program that night, "the British War Office and our Air Force have different ideas on trusting the public."

The Air Force was still smarting over this when Captain

Walter Karig's story, "The Official Truth About Flying Saucers," appeared in the *American Weekly Magazine*.

Contradicting the Air Force, Karig revealed that the Utah pictures were still under study. The UFO's, he said, were apparently solids, traveling at speeds never achieved by earthlings. Moreover, there was every evidence of control by intelligent beings.

The following night I heard from the Intelligence officer who had advised me to call Ruppelt for help. He told me Karig had set off a row almost as bad as the one I caused. But all that the censors could do was to lick their wounds and curse Captain Karig in private. For he had too many powerful friends in the Pentagon and on Capitol Hill.

"And that article by Shapley in the November *Atlantic Monthly* scared the hush-hush crowd," the Intelligence officer told me. "Coming from the number-one Harvard astronomer, it could have made headlines all over the world."

I had already seen the article, taken from Dr. Shapley's new book.

After the officer hung up, I remembered one haunting sentence, which followed Shapley's declaration about the millions of inhabited planets. It consisted of just four words:

"We are not alone."

The strange effect it had on me went far beyond the mystery of the saucers.

On many of those millions of planets there must be some very great good—many of the unknown beings must live by a higher code than the one which governs this earth.

"Men, bees and crows," Shapley had said, "could be ridiculously primitive, compared with life on some planets."

Perhaps under the plan of creation there might be many intelligent creatures unknown to us—some perhaps like ourselves, some different. But regardless of their shapes, they would be endowed with thinking minds, with deep emotions. . . .

The phone rang again, sharply cutting in on my thoughts.

It was the call from Detroit, giving me my first word of the Kimross F-89 disaster. The message jerked me back to cold reality.

What was it Arthur C. Clarke had said? As chairman of the British Interplanetary Society, he had given much thought to the creatures from outer space. I remembered something in his book, *The Exploration of Space.*

"What then if we ever encounter races which are scientifically advanced, yet malevolent?" Clarke had asked. In that event, he said, "astronautics [space travel] might open a Pandora's box which could destroy humanity."

But to offset this, Clarke had added: "With superhuman knowledge, there must go equally great compassion and tolerance."

There were many who would not accept that. The Nazis could be said to be scientifically advanced. But few of them knew the meaning of compassion and tolerance.

Malevolent or compassionate—which would they turn out to be, these creatures from outer space?

Had it been an accident over Lake Superior? Or had that F-89 been the victim of devils bent on destruction?

6 The Hidden Orders

The strange Kimross case, coming at the height of a new crisis, forced the silence group into a desperate decision.

For almost two months, during October and November of '53, the censors had fought to hide the startling saucer discoveries. Then suddenly in November they had been faced with a showdown.

By a Presidential directive, Executive Order 10501, the classification of "Restricted" was officially abolished, effective December 15, 1953.

It was a stunning blow to the silence group, for both JANAP 146 and AFR 200-2 were restricted Defense documents. Unless the censors violated President Eisenhower's directive, it looked as if they would have to reveal these two long-hidden blackout orders on request. Besides this, the President's edict blocked a new plan to explain away the saucers through a so-called "Fact Sheet."

Just before the President's order, this remarkable statement had been drawn up to answer the flood of inquiries. After dragging out all the old alibis—such as hoaxes, birds, mirages, and balloons—this document also attempted to offset the key points I had revealed. In an effort to offset the Gulf of Mexico case, when the crew of a B-29 had encountered a mother ship and three saucer formations, the Fact Sheet stated:

"There have been a small number of unexplained reports involving objects spotted officially and detected simultaneously by radar. The objects appeared at nighttime and had the appearance of simple lights."

The exact nature of the "simple lights" caused by the giant mother ship and saucer formations was not explained. There was not even a hint of the dramatic report by the B-29 crew.

This "simple lights" explanation also contradicted the evidence in other radar reports which Intelligence had cleared for me:

1. An official *daytime* report in 1951 from the White Sands Proving Ground, where UFO's were seen through binoculars, tracked by radar, and filmed with movie cameras.

2. The *daytime* jet chase on August 1, 1952, near Dayton, Ohio, when an Air Force pilot, using gun-cameras, photographed a flying disc.

3. The night encounter at Oneida Air Force Base, Japan, August 5, 1952, when control-tower operators saw the *round dark shape* of a saucer behind its glowing light.

Though the Fact Sheet did not name the Utah pictures, it denied that the Air Force had photographs which proved flying saucers existed.

"A few movie-type films have been received," the statement admitted. "But they reveal only pinpoints of light moving across the sky. The images are too small to analyze properly. Since ownership of these films remains with the persons taking them, the Air Force is not in a position to give them out. The owners may do with them as they please."

To top it off, the Fact Sheet denied all charges of secrecy:

"One misconception is that the Air Force is either withholding flying-saucer information from the public or cloaking it beneath a security classification. This is untrue."

This last claim would immediately be branded as false if

JANAP 146 and AFR 200-2 were made public. Now, under the President's new directive, either the Fact Sheet would have to be killed or the silence group would somehow have to keep the two orders hidden.

There was one obvious way out. Before the December 15 deadline, both orders could be upgraded to "Confidential" or "Secret," though to many this would seem to violate the intent of the President's directive.

With AFR 200-2 this device might succeed, since only members of the armed forces were supposed to know of the order. But JANAP 146 posed a harder problem, for its existence was known to thousands of airline pilots, and some of them might talk.

For three weeks the silence group stalled, nervously weighing the dangers. Then word of the Kimross mystery forced a swift decision. Above all, they felt, the implications of this latest saucer encounter would have to be kept from the public.

As quickly as possible, the Fact Sheet was released to the press—to divert attention from the Kimross disaster.

Now the die was cast. The two blackout orders had to be kept under wraps. To avoid the dangers of upgrading, another plan was devised.

When December 15 passed, with neither order made public, I privately met one of the censor-fighters. He told me what had happened.

"They've stamped JANAP 146 'Declassified on December 12,' and if any trouble comes up, they can point to the declassification. They can do the same with AFR 200-2. But actually they're going to sit on the orders as long as they can. They're not going to release them until they're forced to."

Then he gave me copies of both orders.

"I'm not violating security," he said, "because President Eisenhower has abolished the 'Restricted' category. But you can't make these public because they haven't been officially released." *

The next day, with both documents in front of me, I phoned White at the Pentagon.

"I'd like to have copies of the two declassified UFO orders," I told him.

White was silent for a moment. "I don't know what you're talking about," he said.

"I mean the restricted orders that tell pilots to keep UFO reports secret."

"There are no such orders," White replied. "If you read the new Fact Sheet you'll see all witnesses are free to say what they please."

Ten minutes later I got the same answer from Lieutenant Colonel Moncel Monts, a senior PIO.

"Absolutely not," said Monts. "We're not hiding a thing."

Both men, I knew, were acting under instructions to back up official secrecy. What I didn't know, though I should have guessed, was that they also had been told to report any queries I made. My two calls, I learned later, threw a scare into the top UFO censors. Because I was soon to appear on "Town Meeting of the Air," over a coast-to-coast network, they feared I might expose their evasion of President Eisenhower's order.

Two days after this, Frank Edwards called me.

"I just heard some bad news," he said. "Someone in the Air Force is working up another smear against you."

"Who told you?"

Frank named a Washington correspondent. "He wouldn't say who was back of it, but evidently it goes pretty high. He said the story would break in a week or two."

"Thanks for the warning," I said. "It must be tied in with the Town Meeting program. I'm appearing against a science

---

* The extracts shown in the Appendix, pp. 301 and 312, were taken from *official* copies given to me months later.

editor named J. H. Leonard, and he's already put out a statement that my book is based on 'anonymous sources and unidentified authorities.' "

"Sounds as if the hush-hush crowd has been at work," said Frank.

As quickly as possible I checked on Leonard through New York contacts. Since he had not made a full investigation of the saucers, he might possibly have been misled by someone in the Air Force.

For five anxious days I tried to prepare for the threatened smear. Then I suddenly learned I was aiming at the wrong target.

It was Delos Smith, veteran science editor of the United Press, who was planning to denounce me. Convinced that I had deceived the public, he was preparing three articles for the UP's national wires. With his reputation for careful checking, it could be ruinous.

The news reached me on Christmas Eve. When I phoned Smith, he agreed to hold off until I could see him. But I could tell he believed I was guilty.

Before flying to New York, I called the censor-fighter who gave me the blackout orders that had been declassified but not released. He warned me, however, not to show them to Smith.

"You couldn't get him to keep it off-the-record," he said. "It would be too big a scoop for the UP."

But I had to have proof to show Delos Smith. As a last resort I called Albert Chop and got Captain Ruppelt's address.

"I hate to get mixed up in this," Ruppelt said, when I reached him. "But if somebody *is* framing you, it's a dirty trick. I'll wire you a statement you can show Smith."

On December 29, only hours before the Town Meeting program, I met Smith and UP Executive Editor Ferguson in the latter's office. I started to tell the two men how the ATIC cases were cleared. Smith listened coldly, then he abruptly leaned forward, watching my face.

"What if I tell you a certain Air Force general *swears* your book is a complete fraud?"

Even though I'd been prepared, it was still a shock.

"Who told you that?" I demanded.

Smith shook his head. "I can't reveal that now."

"Then let me meet him with you. We'll see if he dares to repeat it."

Smith and the executive editor exchanged glances.

"The United Press certainly doesn't intend any unjust attack on you," said Ferguson.

"Well, here's proof the general is lying." I took out Ruppelt's telegram. Not only had he confirmed ATIC's clearance of the 41 official reports but also the secret analysis of the Utah pictures and the planned press release."

Smith looked up from the wire.

"How do I know this is on the level?"

"You can phone Captain Ruppelt—I'll pay for it." I gave him the number in Long Beach, California.

Slowly Smith's hostile expression changed.

"Come on out to my desk," he said. He carefully reread Ruppelt's message, then went through the Air Force clearance letter and Chop's statements to Lieutenant Colonel Hugh Day.

"All right," he said, "I'll let you tell your side if I do the series. I'll boil it down to a few questions. You can give me your answers and I'll run them."

"That's a fair deal," I said. "But I'll still meet that general with you any time you say."

Even with this problem settled, there was still one danger. For the unknown general might also have given Leonard the same false information.

Actually, though Leonard had asked the Air Force for help, all they had sent him was a routine PIO letter, with extracts from the Fact Sheet. Apparently they had decided to concentrate their attack through Delos Smith.

As soon as I returned home, I called Colonel Monts and told him about the UP story.

"I want to meet that general," I said grimly.

"No general ever told Smith that," said Monts. "We all know those cases were cleared for you."

"Smith didn't imagine it, Colonel. He was dead serious. And if he quotes this Air Force general——"

"He won't!" Monts broke in. "I'll get Charley Corddry, the UP man here, and see that he puts Smith straight."

For the second time in three months I'd had a narrow escape.

It was an uneasy feeling to know that a general was after my scalp. If I only knew who he was, I might be better prepared to defend myself.

That same day I found that the silence group had again banged down the lid on all UFO reports.

To make it appear that nothing was hidden, a number of old sightings had been kept for inspection at the Air Force Press Desk. But curious reporters, noting the gap in dates, had asked for the latest records.

One of these newsmen was Richard Reilly of the Washington *Times-Herald*. Since early December, Reilly, going beyond Press Desk sources, had quizzed several other Air Force officers at the Pentagon. Then, beginning on December 26, he had summed up their contradictions in three sizzling articles.

When Reilly's articles appeared, the silence group angrily ordered an end to such "irregular" interviews. For, deliberately or not, some Air Force officers had crossed up the Fact Sheet and contradicted top Pentagon spokesmen.

Immediately saucer files at ATIC were ordered closed to the press. Back at the Pentagon, PIO's were told to refuse all requests to see UFO reports, including even those previously released.

7 Cover-up at Quantico

The 1954 New Year had started with everything apparently under control.

But within 48 hours the strange Quantico sightings gave the Air Force a new jolt.

For six nights mysterious red-lighted objects had maneuvered over the Marine Corps base at Quantico, Virginia. A Marine detail had searched the tank park where one of the saucers had hovered, as if for a landing. On January 4 this story broke in all the Washington papers.

For 24 hours 30 witnesses—Marine officers and enlisted men—were kept from talking to newsmen. Then on the following night a curious act was staged at Quantico, apparently by Air Force direction.

As darkness fell, newsmen and photographers were assembled for the "official explanation."

Exactly at 6:40 P.M. an airliner with a flashing red light on its tail approached the base. At seven forty-five several lighted weather balloons appeared above the horizon, apparently released only a few miles away. Five minutes later a bright twinkling star was pointed out to the newsmen. Incredible as it seems, newsmen were told that these objects were what had caused the saucer reports.

To back this up, photographers were invited to photograph the flashing taillights at the Washington airport. Using time exposures during an airliner's take-off, they photographed several flashes of light against a dark background.

None of the papers called this a frame-up. But the Washington *Daily News* came close to it. In its report the *News* said:

"Mysterious red lights which have flown over the Quantico Marine base 22 times in the past six nights were officially explained away today as a new type of aircraft navigation light, but most of the Marines who saw them still don't believe that that's what they were.

"In addition the *News* ran into what seems a deliberate attempt to cover up certain facets of the investigation."

The *News* then quoted the Quantico provost marshal, Major E. D. Pomerleau. Pomerleau said the light was sharply delineated and unlike anything he had seen. Moreover, he had heard no aircraft engine—no sound at all.

"But I have friends and a professional reputation," he told the *News*. "As far as I'm concerned just say it's an aircraft navigation light."

When the *News* story first broke, it contained reports that troops had twice been sent into areas where the saucers had descended. On January 4 the Quantico PIO denied these reports.

"We did at no time dispatch troops," he said.

That evening the Washington *News* uncovered this official record:

"A thirteen-man detail arrived at 11:15 P.M. December 30, from Camp Barrett. It made a search of the area in which the light was first seen."

The second official record, the *News* said, revealed another search by troops on the evening of December 31.

The act that was staged later at Quantico, which I thought to be at Air Force instigation, seemed to ridicule the Marines. But this type of explanation set the pace for 1954. From this time on, whenever important UFO sightings leaked out, they were hastily ridiculed or explained away.

By contrast, at the very same time two foreign sightings were being soberly investigated with no attempt at a cover-up.

On January 1 Captain Douglas Barker, an Australian airline pilot, reported a strange flying object moving rapidly in and out of a cloud. After Barker reported his sighting, other Australian pilots came forward with similar reports. At Melbourne, on January 9, a spokesman for the Royal Australian Air Force made this public statement:

"The flying saucers could be interplanetary. We should be able to fly into space in 40 years. Why shouldn't people on other planets have already reached this stage?"

In South Africa an official radar report was under careful investigation. Near the end of 1953 military radar operators had tracked a mysterious object flying across the Cape Peninsula at 1278 miles per hour. As they watched, the saucer flew back and forth, crossing the cape six times before it disappeared. The report was released—in the public interest—by Major F. J. van Nierkerk, chief radar instructor at the School of Coast and Anti-Aircraft Artillery.

Yet in the United States steps were still being taken to conceal the important reports.

Later in January Captain Ed Stone phoned me one evening as I was preparing for a flight to North Bay, Canada.

"I just got in," he said, "but I'm bushed. How about seeing you early tomorrow morning, before you leave? I have something to talk about."

"Is it about the Kimross affair?" I asked.

"No, it's about the green fireballs. I'll tell you tomorrow."

After I hung up, I thought about the mysterious objects known as green fireballs.

The first flurry of reports had come in December, 1948. Night after night huge projectile-like objects had raced over the Southwest. Absolutely silent, they followed a straight course, then exploded without a sound, casting a brilliant green glare for hundreds of miles.

As reports poured in, the Air Force quickly concluded the objects were not meteors but some unknown type of missile.

Designated as "green flares" by the Air Force, these new objects were reported in an analysis on December 27, 1949. In six cases the green flares were described as traveling at terrific speeds, often against the wind, and obviously under control. In a separate investigation known as "Project Twinkle," several of the strange missiles were tracked at speeds of nearly 14,000 miles an hour. After each silent explosion Air Force crews searched a wide area beneath. But not a fragment was ever found—or at least reported by the Air Force.

But an unofficial investigation had been made public by Dr. Lincoln La Paz, Director of the New Mexico Institute of Meteoritics. Dr. La Paz insisted these were no ordinary meteors. Without indicating their source he hinted that they were an unknown type of guided missile.

The next morning, when I went in to see Stone, I took my file on the fireball cases. We went up to the airport mezzanine, where Stone glanced through the file.

"I've heard most of this. What I wanted to ask"—he hesitated—"maybe it sounds silly, but do you know of any accidents caused by the green fireballs?"

"No, though one did explode after passing an airliner about two years ago."

I dug out the report and showed it to Stone. On November 2, 1951, an American Airlines DC-4 had been flying from Los Angeles to Tulsa by way of Dallas. At 7:15 A.M. the airliner was cruising east of Abilene on Airway G-5. The altimeter read 4500 feet.

Suddenly a bright green object streaked past the airliner at the same altitude and holding the same course. As nearly as the crew could judge, the projectile-shaped device was about the size of their plane. As it raced ahead, the pilots saw a white trail, which they took to be exhaust vapor. The DC-4 was cruising at 220 miles an hour, and it was only a matter of seconds before the strange green fireball had shot ahead. Then, to the crew's amazement, the strange missile exploded, shooting red balls of fire in all directions.

"It was like a Fourth of July roman candle," the First Officer said later.

Stone looked up soberly as he finished the report.

"That's new to me—shooting out those red balls. If they'd been close enough to hit the plane it could have been curtains." Then he paused. "There was a Transocean DC-6 crash off Wake Island last July. Have you heard anything about it?"

"Yes. But I thought it was just a routine accident. I haven't seen the CAB report on it yet."

"It's still held up," Stone said. "But I got part of the dope on it from a Transocean pilot I know. It's a very strange thing. This DC-6 was on a flight from Guam to Oakland. They stopped for gas and to get a weather report at Wake. Then, about 7:00 A.M., they took off for Honolulu. There were 50 passengers and eight in the crew. The captain called in an hour and a half later to say everything was okay. They were cruising at 15,000 feet. That's the last report he made.

"Now here's the odd part. When they failed to call in again, the CAA at Wake started an emergency search. The Coast Guard, the Navy, and the Air Force were all alerted. Then—and this is really weird—Wake Island radio picked up some very strange messages on the international distress frequency. They couldn't make head nor tail of them. While this search was going on, several plane crews and search vessels reported seeing green lights or fireballs.

"Early next morning one of the search ships found an empty life raft, and some bodies floating in the water. From what wreckage they recovered they could tell the DC-6 had either dived in like a bat out of hell or gone to pieces in the air. There wasn't the slightest reason for it. The plane had just been inspected and was in perfect shape. The Transocean pilots say it's a complete mystery to them. They also say that Air Force Intelligence was in on it and the CAB has clammed up."

Stone stopped, looked at me.

"Well, what do you think?" he said.

"I don't know, Ed. The radio messages certainly sound queer. But the green fireballs—could they have been flares sent up from one of the life rafts?"

"Absolutely not. That raft inflated itself *after* the wreck. From the condition of the bodies and the wreckage, nobody could have lived for a second—no matter how it occurred."

"I'll ask Caperton about this," I said. "I hope to heaven it wasn't caused by one of the missiles. That Kimross thing was bad enough, and we know that was connected with the UFO's."

Stone stood up. "I don't want it to be true either. But if there is any danger I think pilots should be told, especially when they're carrying passengers."

As Stone turned away, I went over to pick up my flight reservations. I was flying to Canada that morning. The green fireballs were missiles, I had no doubt about that. But why should one be aimed at an airliner? It would be just wanton destruction. . . .

Two days later, at North Bay, I talked with Flying Officer William Scott, in charge of the RCAF Filter Center. Scott told me he took the flying-saucer reports seriously.

"We've received several for which there is no normal explanation," he said. "Whatever the UFO's are, they're worth our serious consideration."

The next day at Ottawa I met W. B. Smith, head of Canada's flying-saucer Project Magnet. I had known Smith since 1950, when he told me that Project Magnet reports indicated the saucers were interplanetary. During my visit Smith showed me the Shirley Bay flying-saucer observatory. The equipment included an ionosphere reactor, an electrical device for measuring sound, a gamma-ray detector, and a gravimeter.

During my visit I told Smith what I had learned since we last talked.

"There's one thing that bothers me," I said. "Remember, in 1950 we thought the saucers must be remote-controlled—that is the ones which made such sharp turns and speeded up so fast." I told him about the Pearl Harbor report. "This creature which the Navy pilot saw must have been able to withstand a terrific number of G's." (One G equals the normal force of gravity.)

"There have been some new developments," said Smith. "I still believe the discs are using electromagnetic power. Besides the earth's magnetic field there are tremendous forces in space which could be tapped. It has been proved now that the sun is a magnet like the earth. Undoubtedly all suns and planets are surrounded by magnetic fields. There are millions of volts in the cosmic clouds of space. This has been proved by the cosmic-ray bombardment of the earth's atmosphere."

Smith paused. "The new point is this. The discs may create their own gravitational field—that is, they could nullify the pull of the earth's gravity. If this is true, then living creatures on board could withstand sharp turns and swift accelerations. Actually, they would feel nothing unusual, for the force propelling the discs would apply simultaneously to every object and every being aboard. They could turn sharply at 5000 miles an hour and never know it."

But for Smith's background and his important position with the Canadian government I might have discredited the idea. The "anti-gravity shield" had been used as a device in hundreds of science-fiction stories, but I had never taken it seriously. As a pilot I knew of the powerful G forces in even such ordinary maneuvers as pulling sharply out of a dive. More than once I had felt myself rammed down in my seat with my vision blurred, though I had never blacked out completely. The idea of a violent turn at 5000 miles an hour, without even feeling it, was fantastic.

Smith looked at me with a dry smile.

"Don't take my word for it. Ask some of your scientists down in the States—that is, if you can get them to talk. I think you'll find your government is working feverishly on it."

"Well, it is hard to believe," I said. "If it's true, it would certainly change the entire picture."

"Part of the picture," said Smith. "For instance, you might have a being from a planet like Jupiter, where the gravity is two and a half times the earth's. Such a creature would be accustomed to tremendous gravitational pull. Here on earth if he took a step, he might bounce 30 or 40 feet in the air, the way you might do on the moon if you didn't wear weighted shoes. But in a space ship the gravitational field could be made identical with that of any planet. So your Jupiter 'man,' or a creature used to a very light gravity like Mars, wouldn't feel any effects at all."

"Could there be any other effects?" I asked.

"Yes. There's one that ties in with the saucers' silence, why there's no sonic boom when the saucers go through the sound barrier."

"If they're fairly high," I said, "you wouldn't hear a boom anyway."

"Yes, but if the discs do have their own gravitational fields, then you wouldn't hear a sound at any altitude."

"Why?" I asked.

"Because the saucer wouldn't hit the sound barrier with a hard impact like a plane. Instead, the air close to it would be dragged along with it by the gravitational field. So there would be a cushion of air molecules around the saucer when it came to the barrier. Beside this, I believe there will be a corona discharge ahead of the saucer caused by the electromagnetic propulsion. This would lessen the transmission of sound waves."

Next day at the Department of Transport Building I had a brief talk with Deputy Minister Baldwin. He told me that flying-saucer sightings were classified by the Canadian Defense Research Board.

"I'm surprised they didn't keep the Shirley Bay Station under wraps," I said.

"Perhaps it would have been better," said Mr. Baldwin. "It received more publicity than anyone expected."

Mr. Baldwin refused to tell me his opinion of the saucers. "However," he said, "this Shirley Bay Station may give us the answers. At least we're making a serious effort to learn what the saucers are."

After leaving Baldwin's office, I wondered whether I should have asked about the Kimross case, since Canadian flyers had been involved in the search. Instead, I decided to question Smith. As head of the telecommunications section, in charge of radio and TV monitoring, he was naturally an expert on radar.

First, I put it up to him as a hypothetical question.

"Suppose you saw the blips of two aircraft—both at the same altitude—suddenly merge on a scope. What would you think?"

"Obviously the two planes collided," Smith answered promptly.

"If someone told you," I said, "that the two blips were actually from objects miles apart, what would you say?"

"I'd say he didn't know anything about radar," Smith replied. "Why? What's this all about?"

"It was a saucer chase." Then I explained what had happened.

When I told him about the plane's disappearance and the Air Force explanation—that the GCI operators had misread the scope—Smith gave me an odd glance.

"Very curious, very curious," he said. He glanced thoughtfully out into the wintry sky.

"Well," I said, "exactly what do you think happened?"

Smith looked down at his desk for a moment.

"Because of the statements your Air Force has made," he said slowly, "I'd rather not try to answer that."

Following my return from Canada, a new series of events quickly jolted the silence group out of its complacency. The first blow fell on February 11, when the Scripps-Howard papers charged that the Air Force knew what the flying saucers were and was hiding the truth for fear of public panic. At the Pentagon a hot denial was planned and then abandoned—reportedly on the advice of the National Security Council. Apparently they hoped to kill the story by the old trick of ignoring it. But this time the Scripps-Howard papers were ready for a fight.

Two days later they released another story, this one by Jim Lucas, one of their top correspondents, a man with hundreds of important contacts, including officers high in the Pentagon.

In a story headed, "Air Force Still Mum," Lucas bluntly exposed official secrecy. Airline pilots, Lucas reported, were sighting between five and ten flying saucers every night. As examples he cited two recent cases.

The most impressive encounter had been between Seattle and Anchorage, Alaska. Soon after taking off from Seattle two Northwest Airline pilots had been startled to see a huge, round machine flying alongside. A bluish fluorescent glow shone from the side of this strange ship. Through binoculars the pilots could see a number of windows or ports. Cautiously they tried to close in for a better look. Each time the mysterious craft either shot ahead or climbed up steeply, then turned and resumed its former position. This continued until they neared Anchorage, Lucas reported. The pilots, he said, had been questioned for two days by Intelligence before going on to Tokyo. They stated that the object was definitely under someone's control.

In the second case a Colonial Airlines captain, flying near Washington, saw a brightly glowing saucer descend steeply from the stratosphere. It flew parallel to the plane for several moments, then swiftly reversed its direction and climbed back into the night. The captain, Lucas said, was a man of mature judgment, a college graduate, and an attorney as well as a pilot.

Lucas also revealed an Intelligence plan to speed up saucer reporting by airline pilots. At the same time, Lucas disclosed, airline pilots were told to keep their reports from the public. Under the denial and ridicule policy a less famous reporter might have been quickly blasted. But Lucas was known for his accuracy. Attacking him might kick back—evidently someone high up in the Pentagon had given him the story.

On this same day, by coincidence, Dr. Clyde Tombaugh gave the censors another headache. In addition to heading the search for the unknown satellites, Dr. Tombaugh also was president of the Las Cruces, New Mexico, Astronomical Society. At a Society meeting, Dr. Tombaugh gave the Las Cruces astronomers a special talk on the moon, including the recent puzzling changes. At the end of his speech he quietly told the astronomers to be on the watch for flying saucers and to report them quickly and accurately. He predicted an increase in saucer operations.

Since Dr. Tombaugh had not asked for secrecy, several members of his audience passed on this information to other astronomers. The Pentagon learned of it immediately.

To add to the Pentagon worries, the Scripps-Howard papers fired another barrage on Monday morning. This one was aimed at violations of the President's classification order. In the sharpest attack of its kind, the Scripps-Howard papers charged that:

1. Instead of killing the restricted label, many military had upgraded documents to "Confidential" or "Secret."
2. Some security officers had created a new grade—"for official use only." By this device even declassified information could not be released to the newspapers.

Though the article did not specifically mention flying saucers, it was clear to the UFO censors that the attack was aimed at the blackout. Two days later, when the Scripps-Howard papers sent reporter Evert Clark for another dig at the Air Force, he was told that saucer sightings had dwindled to practically nothing.

But, as if to give this the lie, new UFO reports began to break into print.

At 2:00 A.M. on February 21 a saucer with flashing lights was sighted above the airport at Rockford, Illinois. Although flying at a high altitude, it was clearly seen by a CAA operator in the airport tower. Half an hour later it was observed by two squads of deputy sheriffs as it circled over Freeport.

Just 24 hours later Ground Observer Corps spotters sighted 14 flying discs at 15,000 feet over York, Pennsylvania. Warning was immediately flashed to the Filter Center at Harrisburg and from there to the Baltimore center.

As the discs flew south, Ground Control radar quickly picked up their track. But when jet fighters streaked up toward the discs, the formation banked away and climbed steeply into the sky.

To complicate the matter, another saucer—perhaps separated from the group—was sighted over nearby Easton, Pennsylvania. Shortly after this a fire broke out in the woods below as a flaming object dropped from the sky. As quickly as possible, Civil Air Patrol planes circled the area and an Air Force detail searched the woods.

Meantime, word of the York sighting had leaked out to the press. For two hours both the York and Baltimore centers denied there had been any sighting. Finally, under pressure from the press, permission was given by the Pentagon for Baltimore to confirm the report.

Ironically, it was on this very day that the *American Aviation Daily* came out with a planted Air Force story pooh-poohing the saucers.

That night Frank Edwards threw a sharp jab at the silence group. After reporting the formation at York, he threw a sardonic question at the Pentagon, quoting the official explanations which had been given to the *American Aviation Daily*:

"Balloons, meteors, reflections, mirages, temperature inversions, birds, weather phenomena—which of these were the saucers at York, gentlemen? What were your jets chasing over Pennsylvania—birds, mirages, or just plain hallucinations?"

8 Satellite Search

On the first day of March, just one week after Frank Edwards' broadcast, Paul Redell gave me a call. He told me he had flown in from the Coast after a stop at Albuquerque.

"I've got some hot news," he said. "Word has just leaked out about the secret search for the unknown satellites. The censors at White Sands are running around in circles trying to figure out what to do."

The information, he told me, had come through Dr. Lincoln La Paz, director of the New Mexico Institute of Meteorites, who was assisting Dr. Clyde Tombaugh in the search. In the February publication of the Astronomical Society of the Pacific, La Paz had mentioned plans for the satellite search. Quoting Tombaugh as his source, he indicated that special telescopic equipment was to be used.

"But La Paz is in on the project," I said. "How did he dare 'break' it?"

"In the first place, he wrote this article before the project was even approved. Also, he mentioned natural objects like asteroids, and he didn't specify that the search was for artificial satellites."

"Then I don't see why White Sands is so worried."

"They've got good reason to be," said Redell. "The press usually overlooks technical articles like that, but a few days ago reporters started asking White Sands a lot of questions. They wanted to know if the satellites really existed, how many there were, and who they belonged to. Army Ordnance Research—they're the ones in charge—started to deny everything. Then someone—I think it was probably Tombaugh—advised them to make a statement instead of covering up."

"What are they going to say?" I asked.

"I don't know, but they can't hold off much longer. I think the AP is after them now."

Just two days later, on March 3, the story broke. The official White Sands statement admitted the Armed Forces were making a sky-sweeping search for "tiny moons" which we could use eventually as space bases and also for launching missiles in time of war. It avoided any hint that the unknown objects were actually interplanetary bases.

The satellites, Dr. Tombaugh explained, could be following orbits near the equator. There the scarcity of observatories would make them harder to locate. Also, since these fast-moving objects would give off very little light, ordinary telescopic cameras would not reveal them. The only way to locate them, Tombaugh stated, would be to use automatic-tracking cameras moving at the same speed as the satellites.

This statement implied that the satellites were natural objects from outer space which had come in and—uncontrolled by intelligent beings—had assumed the exact mathematical courses necessary to orbit the earth.

As soon as I saw the news story, I called Redell.

"Well, it was the only way out," he said. "The idea of natural objects suddenly coming in and orbiting is ridiculous, and they know it. However, it will cover up the thing for a while."

I had some other questions, but Redell was tied up. We made a date to meet that evening.

That afternoon I learned that the Air Force was blaming me for the increase in UFO sightings. Quoting the Air Force, *American Aviation* magazine made this statement:

"The Pentagon definitely attributes the latest rush of saucer reports to Major Donald Keyhoe's book, *Flying Saucers from Outer Space*."

Only minutes later Bob Stirling of the United Press called me.

"We just got a story from Senator Francis Case," he said. "He wrote Secretary Talbott and asked if they were really hiding UFO information, as you said in your book. General Joe W. Kelly answered for Talbott. Here is what he said:

" 'All information on sighting of aerial phenomena, including our conclusions, is unclassified and available to the public.' "

"Bob, that's absolutely untrue! The lid has been down since the end of December."

"Well, since we're running this, you can answer if you want to."

"All right," I said. "You can quote me: I believe a group in the Air Force is misleading the public. There is a blackout on all UFO reports and the Air Force is still withholding the Utah picture analysis."

That night, when I saw Redell, I told him about General Kelly's attack.

"Well, what else can you expect? You're bucking the National Security Council, some of the Pentagon brass, and God knows who else. This is a big deal, Don, maybe the biggest thing that has ever hit this world. Some of those top people are really worried."

We had gone to Redell's office after dinner. On the way he picked up a late paper with news of the White Sands sky search.

"I bet a lot of astronomers laughed when they saw that," Redell commented. "There may be some very tiny asteroids between us and the moon. But just consider the odds against even one big asteroid coming in from outer space and orbiting the earth."

"How many satellites have they tracked?" I asked.

"They've picked up two visually, for a few minutes at a time, but they still don't have the special cameras. They're also having trouble building the radar-tracking gear; but they'll do it eventually. In fact, they started on three special stations, but they had to stop work."

"Where are they?" I said.

"One's in New Mexico, one is outside of Berlin, and the other, I think, is in Arizona. Let's hope they just stop at tracking them," he added drily. "The next time one leaves its orbit and comes down close, some idiot may order the Nike guided missile batteries to cut loose."

"Wait a second," I said. "You mean these satellites have left their orbits?"

"I'm not positive, but I've reason to believe that one came down to about 60,000 feet, ten days ago, over the Atlantic."

I thought back for a moment. "It was ten or 11 days ago when those 14 discs were seen at York. There were several other sightings about that time too."

"It may be only a coincidence," said Redell. "But it's possible, of course, that the big ship came down for a rendezvous, as in the Gulf of Mexico case the Air Force gave you."

"It's plain they've stepped up their observations, moving those bases in so close." I looked across the desk. "Paul, what do you think is back of all this?"

He hesitated for a second.

"There could be a dozen answers, but there's one I've never heard mentioned publicly, though Intelligence certainly must know it. Do you know about Dr. Fritz Zwicky's artificial meteor experiments?"

"No, but I know that he's one of our greatest rocket designers."

"Well, this goes far beyond rockets. I'll give you the main points on the way back to my hotel. It goes back about eight years."

It was only a few blocks to Redell's hotel and we decided to walk.

In 1946, Redell told me, Dr. Zwicky and several Army Ordnance experts had worked out a plan to bombard the moon, Mars, and other solar system planets, with tiny bullet-like projectiles. Under Zwicky's plan, huge rockets would carry scores of the tiny projectiles high into the ionosphere. Near the peak of the main rockets' flight, special explosives called "shaped charges" would hurl the miniature projectiles up into empty space.

It was calculated that these projectiles would have velocities of 50 times the speed of sound or even higher, depending on the peak of the main rocket's flight. Their tremendously high speeds would enable them to escape from the earth's gravitational pull. Passing through the ionosphere, many of these artificial meteors would become electrically charged, causing them to "flash" on impact with the moon. An analysis of these flashes by spectroscopes would provide a means of exploring the moon's surface, determining its chemical elements and atmosphere. After this, similar tests with larger projectiles would be carried out on Mars, Venus, and the other solar-system planets.

We had stopped for a traffic light at 14th and New York Avenue as Redell finished. He gave me a curious glance, waiting for my reaction.

"Were those projectiles actually fired?" I asked him.

"Yes, I'm fairly certain they were," Redell answered. "The first test failed. That was in December of '46, when they used a V-2 rocket to launch them. But Zwicky said they were going to try again. And they've had eight years."

"Paul, this could be deadly serious," I said. "If there is anyone on the moon——"

"Yes, exactly." Redell waited until we crossed the street. "To get the picture, just reverse it. Suppose projectiles like that suddenly bombarded the earth. Even if they didn't hurt anybody or cause any damage, they would set off a scare. A lot of people would take it for a hostile act."

"You're right, and it's possible their bases might be set up so that even small pellets could cause serious trouble."

"That's not the worst of it," Redell said. He stopped as we passed through a crowd in front of Keith's Theater. "After the first test failed, Zwicky suggested a new firing method. They would launch the projectiles from huge balloons sent up to about 100,000 feet. The tiny missiles would be guided, he said, by electronic controls here on earth.

"Once out of our atmosphere, they would travel at about 25,000 miles an hour," Redell went on. "And here's what worries me. Zwicky said some of them might detonate on contact with the moon or solar planets and possibly set off nuclear explosions."

"Good Lord! Missiles like that could cause real trouble. If they hit an inhabited planet—say Mars—the people would certainly believe we were trying to attack them. I'd think that if they did it to us."

"There's another bad angle," said Redell. "If these tests have been carried out recently, the saucer people may think we're trying to hit their satellites. That's why I mentioned our Nike batteries. So far this UFO race hasn't retaliated, though our jets have fired at them several times. But adding up the projectile angle, jet attacks, and then Nike guided missiles, it could be the last straw. I'd hate to think what might happen."

"But if there's any proof of a base on the moon or Mars the government would surely have stopped the tests."

Redell shook his head. "The damage may have already been done."

After I left Redell, I soberly thought over what he had said earlier about the attack on me.

I had felt, since 1950, that the flying-saucer problem was

of tremendous importance. But until recently I still had seen no proof of hostility. Now, even if the new developments did indicate possible danger, I still felt the National Security Council and the Pentagon were wrong to hide the facts from the public.

The next morning I received a letter from a Yale professor who had asked the Air Force two questions about my book:

1. Did the Air Force actually clear the 41 Intelligence reports Major Keyhoe listed in his book?
2. Were the Utah flying-saucer pictures secretly analyzed, as Keyhoe says? If so, what did the analysis show?

"Here is what the Air Force sent me," he wrote. "Who is lying?"

The Air Force answer was a mimeographed letter with a Department of Defense letterhead:

DEPARTMENT OF DEFENSE
Office of Public Information
Washington 25, D. C.

Dear Mr. ———:

In reply to your recent letter, the publication to which you have reference was not submitted to the Air Force for authentication prior to publication. There is no official recognition and the Air Force does not choose to comment upon it.

It is not our policy, nor would it be possible, to review all publications which have been written on this subject. We continually supply unclassified information to various media, and it is entirely possible that some of this information contained in the publication referred to, was supplied by us.

However, we are in no way responsible for the author's interpretation of this material, and of course, his opinions and conclusions are his own. . . .

Sincerely yours,

Robert C. White
1st Lt., U.S.A.F.

Before calling White I tried to reach General Kelly. I phoned his office twice; neither call was returned. Later I phoned White.

"I'd like to see the last three months' UFO reports, since General Kelly says everything is open to the public."

"There is no new policy," said White. "No one can see those reports."

"Then General Kelly deliberately misled Senator Case?"

"No, it was an error."

"General Kelly knows better than that," I said. "He's the Director of Legislative Liaison and he's supposed to be a top expert on military law. Unless he's incompetent, he certainly should know about JANAP 146 and AFR 200-2, as well as the penalties for violating those orders."

White was silent.

"Well, since it's not true, he should retract it," I said.

"That's up to him. For heaven's sake, don't drag me into it."

"All right. But there's one thing you're in on already— that Air Force letter denying my book was authorized."

"That's not aimed at you," White said quickly. "That was drawn up to answer queries about those writers who claim they've talked with space men."

"That may be, but it's being used against me. I've one letter right in front of me which you signed. I'm not blaming you—I know this was done under orders. But it's absolutely misleading. The Air Force not only authorized my using those Intelligence cases, they invited me in there and asked me to name what I wanted. It was all on the level."

"I know that," said White.

"Then this trick letter should be stopped."

"I—well, all I can do is pass on what you say."

After this I went to Senator Case's office, but he was on the Senate floor. So I talked with Rodney Moulton, his press secretary. I showed him Captain Ruppelt's telegram confirming the declassification of Intelligence reports.

"No one can get UFO reports now," I added. "Pick up the phone and try it yourself."

"I'll tell the Senator," said Moulton.

Before I left I gave him a photostat copy of the canceled Utah press release. It was the first time I had let this out of my hands. I knew the uproar it would create among the silence group, and that it might backfire on me, but I had to take the chance.

When I returned to my home, I checked through the saucer reports for the past month. Most of them were typical:

On January 27, the Sacramento Filter Center had been alerted by GOC observers at Fairfield, California. An official report by six observers described a round object, glowing an orange-red, flying at 5000 feet. After a few moments it tilted straight up and disappeared into the clouds.

On March 8, an identical saucer had been sighted at Laredo Air Force Base in Texas. Traveling at tremendous speed, it too had tilted straight up and vanished. On the following night a silent, oval-shaped machine, glowing with an intense blue-white light, was sighted at Cincinnati. As reported by John H. Stewart, a private pilot, it suddenly accelerated and disappeared. Stewart said the strange machine was as large as a DC-6 airliner.

I was still waiting for action from Senator Case's office when on March 12 the long-delayed Transocean crash report appeared. Though the accident had happened on July 12, 1953, the Civil Aeronautics Board report—SA-280—had been held up for eight months.

This official CAB report confirmed what Captain Ed Stone had told me, and gave some additional details.

On the morning of July 12, the Transocean DC-6, Flight 512, had taken off from Wake Island. When the flight failed to make its second scheduled report, the alarm was flashed at Wake.

"Search activity," the Board report said, "involved the Coast Guard, Navy, Air Force, the CAA Communication centers at Honolulu and Wake, civil aircraft and merchant vessels. Several false starts were made because unidentifiable radio transmissions were heard over the 500-kilocycle frequency (the frequency allotted to international distress calls) which were thought to be associated with the missing aircraft."

No other details were given in regard to the strange messages; whether they were in an unknown tongue or in code was never established.

"During the search," CAB reported, "aircraft and surface vessels reported seeing green flares; however, it was concluded that what was thought to be flares were actually meteors or distant aircraft lights."

Next day the USNS *Barrett* sighted 25 bodies floating in a debris of rubber matting, clothing, luggage, life vests, and life rafts. No one was found alive.

"An examination of the bodies and wreckage," said the Board report, "definitely indicates the aircraft crashed with a high impact force. It is not possible to determine whether mechanical or structural failure occurred. However, if such a failure did occur, it must have happened suddenly, without prior warning to the crew. The fact that the aircraft struck the water with a high impact force, indicates that the crew lost control of the aircraft prior to impact.

"The flight last reported flying at 15,000 feet, but nothing was said to indicate any difficulty. Unless there was a sudden radio failure, it is difficult to understand why in that period of time and distance and from that altitude the crew were unable to advise of any difficulty, unless it happened as stated above [suddenly, without warning]."

The DC-6, the Board found, had been in perfect condition when it left Wake Island. The weather reports indicated no dangerous air turbulence.

"The possibility of sabotage was considered," the report

continued. "An investigation which included a security check of every passenger was made at Guam. No evidence of sabotage was found."

After the facts had been weighed for eight months, the CAB officially admitted:

"The Board is unable to determine the probable cause of this accident."

I put down the report with mixed emotions. Unless vital evidence had been withheld, there was no proof that this crash had been caused by a green fireball. That was a relief. But the strange messages were disturbing. The Board's term —"unidentifiable"—suggested a real mystery. For no radio operator would risk playing tricks on the international-distress frequency.

What could have struck down the DC-6 in the few minutes after that last radio report? Unless the plane had been almost instantly destroyed, the crew would have had time to report.

But puzzling as it was, there was nothing to prove it was linked with the flying saucers. It would probably remain one of the great air mysteries, like the strange disappearance of the Manila Clipper which had vanished between Guam and the Philippines in 1944.

I was still puzzling over the strange messages in the Transocean Airlines disaster when, on March 17, Senator Case sent me the following letter:

United States Senate
Committee on Armed Services
Washington, D. C.

March 17, 1954

Major Donald Keyhoe
Alexandria, Virginia

Dear Major Keyhoe:

We are enclosing the photostat which you left here for us to examine some days ago.

You will be interested to know that yesterday we gave a copy of that release to an official of the Air Force and asked for his comments on it. We will advise you later what those comments are.

With best wishes, I am,

Sincerely yours,

Francis Case

When Senator Case's letter reached the Pentagon, with the canceled press release, it set off the row I had expected. In the first excitement the censors decided to deny it. Next morning I had a call from Rodney Moulton.

"We just heard from Lieutenant Colonel Kendall Young in General Kelly's office. He says the Air Force knows absolutely nothing about that press release—they never saw it before."

"I can prove it's true," I said. "I'd like an appointment with Senator Case."

A little later Moulton called me back.

"Colonel Young made a mistake—the Air Force did prepare that release. They're sending some Intelligence officers over to explain everything to Senator Case."

Five days passed. But the Intelligence officers, Moulton told me, still had not shown up.

"They say they are terribly busy right now," Moulton explained.

It sounded like another run-around from the silence group. There was one way to force it into the open, I knew. If they were still stalling in the first week of April, I could expose this intrigue on the NBC-TV network. For I was scheduled to appear April 5 on the Betty White show in Hollywood.

While I waited to hear from Senator Case's office, the tempo of developments suddenly increased.

On March 22, Dr. Lincoln La Paz burst into print, urging the United States to rush the building of satellites. La Paz pointed out the military value of space bases. Whoever established the first station in space, he warned, would win absolute control of the earth.

That same day the silence group received another jolt. Four flying discs were sighted at Hazelton, Pennsylvania, making close passes at an airliner. As the discs flashed past the plane, the captain hurriedly radioed the CAA. This alarm was immediately relayed to the New Castle, Delaware, Air Force Base. The captain's report to the CAA was quickly covered up. But a civilian observer, Michael Kuritz, had revealed the case to newsmen. Other witnesses, on the ground, confirmed the sighting.

At first a New Castle PIO said the saucers might have been jet interceptors. Knowing the airline pilots would have howled if any jets had buzzed them, one reporter started to call the airline. But the PIO quickly abandoned the jet explanation. Refusing to give any further details, he said the report had been sent to Washington. But at the Pentagon the Air Force denied such a report had been received.

The next sighting put the censors in an even worse spot, for it was made by the Deputy Coordinator for Civil Defense at Baltimore.

At 10:32 p.m., on the night of March 24, Deputy Coordinator Adolph Wagner sighted a V-formation of 13 saucers, all of them glowing with a fluorescent blue light. As Wagner watched them, an airliner approached, heading toward Friendship Airport.

Immediately the formation split. One group made a sharp turn toward the airliner, while the other held its course. A moment later a much larger disc swooped down from the clouds. This machine, Wagner estimated, was at least two and a half times larger than the others. As if on a signal, the two groups turned and disappeared in the night.

I learned of this next morning in a call from Lou Corbin, formerly a lieutenant colonel in the Army Reserve. After sighting a saucer in 1947, Corbin had begun a private investigation. Now, as a news commentator at Station WFBR in Baltimore, he had begun to broadcast his findings.

When Corbin phoned me, he described the official attempt to cover up the Baltimore sighting.

"As soon as I heard of it, I called Friendship Airport and got the tower. I didn't say anything about the saucers. I just asked the controller for the traffic pattern between 10:20 and 10:40. Before I had hardly finished, he broke in on me.

" 'It was a flock of geese! They were geese flying over!' he snapped at me. In fact he almost yelled. He hung up before I could say anything else.

"When I called back I got a different tower man. He said he didn't know anything about it. I found later the airliner was an Eastern plane. I can't get anything from them either. But I can tell you this: Air Force Intelligence is going to quiz Wagner privately today."

But that day the story broke in Baltimore papers. The UFO censors were still angered by this when the Marines provided a new worry. At three-thirty that afternoon Captain Don Holland, a Marine Corps jet pilot, saw a flying saucer descend over the guided-missile range in Florida. After streaking downward, it stopped abruptly at 3000 feet. Momentarily amazed—Holland had always scoffed at flying saucers—he hastily banked to try for a gun-camera picture. Almost instantly the strange round machine took off, accelerating at terrific speed.

A few hours later I was tipped off to this by Captain William B. Nash, the Pan American Airways pilot who had reported an eight-disc formation in 1952. Captain Nash, calling from Miami, told me the story was all over town.

"The Air Force will be burned up," I said. "I'm surprised the Marines let it out."

"Well, someone must have okayed it," answered Nash. "Holland told the Miami *Daily News,* and the UP is picking it up. Also Holland is going on TV tonight."

When the UP story came out next morning, I heard the results from a newsman whose beat includes the Pentagon. Since using his right name would get him into trouble, I'll call him Henry Brennard.

Brennard gave me a graphic picture of the silence group's wrath.

"Boy, are they cursing the Marines! First it was your book, then the Quantico deal in January, and now this story of Captain Holland's. They're going to squawk to the commanding general at Miami."

"That ought to be interesting," I said. "The commanding general down there happens to be General William G. Manly. He's a pretty tough Marine."

If the squawk did go through, it backfired on the censors. For General Manly backed Holland to the hilt, confirming that the pilot had seen a round, unidentified object twice the size of his jet. Giving the exact time and location, General Manly also confirmed Holland's report that the saucer had descended over the missile range and then disappeared at high speed.

All that General Manly withheld was the pilot's name. And since this was in perfect accord with the policy stated publicly by General Joe Kelly, the censors could only suffer in silence.

When the morning of April 3 arrived, without any word from General Kelly, I took off for Hollywood. Eight hours later I was in California, a flight most pilots would have thought fantastic 25 years ago. Perhaps, I thought, I shouldn't blame people who refused to believe in flying saucers.

The night before the Betty White show, Captain Ed Ruppelt and I met at the Hollywood Roosevelt Hotel. I told him of the recent attack on me. Then, hoping he would mention the Pearl Harbor case, I asked Ruppelt if he knew of anything big which had startled the Air Force in August of '53.

He gave me a quick look. "You mean that South Dakota case on August 12? It's the only one I know."

"That's a new one to me. What happened?"

"It was an unusual chase, which shook a lot of former skeptics," said Ruppelt. "A GOC observer near Rapid City reported a strange lighted object, and radar confirmed it. An F-84 fighter was vectored in to chase it. The pilot reported he could see the UFO. And the radar operators watched on the scope as he chased it for over 100 miles. When he ran low on fuel and turned back, the UFO reversed its course and followed him all the way to his base."

"Then another F-84 tried it," Ruppelt continued. "The UFO led him about 160 miles north before he gave up. After he turned back, a Filter Center farther north was alerted and they reported the saucer right on course. It was not a canopy reflection or stars or temperature inversion—there just wasn't any explanation for it."

"That report is certainly convincing. Now that you're not on the project any more, can you say what you really believe?"

He hesitated for a moment.

"Well, I've given both sides of the picture in an article for *True*. It will be out this month."

"What did you conclude?"

"Well, I haven't gone as far as Major Dewey Fournet. He's pretty well convinced they're interplanetary."

"But you still haven't said what you believe," I replied.

Ruppelt gave me a level look. "All right. Here's what I concluded in *True*. If the flying saucers exist, they're interplanetary."

Next day, when I was interviewed by Betty White, I repeated General Kelly's statement to Senator Case—that sightings were not kept secret. Then I told her what I knew to be the truth. Since this was a national hook-up, I knew that both General Kelly and Senator Case would quickly hear of my charges.

As soon as I returned from Hollywood, I checked with Senator Case's office.

"We still haven't heard from General Kelly," Moulton told me. "But we'll ask him again. The Senator wants an answer in writing."

This long silence worried me. I had a feeling they were preparing for an all-out attack. They might even claim the clearance sheet was false, that no ATIC cases had been cleared. If that happened I would need help, and quickly. I had hesitated to ask Ruppelt in Hollywood, for he was still in the Air Force Reserve. But with the situation getting worse, I decided to ask him for aid.

I wrote Ruppelt that if he gave me the proof I needed, I would like to make it public in Cleveland, where I was to lecture on April 14.

Five days later, with no reply from Ruppelt, I sent a long telegram to Air Force Secretary Harold Talbott. After repeating General Kelly's statement to Senator Case, I told the Secretary:

"General Joseph Kelly answering for you stated that all 'saucer' reports in Air Force possession were opened to the public. This answer given the United Press appeared in many papers. Later I was told by your Office of Public Information that General Kelly had misled Senator Case by accident and that the reports were still withheld. Will you please tell me which answer is true.

"If General Kelly's statement was correct, then I again request permission to examine the Air Force sighting reports and to see the secret analysis of the Tremonton, Utah, flying-saucer pictures.

"If General Kelly's published statement was not true, would you please explain why it has not been retracted."

After asking Secretary Talbott to give me an answer for

release at Cleveland, I referred to the Air Force letter about my book:

"This letter implies that none of the material is authenticated by the Air Force. The Appendix to my book contains an official Air Force memo, and a list of forty-one sightings specifically declassified for my use . . . Does the Air Force claim that these Intelligence sighting reports were never released to me and that the official Air Force memo and list are false?

"I sincerely hope, Mr. Secretary, that you will order all the facts of the seven-year 'saucer' investigation to be made public. Withholding this information is not only unfair to the American people but is, I believe, inherently dangerous."

When I took off for Cleveland, there was still no answer from Secretary Talbott. (During his entire tenure of office he refused to answer this wire.)

On my arrival at Cleveland, I found an air-mail special from Captain Ruppelt, confirming that the Air Force had cooperated with me in 1952 and '53, declassifying reports for my use.*

Ruppelt had made five points clear:

1. These classified sighting reports had been cleared for me at the request of Air Force Intelligence and the Office of Public Information. All this information had been declassified by Ruppelt's superiors at the Air Technical Intelligence Center.

2. The ATIC material I listed had been correctly quoted.

3. The Utah pictures analysis had been classified. The press release he had prepared at Dayton had not been made public.

4. The letter by Albert M. Chop to Henry Holt and Company, which the silence group had attacked, was honest and correct in all respects.

"If the reported speed and maneuvers of the reported

---

* A verbatim copy of this letter appears in the Appendix, p. 307.

objects are correct," Ruppelt added, "I also agree that they must be from another planet, as our level of technical know-how is not high enough to build such craft."

Many Air Force officers, he said, agreed on this point. But the official stand was that all the reports were incorrect.

5. Dr. Donald Menzel's "explaining away" theory—that UFO's were sun dogs, halos, light refractions, and so forth—had been rejected by ATIC except in a few cases which had been written off as such.

"This," Ruppelt concluded, "was communicated to you through the Defense Department, cleared by my superiors."

I reread the letter, realizing how much courage it had taken for Ruppelt to let me use it publicly. For it was bound to infuriate some UFO censors, though no violation of security was involved. If General Kelly stuck to his charges, I now had a powerful weapon.

That night I made the letter public during my talk before the Cleveland Aero Club and guests. Afterward, form letters to be sent to Secretary Talbott were distributed among the audience. The Aero Club had included this pointed question at my suggestion:

"Were the ATIC sightings Major Keyhoe lists in his book actually declassified for him as he claimed, or is his claim false?"

Soon after my return from Cleveland, the Kelly-Case affair came to a climax.

After my appearance on the Betty White show, the Air Force broke its promise to send Intelligence Officers to talk with Senator Case. If they gave him the whole story they feared he might not agree to hide the facts from the public. Though informed of my Cleveland plans by the telegram to Secretary Talbott, General Kelly had waited until April 14 to answer the Senator.

A few days later Senator Case's office sent me a copy of the letter. Although they told me I could make it public, for me to have quoted it directly would have required General Kelly's permission. Since a request for this permission has met with silence, I am now paraphrasing the exact wording.

Dated April 14, 1954, the letter contained these statements:

1. It was unfortunate the information given to Senator Case on February 24 was forwarded at a time when the Air Force was revising its report on unidentified flying objects.

2. General Kelly's first answer was superseded by a more recent report, which he had received after writing Senator Case.

3. The canceled Utah picture press release was only a PIO's personal opinion and was not given out because it was not newsworthy.

Since the Utah press release had been carefully prepared by Intelligence officers, this seemed to me a deliberate evasion, if not actually false. But even though General Kelly failed to retract his published statement, his admissions had at least set the record straight for Senator Case.

9 Mystery on Mars

Shortly after the conclusion of the Kelly-Case affair I learned, through Frank Edwards, of a silence-group plan to block reports about Mars.

Since 1947 each close approach of Mars—at 26-month intervals—had brought a sudden increase in flying-saucer sightings. This year, on July 2, 1954, the elliptical orbits of the earth and Mars were to bring the red planet closer than usual—to within 40,000,000 miles of the earth.

From their seven-year records, the UFO censors knew they faced a rapid increase in saucer reports.

Though most of the military encounters might be kept under cover, other sightings were bound to become known. If they equaled the tremendous number in '52—more than 2000 during the Mars opposition—they could set off another wave of hysteria.

This in itself was serious, but in addition the silence group faced a new danger. To observe the red planet as it neared the earth, a 24-hour, round-the-world "astronomers' patrol" had been planned by an international Mars Committee.

Included in this group were prominent astronomers, astrophysicists, and meteorologists of 17 countries, including such countries as the United States, France, Italy, Turkey, India, Japan, Australia, South Africa, Java, Egypt, and Argentina.

Since the Mars Committee plans were first announced,

they had worried the silence group. For this world-wide observation was certain to focus public attention on Mars just at the time when sightings were expected to increase.

Some of the Mars Committee had already admitted that life of some kind probably existed on the planet. Though most of them hedged on the question of intelligent beings, a few—following the theories of Percival Lowell—had privately admitted their belief that such a race did exist.

A final Mars Committee meeting had been scheduled for March 29, to be held in Washington. Headed by the world's greatest Mars expert, Dr. E. C. Slipher of Lowell Observatory, the committee had agreed to answer questions from the press.

If newsmen put pointed questions to these Mars experts, they could easily uncover a mass of evidence indicating that the planet was inhabited. For there was a long history to support such a claim.

From the beginning of recorded observations Mars had been a mystery, with a score of riddles to plague astronomers and excite the imagination. Over a century ago, Sir John Herschel, the noted English astronomer, had announced his belief that Mars was a planet with "continents and seas." Later in the nineteenth century most astronomers discarded Herschel's theory. Though the strange dark areas on Mars were still called *maria* or seas, astronomers believed they were oases, which stood out in contrast against the Martian deserts.

By this time the basic facts about Mars were well known. Its diameter was approximately 4200 miles, compared with 8000 miles for the earth. Because of its smaller size, its gravitational pull was only three eighths that of our planet, so that a 150-pound earth man would weigh, on Mars, only 56 pounds. The Martian year lasted 687 days, with its seasons twice as long as ours. Its atmosphere, believed once to have contained a large amount of oxygen, seemed to have become too rare to support the type of life existing on earth. Because of this and the bitterly cold nights, Mars until 1877 was considered a barren planet, devoid of any life but the most primitive vegetation.

Then, in 1877, an Italian astronomer, Giovanni Schiaparelli, made a startling discovery at Milan. During an unusually close approach of Mars, he discovered a geometrical network of lines connecting the oases and apparently linked with the melting polar ice caps.

Schiaparelli's designation *canali*, which means "channels," was popularly taken to mean "canals." And Schiaparelli himself hinted they might be artificial waterways.

"Their being drawn with absolute geometrical precision," he said, "as if the work of rule or compass, has led some to see in them the work of intelligent beings. I am very careful not to combat this supposition."

During this same close approach in 1877 Mars' two moons were discovered, and named Phobos and Deimos. As the world's astronomers began to watch these moons, they were puzzled by the movement of Phobos, the object closer to Mars. For it followed a peculiar orbit, apparently not in accord with the natural laws of the universe. But with *artificial* satellites then undreamed of, there was no suggestion that it might be a space station, under control of intelligent beings.

Inspired by Schiaparelli's *canali* discovery, Percival Lowell, one of Harvard's most brilliant honor graduates, built an observatory at Flagstaff, Arizona, to watch the red planet. From 1894 to 1915 Lowell and his staff made thousands of observations. After mapping hundreds of canals—the final figure was nearly 700—Lowell dramatically announced:

"Mars is inhabited. We have absolute proof."

The canal network, Lowell explained, was a vast irrigation system built to carry water from the enormous polar ice caps when they melted in the Martian spring. The network lines they had mapped, he said, were not actually the canals themselves, which would be relatively narrow, but were wide fertile belts on the canal banks, like the areas along the Nile valley.

In the Martian winter, Lowell found, the polar ice caps extended almost halfway to the planet's equator. But in summer the south polar cap melted completely, and the north cap shrank to a fraction of its winter size.

Though Lowell insisted that Mars was inhabited by an intelligent race, he added that life there probably would not resemble life on the earth. Lowell's sensational claims were immediately attacked by many astronomers. Some bitterly denied that the canals even existed.

Until 1937 the fight raged on, with little new evidence added. In this year, however, the famous Japanese expert on Mars, Dr. Tsuneo Saheki, reported seeing a strange bright flare on Mars. Though he was careful not to call it a "signal," neither Saheki nor other astronomers could explain it.

In 1939 Dr. Slipher—even then the leading authority on Mars—reported a mysterious change in the Solis Lacus region, a dark area he described as approximately the size of the United States. The change, he reported, indicated a new expansion.

In succeeding years Dr. Slipher and several Mars experts made another puzzling discovery, known as the "blue clearing." Only when Mars is close to the earth is it possible to photograph the planet with a blue filter. At other times something like a hazy blanket surrounds the planet. Continual observations by astronomers revealed that this peculiar haze, or atmospheric layer, served to screen out harmful ultraviolet rays. Without this protection, these powerful rays from the sun would easily pierce the thin Martian atmosphere, probably killing any plant and animal life which existed.

But during Mars' close approaches to the earth it was

found that the strange bluish "haze" disappeared for several days. During these "blue clearings" observation from the earth was greatly improved, and unique blue-filter photographs revealed many details not shown in other pictures.

The usual spread of growth along the canal banks and at the oases stopped during the blue clearing. As soon as the clearing ended, normal growth was resumed. Though the idea seemed fantastic, it was almost as if the blue haze had been deliberately dissipated, perhaps to enable Martians to get a better glimpse of the neighboring earth.

In 1949 Dr. Saheki posed a new riddle for the world's Mars experts. On December 9 Saheki witnessed a brilliant glow on Mars, which lasted several minutes. To have been so brightly visible across millions of miles, the flare would have had to have been tremendous. After rejecting all other explanations, Saheki suggested it might have been an atomic explosion. Refusing to elaborate, he mysteriously said this could be discussed more adequately by the press than by astronomers.

Early the following year Dr. Saheki's curious statements were analyzed by John J. O'Neill, who later disclosed the existence of the moon bridge.

If it *had* been an artificial atomic explosion, said O'Neill, there were only two possible answers: first, that intelligent beings on Mars had exploded an atomic bomb; second, that Mars had been struck by some type of missile fired from the earth, which had set off an atomic explosion.

If O'Neill considered the possibility that this was one of the "artificial meteors" designed by Dr. Fritz Zwicky, he did not disclose it.

"The cause of the explosion," he concluded, "remains a mystery."

The same year, as Mars neared the earth, there was a sudden outburst of flying-saucer sightings.

The following year, on December 8, 1951, Dr. Saheki and

other astronomers reported sighting a new mysterious flash of light on Mars. According to some observers, it seemed to come from a huge, eerily glowing cloud. This report electrified many Mars experts.

In one of the leading American astronomical journals, *The Strolling Astronomer,* it was described as "an extremely brilliant flash, an exploding cloud of brief duration on Mars, certainly one of the most extraordinary phenomena ever recorded by students of Mars."

Then on December 27, many astronomers who habitually had watched the red planet saw another puzzling cloud. This was described by *The Strolling Astronomer* as ". . . the most conspicuous cloud, brilliant and striking, on Mars."

By now it was apparent to most Mars authorities that these could not be ordinary clouds—if they were clouds at all. First, to be seen from the earth they would have had to be gigantic. Second, to appear so dazzling through telescopes, the light source would have had to be equal in brilliance to an A-bomb blast.

The long duration of some observations, and reports that the strange "clouds" seemed motionless, led to a new suggestion. Perhaps the brilliant glare came from enormous glowing areas on Mars' surface. Though most astronomers scoffed at the idea of colossal signal lights, no one could explain the enigma.

This idea gained force the spring of 1952, when, once again, Mars neared the earth. As before, UFO sightings rapidly increased. Again astronomers witnessed the peculiar blue clearing when Mars was in opposition.

Then on April 16, 1952, as Mars was almost at its closest approach, astronomers again saw a mysterious phenomenon: a huge, double cloud that stood 60 to 90 miles above the surface of Mars in the region Eridania. This was so startling that even the conservative *Strolling Astronomer* described it as "the most interesting Martian cloud of all our records."

There were hundreds of other strange reports going back through the years. Some were privately logged at observatories around the world. Others were described in astronomers' journals. Though this mass of evidence was not proof of life on the planet, few of the skeptics could advance another reasonable explanation.

Yet, until the end of March, 1954, when the Mars Committee met at Washington, very little of this was known to the general public.

But the Mars experts could quickly change that, if they decided to talk.

There were three men who worried the silence group. Foremost was Dr. Slipher, who had seen all the evidence Percival Lowell had acquired. Like Lowell, Slipher had dedicated his life to the study of Mars. There were rumors that he, also, was convinced that Mars was inhabited, though he had not admitted it publicly.

As joint chairman of the Mars Committee, Dr. Slipher would have access to Mars reports from all over the world. And he himself was scheduled to make special observations at the Lamont Hussey Observatory, at Blomfontein, South Africa, where Mars, swinging below our equator, would pass overhead each night.

The second man the censors feared was Dr. Harold C. Urey, famous astrophysicist and former member of the Atomic Energy Commission. It was known that Dr. Urey privately agreed with Dr. Harlow Shapley about there being countless inhabited planets—and he had not ruled out Mars.

The third man was Dr. Seymour L. Hess, professor of Meteorology at Florida State University. In 1950, while stationed at Lowell Observatory, Dr. Hess had seen and publicly reported a flying disc. He was the first of the top-level astronomers who dared to risk his professional reputation.

Any attempt to silence these men was likely to boomerang.

The censors could only wait and hope that no vital information would be revealed at the Mars Committee conference.

This conference, on March 29, was directed by Dr. Slipher. At the outset he and the other experts told the press they expected to find evidence of life on Mars.

Dr. Urey added that this would be one of the most startling discoveries in man's history, for it would show that life can exist not merely on the earth but on any planet where conditions are favorable.

The Mars Committee and the government, Slipher disclosed, were working on plans to use artificial satellites from which Mars could be observed. These satellites, he said, would be launched to circle the earth.

But when reporters quickly questioned him about the satellites, Dr. Slipher refused to comment further. Following this revelation Dr. Slipher stated that news bulletins would be released from time to time during the "Mars Patrol."

"What if you find proof that there is life on Mars?" one newsman asked him.

"I'll announce it to the world!" answered the astronomer.

When word of this reached the silence group, there was consternation. News bulletins about Mars could send the entire country—the whole world—into a fever of excitement. If such bulletins coincided with the expected increase in saucer sightings, no one could miss the connection.

The censors' dismay increased when the *Reader's Digest*, in its April issue, published a challenging article called, "Is There Life on Mars?"

"Scientists generally agree," said the *Digest*, "that life *of some kind* exists on the red planet."

Surprisingly, the article implied that there might be intelligent creatures similar to beings on earth. This was based on the widely held scientific belief that Mars at one time had had an atmosphere like our own. The *Digest* explained that as the oxygen content dwindled, an intelligent race could have learned to manufacture its own oxygen.

Also, said the *Digest,* such an intelligent race could have had "millions of years" to conquer the temperature problems. (In April, 1949, the Air Force had publicly suggested that a Martian race might have built underground cities for just this purpose.)

Citing Lowell's long investigation, the article reported his conviction that Mars, gradually losing its water supply, was a dying planet.

Then came the *Digest* comment which shocked the silence group:

"And presumably the Martians, an intelligent race, would be feverishly hunting around for other planets to which they could migrate. Earth was the closest, most suitable neighbor."

In any widely read magazine this would have been seriously disturbing. But to appear in the *Reader's Digest,* to be read by millions, was especially dangerous.

This reference to the "dying planet" tied in directly with the saucer explanation put forth by a high Air Force Intelligence officer, Colonel William C. Odell, which I had mentioned in *Flying Saucers from Outer Space.*

In almost the same words Colonel Odell had indicated that the flying saucers came from a dying planet, and that the unknown space race was surveying the earth to see if it was suitable for a new home.

Now, the censors knew, they would have to block the Mars Committee plans for world-wide publicity. Even more urgent, they would have to stop Dr. Slipher, if possible, from making any dramatic announcement that Mars was inhabited.

The need for this silence was quickly emphasized by the new and startling UFO reports that poured in as Mars approached the earth.

Just before midnight on April 14, United Airlines Flight

193 had almost been hit by an unknown machine over Long
Beach, California. To avoid collision Captain John M. Schidel had whipped the plane into a steep climbing turn. A
passenger, Cose Barber, of North Hollywood, had been
thrown to the floor, his left leg broken. The stewardess had
fractured an ankle.

Hurriedly, Schidel called the Los Angeles tower. But a
quick check showed no other planes in the area. Schidel's
radio report was picked up by a newspaper. When he landed,
however, reporters were kept from questioning him.

My first tip on this came from an American Airlines pilot
just in from the Coast. We had met some time before, when
I was preparing an air-safety article for *Parade* magazine.

"This couldn't have been another plane," the American
pilot said. "It was moving too fast. Schidel told the CAA it
was in sight hardly two seconds. It came out of nowhere,
heading straight at him."

"Did he get a good look?" I asked.

"No. All he saw were blurred lights. It sounds like one of
those 'rotating light' UFO's that Air Force colonel saw in
Japan."

The CAB report, signed by Investigator R. A. Reed, confirmed the near-collision.

"Flight 193 was flying at 5000 feet in a clear sky," stated
Reed, "when an unknown craft abruptly appeared. To date
the other aircraft has not been identified."

But Captain Schidel's statement, included in the CAB
report, made it plain this was no ordinary aircraft.

"It appeared so suddenly," he said, "it was as if it was flying dark and had just turned its navigation lights on. I can
remember thinking—red light on the right and coming fast.
It was in sight just two seconds and made no movement to
avoid me. After disappearing under our nose we never saw
it again."

Air Force Intelligence moved quickly to keep the story

quiet. For by now the weird "pitted windshield" story had hit the headlines, and they hoped to avoid any link with the flying saucers.

This peculiar epidemic had begun in the state of Washington. At Seattle motorists by the hundreds complained about a mysterious pockmarking of their windshields. Police and newspaper switchboards were swamped as complaints mounted. By April 16 thousands of reports were pouring in from as far east as Canton, Ohio.

In many cases small blobs or pellets, of a brown substance, were seen to strike windshields, greenhouses, and jet-plane canopies. When this substance was wiped off, tiny pits were found in the glass and plastic surfaces.

In other cases the pits suddenly appeared in the windshields without the brown substance, many times before motorists' eyes.

The first account I read carried a debunking explanation by a University of Washington professor. He claimed that it was only mass hysteria or windshield marks from flying gravel. But new reports, backed by photographs, quickly knocked this answer flat. For now the strange pockmarks were appearing by the score on cars parked in lots where there was no gravel.

In an emergency message to President Eisenhower, Mayor Allan Pomeroy of Seattle asked for federal help. Laboratory tests, he said, showed the strange substance falling from the skies could be atomic material.

At Canton, Ohio, police revealed that an identical outbreak had begun 12 days before when about 600 windshields had been pitted in Canton and nearby areas. At first the Canton police believed the pellets were being fired from spring-guns. In some cases tiny holes had been drilled through the windshields. But tests with air rifles, stones, and other weapons failed to duplicate the marks. Even while these tests were going on, 63 more windshields were pitted on a guarded parking lot.

As I finished the Canton report I suddenly thought of Dr. Zwicky's artificial meteor experiments. Could these mysterious pittings possibly be linked with similar tests on the moon or the satellites? If Dr. Zwicky's tests had been carried out and the miniature projectiles had struck the moon or Mars, they might have caused retaliation. Perhaps this was a first warning, deliberately harmless, in case we were planning to fire larger and more destructive rockets at the moon and the planets.

The pitting mystery was still in the front pages when a strange UFO report came in from Alaska.

On the night of April 21, a flying saucer had made four quick passes across Cook Inlet at Anchorage, Alaska. Seen through binoculars, it paced a nearby plane for a moment, then raced back over the inlet, its glowing shape clearly reflected in the water. The sighting was immediately reported to Air Force Intelligence at Elmendorf Field.

Despite Pentagon secrecy orders, Intelligence officers told city police that flying saucers had been sighted repeatedly over Cook Inlet for the last three weeks. This strange admission broke as a front-page story with banner headlines in the Anchorage *Daily News*.

Two days later another dramatic report was flashed to Washington.

On April 23, a Pan American airliner, piloted by Captain Jack Adriance, was flying at 20,000 feet between Puerto Rico and New York. Suddenly a call came from another Pan American plane more than 200 miles behind.

A strange flying object, the other captain reported, had just streaked past.

"It's headed straight toward you," said the pilot. "It's round and pulsating with an orange-greenish light."

A few moments later Captain Adriance was amazed to

see the object—or an identical one—flash past his airliner. Cutting in his microphone, he called Captain Ned Mullen, who was piloting another Pan American flight up ahead. In a few minutes Mullen radioed back that the mysterious UFO had just passed him, disappearing in seconds.

When this amazing report, backed by three veteran PAA pilots, reached Washington, it stunned even those who knew of the UFOs' fantastic performance. For the speeds reported were incredible—but for the three crews' confirmation few people would have believed it.

This was a dangerous report and attempts were quickly made to suppress it. But Captain Adriance, astonished by the sighting, told other pilots when he landed, and word soon began to spread. Since he had not made a CIRVIS report, under JANAP 146, the Air Force could not touch him. Luckily the press wire services did not pick it up and few of the public ever heard of this sensational incident.

It was at this time that Captain Ed Ruppelt's article appeared in *True* magazine. Confirming the secret analysis of the Utah pictures, it also revealed dramatic sightings which baffled Intelligence. In addition, it showed that ATIC had rejected Dr. Menzel's natural-phenomena theories, which purported to explain these mysterious cases. But far more striking than this was Ruppelt's summary statement:

"If the flying saucers exist, they are interplanetary."

In the hubbub Ruppelt's article set off, he was accused of violating security—though at the same time the Air Force publicly insisted that nothing was being hidden. Since the Air Force itself had said no security was involved, there was nothing they could do.

Following this series of blows, the silence group made a new effort to keep everything under cover. When questioning UFO witnesses, Intelligence officers were instructed to warn them not to talk. The CAA and the Civil Aeronautics Board were reminded of JANAP 146 and directed to keep all saucer reports confidential. Again, the Army, Navy, and the Marine Corps were reminded that the Air Force had charge of the flying-saucer investigation, and that reports were to be kept from the public.

Some of the silence group believed this would bring the situation under control. But at the Air Force Press Desk there was no such illusion. They knew by now it was impossible to maintain the blackout. Too many people, including high Air Force officers, wanted the facts told. And with sightings steadily increasing, there were bound to be more leaks.

Proof of this was not long in coming. Barely had the new orders gone out when a hasty message from Oklahoma gave the censors a solar-plexus blow. In 24 hours an oil-company magazine would be in the mails with an article called "We Saw Flying Saucers." Based on an official UFO report, the article could blow everything wide open.

The sightings it described had occurred early in '54 at South Cole Creek—a Phillips Petroleum Company project 25 miles east of Casper, Wyoming. At 11:30 A.M. on a Sunday morning eight flying saucers had maneuvered over South Cole Creek. Suddenly, accelerating at tremendous speed, they formed a straight line. Watched by a dozen witnesses, they next descended as if about to land, then swiftly climbed into the sky.

All the observers agreed they flew silently and appeared to be under intelligent control. When one witness, Mrs. Marge Michaelis, reported this to the Casper Air Force Detachment, the commanding officer told her an identical formation had been sighted at the same hour by pipeline workers.

After calling the Pentagon, the C.O. told Mrs. Michaelis he had received important news. He had been told, he said, that "Washington knows what the saucers are."

This was in flat contradiction to the Pentagon's public claims.

That the Pentagon made such an admission was in itself amazing. Realizing the implications, Mrs. Michaelis—who had then been made a GOC supervisor—wrote a complete report for the Phillips Petroleum magazine, *Philnews*.

When word of this article reached the Pentagon, suppression of the magazine was first considered. It could have been done, just as government agents had seized and suppressed an issue of *Scientific American* some time before because of certain comments on atomic-energy developments. But the Phillips Company would undoubtedly protest and thus focus attention on the story. Instead, the Pentagon decided to keep silent, on the chance that the wire services might overlook the story. For the *Philnews* was a specialized trade journal with a limited circulation.

My first knowledge of this came when Henry Brennard drove out to my house that night.

"I've got something hot," he said. He showed me an advance copy of the *Philnews*, sent to him confidentially by someone in the Phillips Company.

"If it's true this is terrific," I said.

"It's true, all right. Some of the Pentagon boys blew their tops when they found out. It backs up the Scripps-Howard story that the Air Force knows the answer and is scared to tell the public."

I was due to take off that evening for a talk at Lafayette College the next day. Before I left I saw Redell and showed him the *Philnews* article. He shook his head:

"God help that C.O. He'll wish he'd never been born."

"I wonder how much the Pentagon does know," I said, "and whether or not the UFO beings are friendly."

Redell got up and closed the door to his office anteroom. "That secretary of mine doesn't believe in saucers and I'm in no mood for wisecracks today." He gave me an ironic look. "It's a queer thing, all the time you've spent on this, you've never really faced it."

"Faced what?" I said, a little nettled.

"Well," Redell answered, "you've said it could add up to the greatest adventure of all time, some advanced race helping us out——"

"Why not? They might teach us things it would take us a thousand years to learn otherwise. Maybe we could end all disease. They'd certainly be ahead of us technically."

"I grant that. But how are they going to teach us? Will they say, 'Here's all the knowledge, now you're free to use it'? Or will they say, 'This is the way *we* do it—this is what's good for you'?"

"You mean we'd be regimented?"

Redell shrugged. "These beings could be the kindliest creatures in the world—from their viewpoint. But to them we might seem like infants that had to be brought up the right way."

I was silent for a moment. "You could be right," I said finally.

"It might turn out perfectly well," Redell observed. "But I like it here the way it is now. I like to do what I want when I please."

10 "Ground All Planes!"

An hour before I boarded the plane for my trip to Lafayette College, word of a terrifying incident in Utah reached me.

At midnight, on May 1, a terrific explosion had shaken the area from Clarkston south to Paradise. Within seconds police switchboards were swamped. At Logan City frightened residents reported their houses were shaken as if by a bomb blast.

From Clarkston to Paradise, a distance of some 25 miles, came reports that a brilliant object had been seen in the sky just before the explosion. Some frightened observers described it as a glowing ball, plunging at tremendous speed. Others said there had been a dazzling flash as the strange object struck the ground.

A quick check was made with Hill Air Force Base and the Salt Lake City Airport, 70 miles to the south. But no plane, military or commercial, had been anywhere near the area.

It was early the next morning before searchers found the crater—a hole 16 feet wide and six feet deep. Earth and sod had been scattered for more than 100 yards.

Dr. Lincoln La Paz was immediately flown from New Mexico to take charge of the excavation. It was hoped that some clue to the mystery would be uncovered.

Whether by coincidence or not, three hours before the

Utah explosion a formation of six flying saucers had been sighted over Port Townsend, Washington. Glowing a bright yellow, the round machines were seen by Sheriff Peter J. Naughton as they circled in echelon.

Quickly Sheriff Naughton phoned a report to Payne Air Force Base near Tacoma. Minutes later he received an urgent call from Payne Field Operations.

"Ground all planes at Port Townsend!" he was told. "Interceptors are coming in with live ammunition."

For at least two years there had been a standing order that pilots could not fire on UFO's unless the saucers proved hostile. Though the instruction from Payne Field did not prove a change in this order, it did point up the seriousness of the Port Townsend incident. Jet pilots would not be preparing to fire rockets at reflections or hallucinations.

To the public the Payne Field command to Sheriff Naughton should have been proof that the Air Force knew the saucers were solid objects. But few people ever learned of this significant affair.

Two days after the Lafayette College talk I flew to Kansas City.

After we took off I went back to the lounge and picked up a copy of *Newsweek*. In its "Periscope" section I found an item which put a new face on the pitted-windshield mystery:

"Dayton, Ohio. The Air Matériel Command is quietly joining other research agencies in trying to determine just what causes pockmarked windshields. A top team of scientists and officers is traveling the country studying the problem. The Air Force regards it with deadly seriousness."

I thought back over the latest reports, trying to find a clue. The strange pits had now appeared in many windowpanes, and the windshield reports had multiplied. At Antioch College, Ohio, a scientist had examined cars with pitted windshields. In many cases, he told the Associated Press, small blobs and dirt coatings on car tops had proved radioactive.

When this report was linked with the possibility of an H-bomb fallout, the connection was quickly denied by the Atomic Energy Commission and the Defense Department. But the Air Matériel Command investigation showed that something strange was falling from the sky.

As we neared Kansas City I started to check over my lecture material. Up to then my seat mate, a gray-haired, serious-looking man about 57, had been absorbed in a mystery book. When I took out a copy of *Flying Saucers from Outer Space* to make some notes, he glanced at me curiously. After a minute or so he leaned over.

"Do you really believe in those things?" he asked me.

I told him I did. He shook his head.

"I'm amazed—please don't take offense—I just can't understand why so many people believe those flying-saucer stories —even some of my best friends."

"Hundreds of pilots and trained observers have seen these things," I remarked.

"Just mass hysteria. And this idea that they come from other planets—why it's absolutely ridiculous."

I opened the book to the Gulf of Mexico mother-ship case.

"Here's an official Air Force report," I said. "It proves pretty conclusively that the flying saucers are space ships" ... I held out the book.

"I wouldn't be caught dead reading that stuff," he exclaimed. "It's all bunk—the Air Force says so."

He went back to his mystery book. It was not my first encounter with a nonbeliever. There had always been some in my audiences, though many people accepted the interplanetary answer. Yet it was inevitable that millions of people would refuse even to consider the possibility.

The reasons, I recalled, had been summed up accurately

by the *American Scandinavian Magazine* on November 15, 1953.

Written by F. Schilp Haman, the article explained the public resistance:

"When anything fundamentally new comes up there are hoaxes, rumors, controversies, name-calling, and even persecutions. . . .

"There have been many blows to the ego of men on this sad little planet, but through it all there persisted the fond belief that mentally we were still out in front, still on top.

"One thing is certain. The human race won't lightly give up the feeling of security it cherishes or the pet superstition that it constitutes the acme of intelligence in the universe. This monopoly of brains it believes it has is a deep-seated, near-religious conviction."

On the return trip from Kansas City I changed planes at Chicago. At the airport I saw a front-page UP story from New Orleans headed, "Moon Road Reported." On the night of May 6 an experienced private astronomer, Frank Manning, had sighted a strange broad line on the moon, running from a break in the rim of the crater Piccolomini. Manning was using a 20-inch Cassigrain telescope with four-power amplification—much more powerful than the average amateur's equipment. But even with this magnification, no ordinary road would have shown up. The "line" would have to be hundreds of feet wide, possibly a tremendous highway or some kind of launching ramp.

At the time I didn't realize how carefully the silence group was watching all moon reports, even those made by private astronomers. Later, with Manning's help, I found out what had happened.

When he sighted the strange "line" Manning immediately phoned Professor Frazier Thompson, an astronomer at Tulane University. In a few minutes Thompson arrived and with several other witnesses observed the strange markings.

At Professor Thompson's suggestion, Manning asked the United Press to notify Harvard Observatory. But bad atmospheric conditions at Harvard prevented a clear view of the moon.

Unknown to Manning and Professor Thompson, the UP at New Orleans had put the story on its wires.

"Maybe it was just a coincidence," Manning told me months later, "but the next day or so a Navy captain and a couple of Intelligence officers showed up. They asked me who else saw the 'road' and a lot of other questions. They were all dead serious.

"Finally I asked what was back of all this. Up to then I hadn't called the line a 'road'—that was the UP story. So I asked the Navy captain why they were upset, if they thought maybe someone was on the moon. But they wouldn't tell me anything."

The UFO censors had good reason to be upset, for Manning's discovery could lead to exposure of the secret moon studies. So far, though several big observatories, including Palomar, were making secret observations for the government, nothing had become public. But many so-called amateur astronomers were highly experienced, and the dramatic moon-bridge announcement by Dr. H. P. Wilkins had caused hundreds of telescopes to be focused on the lunar sphere.

Early in March Dr. Wilkins had reported another surprising discovery on the moon, close to the mysterious bridge. The new discovery, he announced, was the existence of a wide ravine with vertical sides and a perfectly flat floor. This discovery, said Dr. Wilkins, was almost as surprising as that of the bridge.

"That they should exist side by side is astonishing," he added.

In view of his broadcast in December, stressing the artificial appearance of the bridge, this was as far as Wilkins could go without flatly saying these were engineered structures.

Shortly after this, in his new book entitled *Our Moon*, Dr. Wilkins revealed his belief that a vast system of caves existed inside the moon. This huge network, he said, probably extended 30 miles below the surface.

Dr. Wilkins' assertion could not fail to suggest one startling conclusion: that an intelligent race might exist, unseen, inside the moon.

When I reached home I found a puzzling report on the Utah crater incident.

When operations began on May 3, Dr. La Paz had told reporters they would excavate until they found what had caused the crater. "If it's a meteorite," he added, "it must have been a whopper."

Three days later operations were abruptly ended. The following statement was issued:

"In the region from Clarkston to Paradise, numerous persons saw or heard the explosive phenomenon at midnight on May 1. The testimony thus obtained, and material evidence recovered as a result of subsurface investigations, has disclosed that the crater was not produced by a conventional meteorite fall. For these reasons operations have been discontinued."

But no hint was given as to what *had* caused the crater. Nor would Dr. La Paz explain what type of "material evidence" had been recovered.

Quickly rumors began to fly: It was a bomb from outer space . . . an American secret missile had gone haywire and almost crashed into Logan . . . a strange rocket ship had blasted off after landing, its exhaust-jet causing the crater.

Any one of the three would be serious. But to me the most sobering thought was that of an outer-space missile.

That it was an American missile seemed unlikely. The Defense Department would have known what caused the crater and La Paz would not have been rushed to the scene to search for the answer. It would have been easier, simpler, to call it a meteorite and fill in the hole.

As quickly as possible, I checked several Washington contacts who would talk to me off the record. None had heard what caused the Utah crater. But they did fill me in on other recent developments. . . .

On May 4 three policemen at Canfield, Ohio, had sighted a saucer glowing orange-red as it raced out of sight. The following night another group of saucers had been seen over Cincinnati. On May 6 at Heppner, Oregon, a V-formation was seen racing silently across the noonday sky. According to Albert Lovegren, one of the witnesses, the machines were round and slightly "domed" on top. They were flying between 1200 and 1500 mph, with a typical oscillating motion. They seemed to be at least 125 feet in diameter.

That very night two flying saucers reconnoitered Washington, causing a hasty Air Defense alert. Shortly after midnight two UFO's suddenly appeared on the radarscope at Washington Airport Control Center. Speeding in from the northeast, the strange machines made a sharp turn, crossing almost above the Pentagon, and then disappeared toward the south. Forty minutes later, at 1:27 A.M., and again at 2:08 A.M., the saucers reappeared. Each time the mystery ships vanished before Air Defense fighters could approach them. Seen from the Washington Airport tower, and by Airport police, the UFO's showed clearly as large, round objects glowing with a peculiar bright light.

Next day Navy radar near Washington picked up a huge object maneuvering 90,000 feet—about 17 miles—above the capital. Before it disappeared it was tracked down to a 15-mile level—still too high to be seen from the ground. Meantime word of the airport night sightings had been "leaked" to the *Post and Times-Herald*. At first both the CAA and Bolling Air Force Base denied the sightings. But after Washington Airport police disclosed the incidents, the Air Force confirmed them.

All these reports were climaxed by one that occurred on the 14th of May. About mid-afternoon a 16-saucer formation was encountered near Dallas, Texas, by four Marine jet pilots. Flying at 15,000 feet, Major Charles Scarborough first spotted the formation as it raced in above his fighter. Amazed —he had been a complete skeptic—Scarborough hastily radioed the other pilots. An instant later Captain R. L. Jorgenson, flying at 42,000 feet, sighted the discs below. Calling orders to the other pilots, Major Scarborough climbed swiftly toward the saucers. A second later, diving steeply, Jorgenson and Major E. C. White tried to box the discs between Scarborough and his wingman, Captain Charles Stanton. But with a sudden burst of speed the 16 discs raced from under the diving jets. Still flying in formation, the strange machines vanished.

Though the official report was secret, the UFO censors knew the story might leak out if ham operators had heard the excited pilots' radio "chatter." If the story broke, it could be hard to explain away. Ridiculing the Marine pilots would be dangerous, as General Manly had proved.

But what could they say? No one would believe four Marine pilots had had simultaneous hallucinations. To call the saucer formation a "flock of geese" would be equally ridiculous.

The Dallas sighting was still being kept from the public when the following story appeared on the UP wires:

"Amarillo, Tex., May 15—(UP)—Gen. Nathan F. Twining, the Air Force's Chief of Staff, said today that the Air Force has the best brains in the country working on 'the flying saucer problem.'

"Twining said that about 90 per cent of reports of flying saucers are pure imagination. But the Air Force can't explain the other 10 per cent.

" 'We just don't know about that 10 per cent,' he said. 'If they are from Mars and there is a people and a world that far ahead of us, I don't think we have even to worry about it.'

" 'So far,' he said, 'no facts have been uncovered to show that there is anything to flying saucers. But,' he said, ' "some very reliable" persons have reported flying objects that can't be identified.'

" 'We are certainly working on the problem and are not discounting all these reports,' he said.

"Twining spoke last night at an Armed Forces Day dinner at Amarillo Air Force Base."

For months many of the public had had the impression that the UFO investigation was only a small-scale project carried on by two or three low-ranking investigators. Now it was plain that Project Bluebook was mainly a receiving unit for UFO reports, with a large force of scientific consultants, engineers, and Intelligence officers working behind the scenes.

On Monday I was scheduled to fly to New York for a talk at Larchmont that evening. Before leaving I called Captain White and asked about Twining's statement.

"We can't comment," said White, "because we don't know what the general said."

"But it's on all the press wires——"

"They sometimes get things wrong," White broke in. "It wasn't a prepared official statement. He probably was just talking off the cuff."

On a hunch I called Henry Brennard.

"What White told you is the official line," said Brennard. "Twining's office says he will have no further statement."

My talk that night was given before a church group in Larchmont. Because of the religious aspects of the saucer problem, I had been a little uneasy. But no one in the audience seemed concerned at the thought of other inhabited worlds. However, several of the audience later asked me about the published claims of contacts with space men. By this time there were several of these incredible stories in print, none with a shred of acceptable evidence. In my opinion they were hoaxes, delusions, or stupid practical jokes—and I told this to the audience.

Later I discussed this with John Du Barry, a personal friend whom I met after the talk. Du Barry, a former *True* editor, had helped me with my first UFO investigation.

"I don't say there haven't been contacts," I explained. "The Air Force may have secret records of communications or even landings—but I'd have to see proof to believe it."

Du Barry nodded. "So would I. As to these stories, I think they're mostly cheap fakes. Some of them have already been exposed."

"It's an easy formula. Anybody can claim he has met a space man at some secluded spot, or even ridden in a space ship. If he picks a time when nobody can prove where he was, no one can call him a liar."

"What troubles me," said Du Barry, "is the number of people who accept such faked stories. I've talked with a number of them—intelligent people, some of them successful in business—and they really believe it. At least I can see they want to——"

"That's just it, John, they *want* to believe it. I talked to the doctors and staff of Waterbury Hospital at their annual banquet in February. And a psychiatrist there gave me his explanation. He said all these 'contact' books describe kindly space people, beings like ourselves, who come from wonderful worlds where there are no wars, no struggles for existence. They have all the answers—the keys to a perfect life. No diseases, no hard work, just an ideal existence, lasting for hundreds of years."

"I get it," said Du Barry. "What these books are offering is an escape from all the troubles here—the H-bomb threat, financial problems, sickness, and so on. I can see how people would seize on it and hope the UFO race will save them. But it's a cruel hoax."

"Of course, it could happen that way. But it would be worse than a cruel hoax if they turned out to be dangerous creatures."

Flying back to Washington the next day, I remembered my conversation with Redell. He might prove to be right. But I still clung to the idea Arthur Clark had expressed: that advanced space races would be wise and tolerant beings who long ago had abandoned all conflict. Perhaps it was idealistic. After all, what did we really know about the mysterious creatures who controlled the flying saucers?

11 Breaks in the Blackout

Thus far the secrecy policy had paid off. Apparently convinced that the Air Force was telling the truth, the AP and most of the other wire services seldom ran flying-saucer stories.

But on May 31 the spell was broken. When a glowing disc was sighted by the control-tower operators, commercial pilots, police, and residents of cities from Spokane to Portland, Associated Press put the story on its wires. Officers at McChord Air Force Base finally confirmed the report.

Next morning another wire story broke as the crew of a Trans-World airliner sighted a saucer north of Boston. The Paris-New York plane was approaching the city when the UFO raced overhead. Calling Logan Airport in Boston, Captain Charles J. Kratovil reported that a large, bright disc-like object had just passed above his ship. Moments later eight men in the Logan Airport tower also sighted the object.

If this story were to be killed, it had to be done quickly. But Captain Kratovil would be hard to silence—his radio call to the tower had not been an official CIRVIS report.

When Kratovil landed at Idlewild Airport, he was handed an Air Force statement. What he had seen, Kratovil was told, was actually a weather balloon from Grenier Air Force Base in New Hampshire. At the same time this convenient explanation was released to the press.

When he heard the explanation, Kratovil looked grimly at his crew, First Officer W. R. Davis and Flight Engineer Harold Raney. Both men shook their heads. Kratovil turned to a reporter.

"I've been flying 27 years. If this was a weather balloon, that's the first time I ever saw one traveling against the wind. It sounds like a cover-up to me."

His opinion was backed by the Logan tower observers.

That night Frank Edwards put Kratovil's blunt statement on the air. Then he added:

"The Air Force has rushed out another of its brush-off statements. But, having issued so many, they are now getting tangled up with the facts, as I shall show you tomorrow night."

The next morning the Air Force released a claim that only 87 UFO sightings had been reported in '54.

The figure of 87 was incredible. On March 1 the press desk had admitted a tremendous increase in sightings and blamed them squarely on my book. Now, by some peculiar magic, they had erased the increase and reported the smallest number of sightings since 1947.

In his broadcast that night Frank opened up with all guns:

"We are now approaching Mars, and a world-wide watch is being kept on the planet. In spite of official denials, unidentified flying objects are being sighted at a steadily increasing rate. By Air Force order, jets are sent up at once when radar picks up UFO's. These scrambles are then described to the public as 'routine training flights.'

"The Air Force has just released the publicity statement that only 87 sightings have been reported this year. My listeners have sent me over a hundred sightings from the front pages of the nation's newspapers. This does not even include the military and GOC sightings known to the Air Force.

"Since they no longer permit newsmen to see their sightings, the Air Force can issue any figure they like. The Air Force asserts that the flying saucers are balloons, weather freaks, meteors, and hallucinations. If it really believes its own press releases, why is it spending so much time, talent, and money trying to catch something that does not exist?"

As soon as he signed off, phone calls began to pour in.

"Most of them asked about Mars," Frank told me later. "They asked why there had been no reports from the Mars Committee. I didn't tell them, but the Pentagon killed the plan for daily reports. But there's one thing the Pentagon hadn't counted on: the magazine articles already written by these astronomers."

"I've seen some of them," I said.

Later, when I combed through the scores of Mars articles, I could see why they had made the silence group jittery.

In *Collier's,* Dr. Whipple, chairman of the Department of Astronomy at Harvard, had asked, "Is there life on Mars?"

"Our kind of life is not likely," he said, "but there might be a *different* form of life on Mars—a kind that we know nothing about."

In the same issue Dr. Wernther von Braun, the great German rocket expert, pictured man's trail-blazing journey to Mars.

"As the space ship neared Mars," said von Braun, "it would swing into an orbit 600 miles up. As the mother ship circled, unmanned rockets would be sent down to explore the planet before any landings were attempted."

Judging by the evidence, I thought, this is exactly what might have happened *here*. There was no proof, of course, that the unknown satellites came from Mars.

In an article dated April 29, 1954, the Australian *Post* quoted two astronomers who were to observe the red planet from Mount Stromlo Observatory. One of them was Dr. Gerard de Vaucouleurs, a noted French expert on Mars.

"There is something remarkable on Mars," said Dr. Vaucouleurs. "If we could one day conclude there was activity displayed by reasoning minds on Mars, what a prodigious upheaval it would cause in human thought!"

We have not demonstrated, he added, that life could *not* adapt itself to the conditions of atmosphere on Mars, which, after all, are not so different from our own.

After quoting Dr. Vaucouleurs, the Australian *Post* commented:

"This is not only a learned probe for academic information. It is also a hunt for possible enemies from space."

This nation-wide publicity on Mars had raised serious questions when a humorous "space man" story gave the Air Force a break.

According to the author, he had seen a saucer land at a remote spot in New Mexico. As he cautiously walked toward it, a voice came out of nowhere.

"Don't touch the hull, pal, it's still hot."

Guided by the unseen voice, the author said, he had gone aboard and been whisked to New York and back at 8000 miles an hour. During this time the operation of the saucer was explained to him by the unseen space man—who said he was talking by remote control from a mother ship outside our atmosphere.

Reading this fantastic story, I thought of all the hidden official UFO reports—serious accounts by veteran Air Force, Navy, and Marine Corps pilots who had met these mysterious ships. For months now every effort had been made to hide these serious reports or to ridicule the pilots when the stories broke. But here on the front page of a national newspaper was this far more incredible tale, its author treated much less rudely than some veteran airmen who had reported encountering saucers.

When this story appeared, the Air Force refused to comment. Apparently they hoped it would be taken as a typical saucer tale, and thus help to nullify the serious reports.

But the effect was quickly offset by Frank Edwards' latest broadcast, which reached millions of people.

For a long time the silence group had taken Frank's broadcasts in silence, hoping to avoid an open fight. But his exposé that night was the final straw. His next step might be to tell the public of the moon and satellite discoveries. If possible, Frank Edwards had to be silenced.

Two days later I saw Frank in Washington. He had a worried look.

"I've been asked to come to the Pentagon for a private talk. I was approached through Charlie Corddry, the UP man at the Pentagon. He said an Air Force general would give me the inside story on the saucers."

"You mean for broadcast?" I exclaimed.

"No, it's to be off the record. That's what bothers me."

"Don't do it," I advised him. "Insist on having a witness and a signed statement that everything is *on* the record."

Frank nodded a sober agreement.

"Confound it, I'm not trying to needle the Air Force just for laughs. This is a serious business. And I think the public should know. Unless the Air Force can show me I'm wrong, I'm going to keep on."

As I drove home I wondered if the Air Force had ever complained to Frank's sponsors, the American Federation of Labor. No other commentator on a nation-wide network had tried to expose the secrecy policy. Most of them, accepting the Air Force statements at face value, either ignored the saucers or joked about the sightings.

That evening Frank called me.

"That Air Force 'talk' is dead. No on-the-record discussion with a witness."

"Did you find out who the general was?"

"No. Whoever he is, though, I have a hunch he was trying to gag me."

For several days I had been trying to get together with

Redell. We finally met on June 7, two days before I was due to fly to Buffalo for my last lecture of the season. At the Madrillon Restaurant we found a corner table, and I told Redell about Frank Edwards and the silence group.

"If you were in their shoes," he said, "you'd try to stop him, too, the way things are popping."

"You mean the increase in sightings?"

"No. I meant the latest discoveries about Mars. I think there may be proof it's inhabited."

I stared at him. "What kind of proof?"

"Slipher has already sent one report from Africa." Redell looked over at me solemnly. "The canals are artificial."

A couple passing by looked at Redell curiously. I waited until they were out of earshot.

"How did they find out they were artificial?"

"Some of Slipher's pictures, and others taken at Lowell Observatory, prove the canals follow great-circle courses—you know, the shortest distance between two points on a globe. If they were rivers they'd meander all around the way ours do on earth. No natural waterway could follow great circle courses like that. Also, the artificial network connects up with a lot of those dark areas which Percival Lowell called oases."

"Then this proves it!" I said. "Mars is inhabited."

"Not so fast," said Redell. "Whoever built them may have died long ago. The whole race may have gone. The canals may be filling automatically as the polar caps melt."

"But there's even a better chance that Mars *is* inhabited. No wonder the silence group is worried."

"I think the Mars Committee has learned a lot more," Redell added. "Lowell Observatory is using a new electronic camera. In some ways it's far better than the 200-inch at Palomar."

This camera, Redell told me, had been developed at Johns

Hopkins University where the work had begun several years before.

"I don't know exactly how it works," Redell told me. "But I do know that it amplifies even a faint light that ordinary cameras would miss. The image shows up two or three thousand times brighter than on the ordinary telescopic camera plate."

"Couldn't they use that on the satellites orbiting the earth?"

Redell looked at me oddly.

"*The* satellite—the other has either changed its orbit or is outside of our tracking range. At least they've lost sight of it——"

"Could it be down lower, closer to the earth?"

Redell hesitated. "I don't know. I simply heard that they'd lost it. Their tracking gear isn't fully developed, so it could be a mistake. That's why this new electronic camera can't be used on the satellites just now. It would have to be connected with special apparatus that would track the satellite at the same speed it was moving."

Before we separated, Redell showed me a Scripps-Howard story which had appeared that day. "Interest in flying saucers has reached the ho-hum stage," Captain White was quoted as saying.

"Look at the last part," said Redell.

I read the final paragraph:

"Radar operators at National Airport, who startled the nation in 1952 with reports of strange objects seen on their screens, saw several again recently. But a check revealed what they saw was a plane practicing landings at nearby Andrews Field."

"That's ridiculous," I said. "None of those CAA radar controllers could be fooled like that."

"Well, you know what it means. They've tracked saucers

over Washington again. This was just planted in case the story leaks."

On my way home I stopped at the airport to pick up my Buffalo plane reservations. Afterward I looked up one of the airport radar controllers. He told me that all the controllers were bitter about the "ho-hum" story.

"I can't talk about the sightings that night," he said sourly. "We're under JANAP 146. But you've been in the tower and at Control Center. You've seen us bring in dozens of planes in soupy weather, one right after another. How could we do it if we couldn't identify a plane practicing landings at Andrews Field? If we were that stupid, we'd be crashing airliners all over the place."

It was not the first time these expert radar controllers had been ridiculed. In 1952, in explaining away the mysterious Washington UFO formations, Air Force officers implied that the Control Center men had misread their scopes. Later CAA top officials, instead of backing up their own men, had sold them down the river in an amazing document called Technical Directive Report 180.

Carefully avoiding any explanation of the important Washington sightings, TDR 180 singled out a few other occasions when there had been blips caused by "temperature inversions." In effect, branding its traffic controllers incompetent, CAA top officials then implied that *all* the flying saucers seen on radarscopes were identical "phenomena"—just as the Air Force later crucified its GCI operators in the Kimross case.

When I reached home, I found I had had a long-distance call from Lou Corbin in Baltimore. When I called back, he told me he was planning a special broadcast on flying saucers.

"It'll be on June 9," he said, giving me the hour. "I can't tell you the details, but the Air Force is due for a surprise."

I told him I'd listen in. But after I hung up I realized I

would be on my way to Buffalo. I phoned Frank Edwards and asked if he would check the broadcast.

"Sure. Maybe it'll be something I can use."

On the afternoon of the 9th, just after I checked into the Statler, Frank called me.

"Boy, did hell pop today! This guy Corbin did a real job on the silence boys. First he quoted the Eastern Defense Headquarters in New York—they told him UFO reports were classified. Then he pinpointed General Twining's speech about saucers possibly coming from Mars, and asked if it was meant to condition the public.

"But here's the payoff. Colonel Frank Milani, Baltimore's Civil Defense Director, was on the program. Milani really blasted the Air Force secrecy on UFO's. Here is what he said:

" 'It is a calculated risk to assume that the so-called saucers do not constitute a threat to the welfare and security of our citizens. We are given to believe they are not hostile, but information on Unidentified Flying Objects is classified, unavailable even to the office of Baltimore's Director of Civil Defense.' "

"Then he hit the Air Force contradictions," Frank went on. "He wound up by demanding that they end the secrecy. The press wires grabbed the story, and the silence group's boiling. It caught them flatfooted. Up to ten minutes ago the Pentagon didn't even have an answer."

But Milani *had* to be answered. He had knocked the "hohum" story flat and exposed the deception.

When I landed at Washington the next evening I found that the Air Force had lashed back, practically calling Colonel Milani a liar. In a hotly worded statement, an unnamed spokesman denied that any reports were classified. He added savagely that the Civil Defense Director could have any flying-saucer report in the Air Force files.

(Six months later, on December 6, 1954, Colonel Milani

wrote me that he was still unable to secure official UFO reports.)

When I called my home, my wife told me Frank Edwards had left an urgent message.

"He wants you to come to the studio if you can make it before nine-thirty."

At the Mutual station I found Frank hard at work on his program script.

"I wanted you to help me figure an answer to this Air Force smear on Milani," he said. "But I just got this—and it's dynamite."

He read off a paragraph from his script:

"A high Air Force Intelligence officer today admitted the Air Force is now receiving 700 flying-saucer sighting reports a week. The admission was made by Colonel John O'Mara, Deputy Commander of Intelligence, ATIC, Dayton, Ohio."

"Holy smoke!" I said. "Are you sure O'Mara said that? He's supposed to be one of the key men in the silence group."

"This was a slip—the Pentagon doesn't even know it yet. Leonard Stringfield just phoned it in from Cincinnati. He will take an oath he heard O'Mara say it."

I knew Stringfield. He had been in Air Force Intelligence during the war and was now an advertising executive. Since 1950 he had carried on a private investigation of the flying saucers. During the past few months he'd published a UFO bulletin known as CRIFO, Celestial Research, Investigation of Flying Objects.*

From the first issues, and after talking with him, I knew Stringfield was making an honest investigation.

"But 700 sightings a week!" I said. "I knew there was a big increase, but—sure he didn't say 700 a month?"

"No, I checked back."

I reread the script paragraph.

* This is now known as the CRIFO ORBIT, address: 7017 Britton Avenue, Cincinnati, Ohio.

"Frank, the pressure on the UFO censors must be terrific. If it keeps up like this, it's almost bound to break open."

"Well, here's another headache for them. *Collier's* just came out with a story about 'Flying Saucer Balloons.' Their writer, Charlotte Knight, went to Air Force bases all over the country, asking for official information. Here is what she wrote:

" 'Officers at the Air Research Center in Cambridge, and at some other Air Force bases, insisted that ninety per cent of the "saucers" reported were merely huge balloons released by the Air Force and Navy. The other ten per cent, they said, were mirages, ice crystals, or other weather phenomena.' "

"This flatly contradicts the Pentagon analysis," I said. As Frank finished his script, I looked at the article:

"Every balloon launching is carefully co-ordinated with the Civil Aeronautics Administration and the Air Defense Command, so the pilots flying in the vicinity can be warned beforehand. In areas near heavy commercial flying, CAA recommends a launching hour when traffic is at a minimum.

"During the ascent warning lights on the instrument package blink on and off continuously. If the balloon leaks and does not rise above 50,000 feet within a set time, automatic mechanisms cut it down."

The article further stated that all of these huge balloons carried automatic transmitting devices. With radio-direction finders, and radar tracking, the position of these huge balloons can be determined accurately.

This wrecked a commonly used Air Force explanation: that many saucers were actually huge balloons which could not be identified. The latest case of this had been on June 2, when a huge round object hovered over Kansas City for three hours. The Kansas City *Times,* checking an Air Force claim that it was a balloon, was told it could not be identified by either the Navy or the Air Force.

In his broadcast that night Frank quoted O'Mara's startling admission, the trick answers given the *Collier's* writer, and then repeated Colonel Milani's demand for an end to secrecy.

For the second time in two days the harried Air Force PIO's were caught off guard. Colonel Milani's attack had been bad enough. But O'Mara's ill-timed slip could be ruinous. There was only one thing for the Air Force to do: brand it as false.

Newsmen were told that Frank's report had no foundation, that O'Mara had made no such statement. To date, the Air Force angrily repeated, 1954 sightings had averaged less than 18 a month.

Undoubtedly, Intelligence by now was burning the wires to Dayton, ordering all ATIC officers, including O'Mara, to keep mum about the prodigious increase in UFO sightings.

Apparently under Colonel O'Mara's instructions, an official answer was released by Captain Charles Hardin of Project Bluebook:

"Colonel O'Mara's words were misinterpreted," Hardin told the editors of a flying-saucer publication. "What he meant to say was that if all the sightings were reported to the Air Force, they would total about 700 a week."

O'Mara's attempt to get himself off the hook proved to be another blunder, for it actually confirmed an amazing leap in flying-saucer sightings.

12   "Shadowed from Outer Space"

It was not yet midnight on June 12 when a hurried report from a Ground Observer Corps post came into the Baltimore Air Filter Center. A huge glowing object, flying at high speed, had been sighted between Washington and the Atlantic coast. Swiftly, the Filter Center came to life as other reports poured in. In a few moments another call came in—this from a GOC post in Delaware. The unknown had now stopped. It was hovering a few miles northwest of the capital.

Now, with reports from 100 miles around, it was clear this could be no aircraft flight. Hastily the Filter Center supervisor buzzed an Air Defense Command radar station a few miles from Washington. There Ground Control had already caught the unknown on its scope. One look, and they knew this was no plane.

The blip was huge, larger than that of a Constellation airliner.

The unknown was hovering at 79,000 feet. Nothing but a supersonic test plane could reach that tremendous height. And there were only a few of these in existence—tiny craft capable of but a few minutes' flight. Besides this, only a helicopter-type of aircraft could hover.

Quickly a scramble order went over the Air Defense wire. Though no jet could possibly reach that altitude, there were standing orders to pursue all UFO's.

Meanwhile, teletype reports of the sighting were clattering into the offices of the Air Defense Command, ATIC, and the Director of Intelligence at the Pentagon.

At the Filter Center another report came in, this one from a Wilmington post. The supervisor stared at the UFO marker on the big plotting board. The saucer was almost 80 miles from Wilmington. To be visible that far, it would have to be gigantic.

For nearly an hour the mysterious craft floated silently in the sky between Washington and Baltimore. At its high altitude it was in position to spy on both cities and all the nearby airfields. Finally, climbing steeply, it disappeared into the night.

Dozens of volunteer GOC spotters knew of this sighting, as well as the Filter Center plotters. Next day the UFO censors held their breath. But no one talked, and the blackout held.

From all the reports Intelligence officers knew the saucer was huge enough to be a mother ship. It could be the one which the B-29 crew had sighted over the Gulf of Mexico, or even the missing satellite.

To some that silent watch in the night was ominous. Why had the saucer hovered near Washington? Could the unknown creatures be preparing to land?

The tension caused by this report had just begun to subside when, on the night of June 14, the strange visitor returned. Again reports flooded the Baltimore Air Filter Center—excited accounts of the huge object, glowing orange-red, hovering over Washington and Baltimore. Again the jets were scrambled and Air Defense Commands alerted. This time the giant saucer remained for two hours, flying between the two cities, while the jets circled helplessly far below.

Though there were Nike rocket bases from which deadly defense missiles could have been launched, not even a Nike could have reached the hovering giant.

As before, the huge craft ended its surveillance abruptly, disappearing from radarscopes before its speed could be measured.

This time the story leaked both in Washington and Baltimore, but the news did not reach the papers for almost a month. Even then the official admission was so vague and brief that few people realized the truth.

The day after the second sighting I learned of these two reports. It was not the first time that a mother ship had hovered over a large American city. Ten times, from August 19, 1949, to March 10, 1950, an enormous disc-shaped craft had been sighted over Cincinnati. Each time it had been picked up by an antiaircraft searchlight. On three occasions the large ship was seen to launch smaller objects; in one case two groups of five saucers were picked up by the beam.*

As I thought about these sightings, I wondered—and not for the first time—if I could be wrong in probing this mystery. And yet in 1952 Air Force Intelligence had fully cooperated with me. Since then more than one Air Force officer had urged me to tell the whole story.

In spite of this I felt a growing uneasiness. Could the silence group be right after all? Had they found something too frightening to tell the public? Which was better; to close our eyes to possible danger, or to face it and perhaps find a solution?

Colonel Frank Milani had demanded an end to secrecy. And I knew that Val Peterson, Director of all Civil Defense, must have backed him up. A few months before, commenting on the H-bomb danger in *Collier's*, Peterson had said that only an informed public could hope to meet this threat. The same thing, I felt, should apply to any saucer threat.

Dangerous or not, the saucers operations were increasing rapidly.

* From the log of Sergeant Donald R. Berger. For detailed report see Volume I, No. 5, CRIFO.

By now, saucers had been sighted by the public in many states.

In the Scranton-Wilkes-Barre area, thousands of people had watched Air Force jets try to box in a flying saucer. For several minutes the disc-shaped machine circled swiftly overhead as the interceptors tried vainly to reach it. Then, changing course, it streaked off into the night.

During the next few days newspapers reported sightings in Knoxville, Tennessee; Warren, Pennsylvania; and Coldwater, Michigan. At Coldwater, police said a saucer had passed low over the town. When questioned by Intelligence officers from Selfridge Field, policemen claimed the object was 20 times brighter than the landing lights on most planes.

Next day another story broke at Bend, California. Landing after a flight from Missoula, Montana, pilot Dudley Bolger reported seeing two saucers over Oregon. Flying parallel to his plane, they passed at terrific speed, vanishing in less than five seconds. The machines' bright glow could not have come from the sun, for heavy clouds covered the sky.

At Seattle a formation of six discs was spotted by firemen. But the UFO's were gone before jets could be alerted.

At Point Mugu Naval Base in California, an unknown machine had been seen circling high above the Santa Barbara Islands' missile installations. There was one unusual detail in the sighting. Every ten seconds the UFO gave off a dazzling orange-white light, which could be seen from Point Mugu to Los Angeles and even from ships at sea. That night Air Defense, the Coast Guard, and Civil Defense remained on the alert, but the saucer did not return.

In local papers sightings made headlines at Newburyport, Massachusetts; Beloit, Wisconsin; Harriman, Tennessee; and Coshocton, Ohio. At Point Huron, Michigan, the *Times-Herald* ran a banner headline: "Strange Light Observed in Sky," and with it a photograph of a round object seen just before dawn.

Another saucer was seen at Salt Lake City, its speed estimated at 1000 miles an hour.

A few hours later another disc appeared over Hackensack, New Jersey, and hovered there for ten minutes. On the following day sheriffs in Pierce and Skagit counties, Washington, reported that a glowing sphere had maneuvered over the area.

Just as our Air Force thought to brand saucers as illusions, the Royal Australian Air Force urged citizens to report all UFO's quickly for careful evaluation. Unknown to most Americans, sightings had also mounted in Australia, New Zealand, and New Guinea.

The RAAF request came one week after a syndicated news article in the United States had denied foreign sightings.

"No other country," the article said, "is bothered with these celestial dishes."

The UFO censors were still smarting over this upset when a story cabled from England announced that British Air Marshal Lord Dowding believed the saucers to be interplanetary machines.

To attack Marshal Dowding was dangerous. As leader of the Battle of Britain in World War II, he had been one of Britain's great commanders, as well as a popular hero. To hint that he had been misled and to suggest that he had no evidence was out of the question, for it might quickly backfire. Marshal Dowding had access to the Royal Air Force UFO reports. Officially the silence group dared not comment. Privately they branded the story a rumor.

In the last week of June, Bob Stirling gave me a call.

"Did you know the armed services had men tracking asteroids?"

"They called them small moons back in March," I answered.

"I don't mean the satellite search. This is a statement from Dr. Frank Edmondson, Director of Goethe Linke Observatory in Indiana. He just announced the discovery of some new asteroids—and he's been working with the armed forces."

"It's news to me. Thanks for the tip, Bob."

I hung up, wondering what was back of this search for asteroids.

Hundreds of asteroids had already been located in our solar system. Many astronomers believed them to be fragments of a planet which had exploded long ago. Some were large enough for space bases—one, in fact, was 480 miles in diameter.

But why the sudden armed forces' interest when this information was already available through astronomers?

One answer occurred to me instantly. The so-called "asteriods" they were tracking might actually be space ships. Training military men to track them would help to keep the information under wraps.

But if this were so, why had Dr. Edmondson released the story?

Something jogged my memory. Checking a file, I found that Dr. Edmondson was one of the few great astronomers who had not ridiculed the flying saucers back in 1949.

Many saucer reports, he had said, are probably errors, ". . . but there is a residue from reliable reports which is hard to explain."

That night a telegram from Huntington, West Virginia, informed me that strange lighted objects had raced over the city.

Later I learned that Air Defense had been alerted in several parts of the country as UFO's maneuvered over Davenport, Iowa; Everett, Washington; and La Plata, Missouri. Sightings at Chicago and over Butte, Montana, had been reported in the papers. In the latter case, though CAA tower men reported seeing an enormous saucer, the Air Force once again rushed out its "unidentified balloon" answer.

But a bigger story was yet to come. It had been hidden for two days.

Just after eight o'clock, on the night of June 23, a dramatic chase began over Columbus, Ohio. Flying an F-51 Mustang fighter, Lieutenant Harry L. Roe, Jr., was en route from Columbus to Dayton when a saucer raced down through the twilight sky. Roe, a National Guard pilot, had never believed in flying saucers. Yet this, he quickly discovered, was no normal aircraft.

Trying to see the shape behind the brilliant white light, Roe made swift right and left turns. Each time the strange machine stayed with him. Again and again he tried to get a silhouette, but the saucer managed to remain against the darkened part of the sky.

As he picked up his course to Dayton, Roe radioed the CAA tower at Vandalia Airport.

"I'm being chased by a white light. I'll circle the tower so you can see it."

As the F-51 flew over the airport, Traffic Controller George Barnes focused his binoculars on the brilliant object, but the glow hid the shape behind it.

Dropping his flaps, Lieutenant Roe "chopped" his throttle to slow down quickly. With perfect precision the strange machine matched his move.

Then, as Barnes watched from the tower, the UFO abruptly abandoned the chase. In a flashing turn, it passed the F-51 and swiftly vanished toward the southeast.

Within minutes Barnes' report had reached Intelligence at Wright Patterson Field a few miles away. When Roe landed, he also reported the chase to Wright Patterson. He was told to keep it secret.

But a score of people at Vandalia and Wright Patterson knew the story. And on the 25th rumors reached the Associated Press. Assuming the Air Force had released the story, Traffic Controller Barnes confirmed the report. Roe, faced with Barnes' statement, admitted the encounter. He also told reporters he had been silenced.

More than any story in weeks, this worried the UFO censors. Until then the blackout had hidden most reports by military and airline pilots. Again the CAA was angrily told to block all leaks.

The next morning, however, an unusual report nearly dwarfed Lieutenant Roe's story. At 12:40 A.M. on Saturday, the 26th, a blinding glow—like an enormous floodlight—suddenly appeared over the Atomic Energy Commission's test station in eastern Idaho. Coming with the suddenness of an explosion, it dumfounded night-shift workers who had just left the AEC plant.

Two of the witnesses, Kelly Brooks and A. L. Taylor, reported that the light remained motionless in the sky for several seconds, illuminating the ground for six or eight miles around. Then, rising at tremendous speed, it vanished.

Several times in the past three months identical lights had "exploded" over the AEC plant. They were said to resemble gigantic flash bulbs. Until now this had been kept secret by the AEC. Hastily efforts were made to hide this incident too.

But the startled AEC workers were not under blackout orders. Within 30 minutes night-shift workers had phoned the Idaho Falls *Post Register,* and now the AP had it.

Like Lieutenant Roe's story, this report was dangerous. It revealed what the Air Force had known for some time—that UFO's were hovering over our atomic energy plants.

Only a few hours later another dramatic story almost leaked out. But it was bottled up for nearly a month.

At 7:27 A.M. on June 26, Air Defense radar picked up an unknown object flying high over Ohio. Jets were about to be scrambled when Ground Control saw that the UFO was now flying above a United Airlines plane near Columbus.

Hurriedly alerting the captain, Ground Control asked him what he could see.

If a UFO censor had been aboard the DC-6, he would have had an anguished moment. For the captain, switching on the loud-speakers, told his 60 passengers of the request.

"I'll make a wide circle," he said. "We'll be banked so that you can look upward and see the object too."

As he circled at 20,000 feet, the passengers stared up at the UFO glowing in the sun. It appeared to be a metallic object, oval in shape. Even former skeptics among the passengers were convinced it was a flying saucer.

Though the pilot never explained why he told the passengers, it is likely that he wanted witnesses to corroborate his story in case he was ridiculed later.

When the plane landed, the crew was warned not to talk. But there was no way to stop the 60 passengers from spreading the story. For two days censors braced themselves, expecting it to break. Yet no one called the press, and not until late July did it appear in the papers.

By then the mysterious events during the close opposition of Mars had already overshadowed most sightings.

Just before the opposition, on July 2, sightings had risen to a peak. Nervously Air Force Intelligence counted each leak. The published reports had been few. Luckily, most sightings had been at night, and mystery night lights were easier to explain away than solid metallic discs seen in daytime.

The 30th of June had begun quietly for the Air Force. There was only one important news break. At Salt Lake City, the *Desert News and Telegram* stated that hundreds of persons had watched two orange-red discs maneuver through Utah skies.

Most of the UFO censors now believed the blackout would hold. The one thing that could most easily wreck it—another encounter by veteran pilots, headlined in all the papers—had for some time been avoided. (There had, of course, been scores of such sightings, but few of these had been revealed.)

Then, on the evening of June 30, the censors were startled by a cabled report from London. The story was immediately headlined from coast to coast.

At 5:00 P.M., the previous day, the British airliner *Centaurus* had left New York's Idlewild Airport for a scheduled flight to London. Operated by the BOAC (British Overseas Airways Corporation), this was a luxury plane, a double-decked Stratocruiser equipped with berths and a cocktail lounge. In command of this million-dollar ship was Captain James Howard, a quiet, competent pilot, 33 years old. During the war Captain Howard had been a bomber pilot of the Royal Air Force. As a BOAC pilot he had crossed the Atlantic 265 times.

Under Howard's command was a crew of 11, all veterans of the Atlantic "champagne and caviar" run.

Flying at 19,000 feet, the *Centaurus* crossed the St. Lawrence River, cruising at 270 miles an hour. In 45 minutes it was due to land at Goose Bay Air Force Base in Labrador to refuel for the ocean crossing.

As Captain Howard was checking his arrival time, a dark object appeared a few miles to the left. Flying parallel to the plane, it was clearly visible in the light from the setting sun. Maneuvering around this mysterious craft were several small, round objects. For a few moments Captain Howard and his copilot, First Officer Lee Boyd, watched in amazement. Until then Howard had been skeptical of flying-saucer reports, and Boyd had been only half convinced.

The smaller saucers appeared to be flying in and out of the larger ship, though the pilots could not be sure.

Suddenly the mother ship changed its position, making it appear to change shape, just as an airplane, seen from different angles, assumes varying shapes.

Both Captain Howard and Boyd were convinced that the objects were solid. And from the way the six small UFO's maneuvered, circling and apparently boarding the mother ship, they were obviously under intelligent control.

Calling Goose Bay Air Force Base, Boyd reported the strange formation. Within seconds two U. S. Sabrejet fighters were scrambled to meet the *Centaurus.*

By now all the crew and some of the passengers had seen the saucer formation. Had this been a cargo flight, Captain Howard might have risked a closer approach. But with the lives of the crew and 51 passengers to consider, he decided against it.

The mother ship and its smaller saucers were still flying parallel to the *Centaurus* when one of the Sabrejet pilots radioed the airliner from a point 20 miles away. The saucers, Captain Howard told him, were still pacing his plane.

"I'll be there in two or three minutes," the Air Force pilot answered.

Then a strange thing occurred.

Quickly the six smaller craft merged with the mother ship. Accelerating at tremendous speed, the larger machine vanished in a matter of seconds.

Captain Howard and the first officer stared at each other. For over 15 minutes the formation had kept pace with the *Centaurus,* probably watching it with high-powered instruments. It could hardly be a coincidence that the six UFO's had hastily boarded the mother ship and fled at the precise moment when the Sabrejets approached. Either their instruments had picked up the oncoming jets or they had heard the radio reports.

When the Stratocruiser landed at Goose Bay, U. S. Air Force Intelligence officers questioned the crew. By midnight, after the delayed airliner took off, a secret report had been flashed to the States.

The first flash reached the Pentagon just before midnight.

By morning the full story was known by all the top UFO censors, the National Security Council, and the Central Intelligence Agency. What they had feared most—a significant encounter by veteran pilots—had finally occurred. This could be the spark that would set off the explosion. Did they dare ask the British Air Ministry to silence the crew? The British would undoubtedly resent such a move. It was better not to risk it, and simply hope the Air Ministry would see the need for secrecy.

The day passed with no word. For a while the silence group breathed easier. Then the UP story broke.

Late that afternoon Bob Stirling called.

"Don, I've got a terrific saucer dispatch."

In his first brief report Captain Howard had given few details, but the main facts stood out: The *Centaurus* had been followed for 80 miles by a mother ship and six smaller saucers, and the formation had fled when interceptors approached.

Stirling had barely hung up when Frank Edwards phoned. He had just seen the story on a UP ticker.

"I got the Pentagon," he said. "The PIO's said they had absolutely no word on it."

"They're covering up," I said. "You can see why. This thing could wreck the blackout."

That night Frank and other newscasters featured the first BOAC story. Next morning it was headlined throughout the United States.

The UFO censors had one small ray of comfort. There had been no link with Mars, and none of the crew had called the UFO's space ships. If nothing more came out, the story might die overnight. But a new story from London rapidly killed that hope.

Instead of silencing the crew, the British Air Ministry admitted it was making a serious investigation. All 11 members of the crew had signed a report agreeing on the details.

Twelve passengers also had confirmed the sighting—the others had been either in their berths or the cocktail lounge during the hour of the excitement.

Captain Howard was unwilling to speculate about the weird machines, but the statement released by the Air Ministry showed clearly what he believed.

"They flashed into sight suddenly and they were obviously not aircraft," Captain Howard had said. "I could swear they were solid. For 80 miles they flew parallel to the Strato-cruiser. It was one large central object, and six smaller objects maneuvering about it. At first it seemed shaped like a jellyfish. Then it appeared the shape of a dart."

Within hours of Howard's statement, First Officer Boyd publicly stated the objects were undoubtedly space ships. Like his captain, Boyd had a distinguished record. During the war he had been a squadron leader in the famous Path-finder Force, and he held the Distinguished Flying Cross and bars. He also was a veteran of the transatlantic run.

"What we saw was solid, maneuverable, and intelligently controlled," Boyd told the newsmen. "We had a long time to watch them. It was hard to judge accurately, but I believe the big ship was about twice the size of an average house, and the smaller ones the size of our Stratocruiser."

In the same press story Navigator George Allen backed Boyd's story: "I am absolutely convinced that the objects we saw were a base ship with a number of satellites."

Other crew members—Douglas Scott, radio officer; Daniel Godfrey and William Stewart, engineer officers; and Stewardess Daphne Webster—gave identical reports about the weird formation.

In a significant footnote one paper, *The Daily Express,* had added:

"Mars is closer to the earth this week than at any time since 1939."

The BOAC story had to be spiked, and quickly. But how

to do it? The ridicule trick was out—these pilots and the crew were too experienced to be labeled fools. The hint that they were deluded would anger millions of British people, and the Air Ministry might even release a full report.

At noon the UFO censors were still in a frenzy of uncertainty, stalling the press with "no comment." There was one possible out—call the space ships a mirage. It had worked before, but never against such highly competent observers.

Then, before a decision could be made, a tragic report from Griffith Air Force Base stunned the UFO censors.

That noon an F-94 Starfire jet had been scrambled to check on an unknown near Utica, New York. When the strange blip first showed on Air Defense radarscopes, the usual swift check had been made. But no aircraft was scheduled to be at that point. Guided by Ground Control, the pilot climbed steeply while his radar observer watched the rear cockpit scope. By now the pilot could actually see the unknown—a strange gleaming object moving swiftly above. Pulling into a tight climbing turn, he started to close the gap.

At the same time his radar observer started to call the unknown. There was no response.

Until that moment the Starfire's jet engine had been working perfectly. Suddenly, as the plane streaked toward the UFO, a wave of heat mysteriously filled the cockpit. It was like the blast of a furnace. Half dazed, the pilot ran his eyes over the instruments. There was no sign of trouble, but the stifling heat was increasing each second.

Frantically he looked around. The radar officer's face was a blur in the waves of heat. At any moment it seemed the whole plane might burst into flames.

"Bail out—bail out!" he shouted.

He jettisoned his canopy and seized the ejection lever. He felt the jet jump as the radarman bailed out. Half blinded by sweat, he got a glimpse of the unknown machine as it passed overhead. There was one final blast of heat. He pulled the ejection lever and was hurled out of the cockpit.

Moments later, his senses still blurred, he saw the radarman's parachute below him. Looking back at the F-94, he groaned. The jet was plunging straight into the village of Walesville, New York. As he watched, horrified, it crashed in the heart of the town and burst into flames.

After its headlong plunge, the F-94 struck two buildings and careened into a car. Four people were killed, two of them children, and another was seriously injured. As swiftly as possible, Griffith Field officers located the two airmen and pieced out the strange story. Still dazed, neither man could accurately describe the unknown machine, nor could they explain the sudden mysterious heat which had forced them to bail out.

By Air Defense orders interviews with the pilots were forbidden. But the story of the crash spread quickly. In some radio broadcasts the unknown object was called a flying saucer; in others, an unidentified aircraft.

At the Pentagon, Air Force PIO's admitted the strange accident, but said they had no details. Meanwhile, the story of the mysterious heat had leaked out in the Walesville area.

No sooner had this reached the Pentagon when other saucer reports began to jam switchboards in Utica, Rome, and Frankfort, New York. Hovering at 20,000 feet, a silverycolor disc was seen by thousands.

Significantly, in the light of the Walesville incident, no jets were scrambled to investigate the saucer. For four hours it remained motionless over Utica, glowing brilliantly as darkness fell. Among the hundreds who sighted this mysterious machine were John Kosar, a mechanical engineer; his wife; M. Kolfak, a teacher; and Ernst Standacker, a textile engineer. By reports sent to me later, they described the UFO which they had watched from Shandaken, New York.

Just after eight o'clock, they told me, the UFO appeared

high in the twilight sky. Seen through binoculars, the oddly glowing machine appeared to be revolving in a counterclockwise direction. After 35 minutes it suddenly climbed upward and disappeared. About this time a Mohawk Airlines captain sighted the saucer at 20,000 feet.

At the Air Force Depot at Rome, New York, Colonel Milton F. Somerfelt told newsmen the object seemed to be a balloon. If it were still there next day, a plane would be sent up, he said.

Meanwhile, a flying saucer had been sighted over Mobile, Alabama. Streaking in from the Gulf of Mexico, the weird machine dipped low over Mobile Bay, circled the city once, and disappeared on a northeast course.

At nearby Brookley Air Force Base the switchboard quickly lit up as reporters and the public sought an explanation.

To deny the sighting, which had been witnessed by hundreds, could fan suspicion of some hidden danger. There was no time to confer with the Pentagon. A statement was hurriedly released by Major James Zicherelli, the senior PIO.

The strange object, said Zicherelli, had been tracked by radar and seen visually from the Brookley Field tower. The evidence, he added, showed it was "definitely under control." Avoiding the outer-space answer, Major Zicherelli said it was apparently an unknown type of aircraft.

That afternoon I had gone to the Mutual station in Washington to discuss the BOAC case with Frank Edwards. While I was there the story on the Walesville crash came in over the UP wire. It described the mysterious heat and the jet's intercept mission.

At Frank's suggestion I called the Air Force press desk and asked a PIO about the F-94 disaster.

"Did you identify that unknown?" I asked him.

"I can't answer that. It's a classified Air Defense report."

"If it was an unidentified plane, as your release says, why should it be secret?"

"Air Defense won't release it," he repeated.

"Well, what caused that sudden heat in the cockpit?"

"We don't know the answer. It could have been engine trouble. It didn't burn until it hit."

"That crash killed four people," I said. "Unless it was on fire, what could have made the crew bail out that fast with half a dozen towns below?"

There was a long silence.

"I don't know," the PIO said. "I honestly don't know."

It sounded as if he were telling the truth. Perhaps the facts were being kept from all but a few at the top level.

Coming on top of the flurry of sightings, the Walesville disaster pointed up the need to kill off saucer publicity.

Next day, quoting a message from the Navy ice-breaker *Edisto*, the Pentagon stated the *Edisto's* officers had seen the same "mirage" at Ungaba Bay, Canada, hundreds of miles from the BOAC encounter. In wording, the *Edisto* description was almost identical with Captain Howard's report to Intelligence:

"The object appeared to change shape like a jellyfish swimming to the westward. It also appeared as a dart at times."

Based on this report, another statement was released by the Northeast Air Defense Command:

"The sighting has been evaluated as an unknown natural phenomenon, possibly a mirage."

To anyone who knew the facts this answer would seem fantastic.

That the men on the *Edisto*, miles away, should have seen an identical formation at almost the same time as the BOAC crew, was incredible enough in itself. That their report should have been worded exactly like Captain Howard's seemed almost beyond belief.

Since the *Edisto* could not be reached by the press, no close questioning was possible.

But weeks later Captain Howard quietly punctured this convenient answer.

"At 19,000 feet, a mirage of what? Our own aircraft? No. That would be a reflected shadow. The shadow must fall *on* something to be visible, and there was nothing. The light from the setting sun could not possibly throw a shadow *toward* itself."

Captain Howard disclosed his opinion in the London *Sunday Dispatch*. In an article called "We Were Shadowed from Outer Space" he said there was only one explanation:

"It must have been some weird form of space ship from another world. If so, then another world was watching the *Centaurus* that night in June—watching, waiting maybe, for what? One day we shall know, and that day, I am sure, will be pretty important for the human race. I hope I am here to see it."

13 The Wilmington Exposé

Even as the nation's presses rolled with the Air Force brush-off of the BOAC sighting, reports were snowballing.

At Albuquerque a formation of nine saucers was seen high over the city. After hovering for a few moments they raced away, tracked at 2600 miles per hour.

In the next 48 hours saucers were seen over Berlin, where 300 witnesses watched a formation of glowing discs; at South Dartmouth, Massachusetts, where a huge disc, 200 feet in diameter, streaked through the evening sky; at Arcata, California, where an enormous UFO hovered for 15 minutes while a group of smaller glowing saucers circled around it; at Winthrop, Maine, where a saucer was vainly pursued by two Air Force interceptors; and at Wilmington, Delaware, where GOC observers saw a green-lighted saucer racing southeast of the city.

But few of the local reports went on the press wires. The tension at Washington was easing slightly when the moonroad story came back into the papers.

Since Manning discovered the road in May, scores of telescopes all over the country had been trained on the Piccolomini crater. But except for a few days when conditions were favorable, the strange markings could not be seen.

On the night of July 6, however, the "road" was clearly

seen at Darling Observatory in Duluth. It was first picked up by Raymond Matsuhara, who was using a nine-inch reflector telescope. The peculiar marking was also seen by curator Frank Halstead and a score of others at the observatory.

Halstead's published announcement gave the UFO censors a double jolt. As he was a professional astronomer, his words carried weight. But even worse, Halstead was convinced that the saucers were space ships. In a Duluth *Tribune* story, picked up by other papers, Halstead made this statement:

"The government knows what the saucers are but it fears panic if it reveals the facts. . . . Many professional astronomers are convinced that the saucers are interplanetary machines . . . I believe they come from another solar system, but they may be using Mars as a base."

At Washington, Frank Edwards broadcast Halstead's opinion. As I listened, I wondered how many other astronomers knew the truth, and what would happen if they suddenly defied military pressure and revealed the facts. Dr. Shapley had paved the way, Wilkins had gone even further, and now Halstead was risking his reputation by putting it into plain words.

Just after Frank signed off, the phone rang. It was Captain Ed Stone, calling to tell me of something important he had heard just before his flight to Washington. I drove in and picked him up at the airport.

"Maybe you've already heard this," he said, looking at me soberly. "It's about that jet crash at Walesville, New York."

"I know what the Air Force said. They insist the jet was chasing an unidentified aircraft——"

Stone shook his head. "Obviously that's a cover-up." He hesitated for a moment. "Some of the Walesville people are pretty bitter, especially the relatives of the ones who were killed. But if they knew the truth, they wouldn't blame the pilots."

"I know that. Even the Air Force said the heat was unbearable. Do you have any of the details?"

Stone looked somberly ahead as I turned from the airport road into the Mount Vernon highway.

"I know this; it came from outside. It was so fast, the crew told Intelligence, they didn't have time to think. You're a pilot—you know you'd never bail out over a town like that if you could possibly stick it out."

"Unless the ship was on fire——"

"Even then," said Stone, "pilots have stuck long enough to get away from cities, and some poor devils have even ridden them down. But these guys were hit so suddenly, they were almost out of their minds. One second everything was normal, then suddenly it was like an inferno. Whatever hit them, it must have come from that saucer."

"You think it was some kind of heat beam?"

Stone leaned over to reach the ash tray. Under his pilot's cap his silver-gray hair shone in the glow of the dash light.

"It must have been that. But why? *That's* what scares me. And when you tie it to the Kimross case——" He stopped for a moment. "Maybe that's what happened to the F-89 crew. A heat beam could have made them bail out over Lake Superior. And the jet could have flown on into the UFO."

"I don't know, Ed. I've had some strange ideas about that case, but I can't find any proof at all. One major told me it was not smart even to discuss the matter."

I had intended to drop Stone at his hotel, but he asked me to come in.

"I can't get this out of my mind," he said. "Anyway I've got something else to tell you."

After he checked in we found an all-night restaurant. Over

our coffee Stone told me that he finally had worked on that Pearl Harbor incident I had asked him to check.

"You were right. Something queer happened on the night of August 6. Here's the story they gave out. Some Navy jet pilot suddenly went nuts while on patrol. He buzzed Waikiki Beach. Then he cut in his mike and started yelling at the Naval Air Station tower. When he landed, they grounded him and hushed it up."

"Who told you that?" I asked.

"A DC-6 captain on the Honolulu run. That's what he was told when he started nosing around. We both agreed it sounded fishy."

"If a jet had buzzed Waikiki Beach," I said, "it could never have been kept secret. The police and city officials would have screamed—and we'd have seen the story in headlines here in the States."

Stone called the waiter and ordered more coffee.

"What do you think they're hiding?" he said.

I told him the original story about the Navy pilot who claimed to have seen some kind of creature.

Stone swore under his breath. "This thing gets worse and worse," he said. "It's like a nightmare."

"It may sound silly now," I answered, "but I still say this space race may not be hostile. I know how bad things look, after the Kimross and Walesville crashes. But remember this —both times armed jets were chasing the saucers just as in the Mantell case."

"Have we actually fired at the UFO's?"

"In 1949 the Air Force told me they had been ordered to 'get' a flying saucer by any possible means. This was admitted by an Intelligence officer at the Pentagon—Major Jere Boggs. In front of General Sory Smith, Boggs told me that one Air Force pilot had fired at a saucer over New Jersey. Later on I found that fighters had fired at a UFO over Luke Field in 1945. And recently I've had a dozen reports that Pacific convoy gunners fired at saucers circling their ships in World War II."

Then I told Stone about the Port Townsend case when planes had been ordered grounded before armed fighters came in.

"Where do you think these creatures are from?" he said. "Mars?"

"The way sightings have jumped each time Mars approached us—yes. I'm convinced they're at least operating from Mars, and from the moon as well."

"*The moon?*" said Stone. "You mean there's evidence of a base there?"

I told him about the discovery of the strange bridge, Frank Mannings' moon road, and the secret studies now being made.

"It sounds unbelievable," Stone said finally. "But that bridge—from Wilkins' and O'Neill's description it couldn't possibly be natural. That means somebody has been on the moon for over a year."

"Maybe even longer," I told him. "It's possible that the moon has been occupied for centuries."

"But that's fantastic," Stone replied.

"That's the way it hit me too, at first, but I can't get around the evidence." I gave him the details of the earlier observations, including the authoritative survey made by the Royal Astronomical Society from 1869 to 1871. Bringing him up to date, I told him about the tunnel exits which had been discovered, and of Dr. Wilkins' cavern-network theory.

"Good Lord," Stone said. "We've always been told the moon was a barren rock—that life could not possibly exist there. And now, underground cities!"

"The tunnels may be natural," I commented, "but it's not likely. Actually, there's nothing impossible about underground bases or cities. That's exactly what *we've* been planning for the moon."

Stone lit a cigarette, looked at me through the smoke.

"Maybe that creature story is right. A moon race couldn't possibly be like us. But wait a minute! How does Mars tie in with all this?"

"Maybe it's not tied in, though I think it is. There could be two separate races—or the same race could have occupied both Mars and the Moon. If they're separate races, maybe one has developed space travel and the other hasn't. Unfortunately the facts lend themselves to the most incredible tales."

I showed him a recent press wire story from Garsson, Canada. On July 7 a Canadian miner had reported encountering a monstrous space man, 13 feet tall, with six arms and strange burning eyes. According to the miner, the hypnotic effect caused him to faint. When he recovered, the saucer and the space man had disappeared.

Stone snorted. "Why do newspapers print stories like that and yet shy off from serious UFO reports?"

"Most papers honestly believe the Air Force releases. Since they don't think anything is being hidden, it's easy to fall in with the 'ridicule policy.' "

"But the cover-up is so obvious now," protested Stone.

"To you, yes, and to anyone who has really investigated. That goes for a few papers too—some of them have gotten suspicious."

"There's one thing about this Garsson story," Stone observed. "Notice it says a Royal Canadian Air Force officer checked on it. Here is what he says: 'It did not conform as it should with what we know.' "

Then he pointed to the next line. "It says here that when reporters asked what he knew, the officer said that it was classified and he couldn't talk about it."

"That sounds as though the RCAF knows what the saucer people look like."

"If they *are* people," Stone said soberly. "I just can't believe evolution on another planet would produce beings exactly like us.

"And that goes for the moon too," he added. "With the terrific temperature changes on the moon, any being like us would almost have to go underground."

"You're right. For 14 days the exposed areas are almost as hot as boiling water. But during the long night the temperature drops to about minus 160 degrees. It would take a pretty weird creature to stay in the open and adapt itself to those changes."

"On top of that there is the G effect," said Stone. "With the moon's gravity only one sixth of ours, any creature evolving up there would be bound to be different."

Stone stood up, looking at me with a rueful smile.

"I wish to heaven the Air Force was right and all this was just our imagination."

We walked toward his hotel where I had parked. Just before I left him he gave me a somber glance.

"Suppose you were an airline captain with a ship full of passengers, and a saucer made a pass at you. What would you do?"

"Probably fly straight and pray the thing would leave."

"I don't know," muttered Stone. "I think maybe I would land fast, if I could reach a field."

He was silent for a few seconds.

"This damn secrecy! If they'd only tell us the truth."

The Garsson space-man story, printed all over the United States, gave the UFO censors a brief breathing spell. Then, apparently by coincidence, another news story appeared which mocked at saucer believers. The article stated that a flying-saucer project at Ohio Northern University had been closed for lack of UFO reports, "with the saucer business coming to an ignominious end like a car running out of gas." What it failed to explain was that the project closed because the United States Air Force refused to release its thousands of hidden reports.

But the effect of these mocking stories was short-lived. Unknown to the silence group, careful plans were being made to release vital reports confirmed by the Baltimore Air Filter Center. Even before Colonel Frank Milani's fiery blast at the censors, other Civil Defense officials and some Air Force officers had been trying to end the blackout.

On the 8th of July I learned that a daring step was about to be taken. Unless the UFO censors were tipped off at the last minute, a big story would break the next day in the Wilmington *Morning News*.

To publish the actual Filter Center reports was impossible, as these were classified. But there was a loophole, for certain Ground Observer Corps logs duplicated these reports. After a check it had been found that the Wilmington GOC log contained the most impressive evidence.

On the morning of the 9th the Wilmington news story broke. Headlined "100 Flying Objects Spotted Here," the story at one stroke revealed a mass of dramatic sightings, disclosed the Air Force's concern, and exposed the blackout.

Only a month before, in the "ho-hum" story, the Air Force had admitted to but 429 sightings for the entire country in 1953 and 87 for the first five months of '54. Yet by the official GOC record there had been over 100 sightings in Wilmington alone, 40 of them during the first five months of 1954. Obviously the Air Force statistics were misleading.

In this article, for the first time, the public was told of the mother-ship sighting on April 18, 1953. At 11:15 A.M., a huge mysterious machine shaped like a rocket had flashed high above Wilmington, flying a northwest course.

The GOC log also disclosed the carefully hidden reports of June 12 and 14, 1954, when a giant UFO had hovered between Washington and Baltimore.

"Confirmed by Air Force," read the GOC log. "Air Force

told observers to keep constant watch—object 70 miles from Wilmington and 15 miles in the air. Thought to have been the one which hovered over Washington on June 12. Baltimore Filter Center had it on radarscope for over two hours."

Equally serious, from the UFO censors' viewpoint, was the final GOC report dated July 5, 1954. At 9:39 P.M. another flying saucer had raced over Wilmington. As it passed overhead a blinking green light was seen by two GOC observers, Robert O'Connor and Frank Garosi. At nine-forty, one minute after they reported to the Baltimore Air Filter Center, the Air Force confirmed this object as a UFO.

When official Washington learned of the Wilmington news story, repercussions echoed from the National Security Council on down to the Air Force press desk. The men back of the story expected an uproar, though they had carefully followed the published June 10 policy. That policy, stated in answer to Colonel Milani's charges, had asserted that no saucer reports were classified, that all were open to Civil Defense. As the storm broke, the censor-fighters hoped this would be the opening wedge for reporters and radio commentators who were already demanding the whole story.

Just before noon Henry Brennard called and told me what had happened.

"The Pentagon's already got a dozen requests for other cities' GOC logs. They're in a hell of a spot. If they let out one, they'll have to release every GOC log in the country.

"Here's another point. The story says 98 per cent of the saucers have been sighted at night. If you figure the admitted daytime sightings as two per cent, you can see they must be getting hundreds of reports each week. Colonel O'Mara's 700 figure must have been accurate."

"What is the Air Force going to do?" I asked him.

"They've already done it. They slammed down the lid on all GOC logs. Civil Defense has been told to keep its observers from talking."

"That's going to be tough. Those people are volunteers and not under military orders."

"Yes," said Brennard, "but they can put the heat on them. I'll give you a hundred to one that no more logs will be released."

A few hours later Lou Corbin proved Brennard was right. Following up the Wilmington story, he had tried to get UFO reports from both the Baltimore Filter Center and a Maryland GOC post. Each time he had run into a stone wall.

I had just finished talking with Corbin when Frank Edwards phoned.

"This Wilmington story does it!" he exploded. "Imagine it: a hundred sightings over one town and they keep it secret all this time. I'm going ahead with that special broadcast we planned. Mutual will go for at least one special program, maybe even three. Will you help me work up the scripts?"

"You can have anything in my file. Are you sure your sponsor won't kick about this?"

"They've gone along with all the other saucer broadcasts. They know a lot of people tune in just to hear about flying saucers, since I'm the only one on a national network who touches the subject. George Meany, President of the AF of L, even okayed a saucer article in the AF of L *News Reporter*."

For the next three weeks Frank and I worked out the special broadcast. There was no lack of ammunition. Aside from a mass of new sightings there were two significant developments.

On July 23, under Air Force pressure, the Navy issued a new UFO order. Though not a word appeared in the press, I secured a copy covering the Washington area. Issued by the Potomac River Naval Command, it was entitled PRNC 3820.1—Code 03.

Signed by Admiral T. B. Hill, this directive ordered immediate reporting of unidentified flying objects. Using the code word "Flyobrpt," reports were to be phoned or tele-typed to the following:

1. The Director of Air Force Intelligence
2. Air Technical Intelligence Center
3. C.O., Air Defense Command
4. C.O., Eastern Air Defense Command
5. Director of Naval Intelligence
6. C.O., Eastern Sea Frontier
7. Commandant, Potomac River Naval Command.

To insure secrecy on the reports, the directive cited JANAP 146, AFR-200, and two previous Navy orders, OPNAV 3820 and Directive 3820.2 by the Commander of the Eastern Sea Frontier.

At first, when this new directive came out, it appeared to complete the blackout. No longer need the silence group fear disastrous leaks from Navy and Marine Corps pilots.

Suddenly, however, the censors discovered that the Navy directive was unclassified. If made public, it would force them to reveal AFR-200, which contained the secrecy order and showed the serious official concern over the flying sau-cers.

It was too late now for the Navy to classify the order. Cop-ies had gone to all PRNC commands. Quickly the Air Force ordered a new edition of AFR-200 without the "restricted" label.

The second development had come just two days after the Wilmington story.

In an interview cabled from England, Air Chief Marshal Lord Dowding confirmed earlier rumors of his belief in fly-ing saucers.

"I am convinced the flying saucers are real," said the vet-eran RAF leader. "I believe they are machines controlled by intelligent beings from another planet."

Following this, Marshal Dowding explained his reasons in a story carried by the London *Dispatch*. Citing more than

10,000 reports, he stated that saucers could not be secret weapons made on earth. Confirmed speeds of over 9000 miles an hour, in a thick atmosphere, were on record. No metal, no material on earth, he said, could be driven through the air at such tremendous speed without destructive change.

For the first time in recorded history, Marshal Dowding added, intelligent communication with other planet races now seemed possible.

Our space visitors, he concluded, might come from different planets, with varying motives. He gave a sober warning against attacks by planes or ground guns, saying this could turn neutral curiosity into deadly hostility.

When Frank Edwards and I met to select sighting reports for the broadcast, I first showed him the Navy directive. He had already seen my copy of JANAP 146 and the restricted edition of AFR-200.

"This should do it," Frank said crisply. "It proves the official secrecy. Next we'll quote Captain Ruppelt's letter to you proving that Intelligence cleared these cases you listed—and then that Air Force letter denying it."

Selecting the sighting reports was a difficult job. Frank had already chosen a few key incidents, such as the Kimross and Walesville cases. Together we went over the more recent reports.

Since July 7 sightings had been confirmed at Vernon, Texas; Roseau, Minnesota; Philadelphia; Oakland; Miami; Los Angeles; Yonkers; as well as in Holland, England, and at Capetown, South Africa.

On July 11 a flying disc had paced four Air Force jet bombers over Hunterdon, Pennsylvania. Two days later an ex-pilot in Norfolk sighted a huge disc, 200 feet in diameter, racing silently at 3000 feet. On the 29th a Dutch shipmaster gave officials a detailed report of a saucer he had seen 80 miles from New York, hovering over his ship.

There were scores of other sightings, but one stood out

from the rest. It provided another link in the chain of "cover-up" evidence. At 7:20 P.M., on the night of July 23, four large saucers were spotted over Franklin, Indiana, gleaming like metal in the twilight. They were immediately reported to the South Bend Filter Center by Robert D. Wolfe, Chief of the Johnson County GOC. In less than two minutes jets from the 97th Interceptor Squadron at Dayton raced toward the scene. Meanwhile, word had reached Burk Friedersdorf of the Indianapolis *Star*.

By the time Friedersdorf reached the GOC post, three of the saucers were zooming into the night. The fourth, described by Wolfe as about 500 feet in diameter, was maneuvering slowly and glowing brightly in the darkness, south of Franklin.

Just as Friedersdorf came into the GOC post, two Air Force jets reached the area. Wolfe had no time to order the reporter out—the pilots were already asking directions through a ground hook-up with the South Bend Filter Center. With Friedersdorf calling off bearings, the Chief Observer guided the jets toward the saucer.

As one jet dived over the UFO, the strange machine suddenly began to climb. The two pilots raced up beside it, then suddenly veered away and headed back to Dayton.

When Friedersdorf called Dayton, the 97th Squadron officers denied sending the two jets.

But Friedersdorf insisted that he had seen them. He said, "I was at the GOC post; I helped the Chief Observer vector them in."

There was a hurried conference at the other end. Then Friedersdorf got his first lesson on the blackout.

"The incident is officially denied," said the Wright Field officer. "It is a classified matter."

"I'll use this news story," Frank decided, "and I'll ask the Air Force to explain what happened."

"Are you going to use the Pearl Harbor 'creature' story?"

Frank hesitated. "No, I'd like to have more on it first. But I'll cover everything else: the satellites, the moon discoveries, the sudden clamp on the Mars Committee report, along with all the key points of the past year. I'll call you in a couple of days to look over the final script."

"Frank, if this doesn't kill the blackout, nothing will!"

"The Air Force will *have* to talk," he said. "I privately sounded out some other commentators and a couple of wire service boys I know. They all say they'll carry it. They say it's bound to be a front-page story."

That evening, as if by perfect timing, a press report from Germany gave Frank a final punch story. Hermann Oberth, the great rocket expert and space-travel authority, had just announced his belief that the saucers were space ships. Like Air Marshal Dowding, he said he was convinced we were being visited by an advanced race from another world.

For two or three days I waited to hear from Frank Edwards. Finally he called.

"Don, it's happened," he said. "I've been muzzled!"

"*Muzzled?* You mean the Air Force——"

"I don't know. George Meany told me I'd have to have a censor at my elbow every minute."

"They must have found out about the special broadcast."

"You're probably right, though there were some other angles too. The Air Force isn't the only agency that wanted me silenced."

"Did Meany mention the saucers specifically?"

"Absolutely. He told me I was not even to mention them, except to quote press wire reports. Even then I couldn't comment on them."

"But the press wire stories have almost died out!"

"That's what I told Meany. He said, 'Never mind, that's an order, and there will be a censor at your elbow to see that you carry it out.' "

"What are you going to do?"

"I'm going to resign—that's all I can do. They knew that when they pulled this censor trick."

But though he was temporarily silenced, Frank had not abandoned hopes for his special broadcast.

"I'm talking it over next week with another network," he told me.

Then a strange thing happened. The Pentagon offered Frank a mysterious hush-hush job.

"On what?" I asked him.

"All they would tell me was that it was terrifically important. They said I'd be helping to prepare the public for something. I know," he said, "it sounds like the saucers, but would they actually get me off the air and then give me this? I'd be of bigger help to them on the network."

"It sounds like a trap," I said.

"I'll soon know. I'm to call this general back tomorrow."

It was two days before I heard from him again.

"I just got back from New York. That network backed down on the flying-saucer deal. I think they were told to, because at first they were all for it."

"What about the Pentagon offer?"

"I think it was an attempt to gag me," Frank said shortly. "This general told me I'd have to sign a two-year contract. During that time I couldn't broadcast or publish a word on any subject without their permission."

Before he hung up, Frank added: "You better watch your step, Don. Those guys are playing for keeps."

14 The Burning Road

Three weeks after Frank Edwards went off the air, I made a date with Lou Corbin for a conference in Washington. When he called me from Baltimore, I told him the inside story about Frank.

"They may try to stop you too," Corbin said.

"I know that, but I've got to take that chance."

Corbin and I had been planning a meeting for some time. Then four new developments speeded it up.

On the 12th of August the Air Force had quietly declassified AFR 200-2. The Pentagon rumor was that General Twining had forced this action. The declassification was obviously linked with the Navy's July 23 directive, but there was no way of proving it.

Soon after this the British Air Ministry had reversed its policy on the BOAC case and refused to offer any further comment.

This was quickly followed, on August 23, by a news story that jarred the UFO censors. Quoting *Aviation Week*, the AP revealed the discovery of two unknown satellites. The satellites had been labeled, however, as "natural" objects:

"Pentagon scare over the observance of two previously unobserved satellites orbiting the earth has dissipated with the identification of objects as natural, not artificial, satellites," the article said. "Dr. Lincoln La Paz, expert on extraterrestrial bodies of the University of New Mexico, headed the identification project. One satellite is orbiting at about 400 miles out, while the other was tracked at 600 miles."

Through the AP, Dr. La Paz had immediately denied the story, even refusing to admit any connection with the satellite search. But *Aviation Week* was no fly-by-night magazine. I learned they had carefully checked the facts. I had a strong suspicion that Dr. La Paz had been told to plant the "natural object" story to offset rumors of orbiting space bases, and he had retracted his story when *Aviation Week* unexpectedly disclosed Pentagon fears over the two satellites.

The fourth incident, on September 1, came in the form of a brief announcement by Deputy Minister Baldwin in Canada.

The Shirley Bay flying-saucer observatory had been closed, he said, because no flying saucers had been recorded.

Corbin and I met at the Willard Hotel in Washington. Until then he had been to me only a vibrant voice from Baltimore. He proved to be a stockily built man, somewhere in his thirties, with an easy smile and a quick efficient manner. Over a luncheon table he produced a formidable list of questions.

"What do you know about the La Paz story in *Aviation Week?*" he said. "Why did he deny it?"

I gave him my opinion as to why it had been retracted.

"I have a hunch you're right. Anyway, I'm going to try to get the satellite answer tomorrow. Captain Howard T. Orville will appear on my program tomorrow. As you know, he's the head of the President's Weather Control Commission. I've talked to some astronomers privately, and they say it's almost impossible for two natural objects to come in like that and start orbiting the earth. I'm going to put it up to Captain Orville."

I jotted down the broadcast time as Corbin looked at his question list.

"You know W. B. Smith, the Shirley Bay Project chief," he said. "Is that closing announcement on the level?"

"I doubt it. Smith wrote me last month that they'd had a startling gravimeter reading on August 8. He said the sky was overcast so he and the staff couldn't see what caused the needle to jump. But he's positive there was a space ship overhead."

Corbin's heavy brows went up.

"So the Canadians are covering up too? Well, one final question for now, and then I've got something for you. What do you think of this burning-road mystery in California?"

The burning-road incident had occurred in Woodside, California, on August 28. At four o'clock in the afternoon farmers living near Portola Road heard a loud explosion from some unknown source. Immediately afterward a 270-foot section of Portola Road's macadam surface was found ablaze. The fire was originating from dozens of strange metal pellets.

Half an hour later, when firemen reached the scene, the surface of the road was almost boiling under the intense heat. Later, Fire Chief John A. Bolpiano tried to pick up one of the pellets. But even then—45 minutes after the fire had been discovered—the metal was too hot to handle.

The burned area was in precisely the shape of a rectangle, 70 by 270 feet. Mystified, Fire Chief Bolpiano notified the Air Force and the Army, but Intelligence officers and demolition experts could not explain the cause of the fire. A suggestion that a jet plane's turbine had exploded and showered the road was quickly abandoned when a check showed no jet had had such an accident.

For almost two days Intelligence officers and scientists admitted they were baffled. The fragments of the mysterious pellets were taken away for analysis.

Then suddenly an answer was made public—an explanation as fantastic as the mysterious fire itself.

According to the story given the press, a tar bucket had fallen from a truck and shattered, the fragments of hot metal starting the fire.

"I just don't believe it," I said to Corbin. "A fall from a truck couldn't possibly shatter the contents of a tar bucket over 270 feet. It would have to be dropped from a height of at least 100 feet. Even then the pieces would scatter in a circle, not in a rectangle. And no tar bucket ever got hot enough to set that road on fire."

"Okay, it's a cover-up," said Corbin. "Then what really caused it?"

I shook my head. "I don't know, but it sounds as though it must have been intelligently directed to make that rectangle."

"Even so," said Corbin, "there's no proof it's linked with the saucers."

"Let's hope it isn't . . ." I replied.

Corbin paused for a moment. Then, "I have a strange report for you," he said. "There was a jet crash near Chesapeake Bay about two weeks ago. It was a queer thing. While a crash boat searched for the pilot's body, its captain sighted a UFO overhead. Right after that the pilot of an F-51 search plane bailed out, after yelling on his radio that he had hit something and was spinning around.

"As you know, I've got a lot of Air Force contacts, so I heard about this next morning. Now here's the queer part. The pilot's squadron commander swore he'd hit another F-51 in mid-air. Yet even though the first F-51 was almost demolished, this squadron commander said the other fighter had only a few scratches on it. When I called to ask him about it, he refused to let me talk with either pilot. 'It's a classified inquiry,' he snapped and banged down the phone."

"You think they may have put a few scratches on an F-51 just to back up the story?" I asked.

"I won't say that," replied Corbin. "But it's certainly a peculiar affair."

The next day Corbin followed his plan to question Captain Howard Orville about the satellites. Captain Orville, a retired U. S. Navy officer, was warned that his answer would be recorded. Corbin asked:

"Do you know of any condition under which two such objects could enter the earth's atmosphere and pick up orbits 400 and 600 miles out?"

"No, not that I know," answered Captain Orville. "Your doubts are well justified."

"If there are two bodies circling," Corbin went on, "then they would be unnatural, or not natural?"

"If that should be true," replied Orville, "military security would prevent discussion."

After reminding the captain that his replies were "on the record," Corbin asked: "Then it's not impossible that the two bodies, if they are there, might well be space stations?"

"Well, that's an interesting thought," Orville responded. Then he amplified his first answer. "I don't know of any set of circumstances that would account for two bodies orbiting around the earth."

"But we still have the puzzle of *something* circling the earth?" Corbin persisted.

"Yes—yes," Orville told him.

When word of Captain Orville's statement reached the Pentagon, the UFO censors expected a big news break. But this time luck was on their side. Apparently none of the Baltimore papers had caught the broadcast.

"I could have tipped off the papers," Corbin told me later, "but I didn't want Orville to think it was a frame-up."

For two weeks after this there was an odd lull in saucer reports. Then, in mid-September, the UFO's returned in full force.

At 9:00 P.M. on September 18 one of the strange green

fireballs streaked over the Southwest, frightening thousands of citizens. Racing at about 20,000 feet, the brilliant green missile threw a weird emerald glow over Colorado, New Mexico, and parts of Texas. At Albuquerque the AP reported that the mysterious fireball had fouled up radio and TV transmission, rattled airplanes flying through its trail, and "scared the wits out of many New Mexicans." Skies were reported to have been as bright as day when the missile flashed overhead. Blinding as a searchlight at its greatest intensity, the object left a luminous cloud visible for 30 seconds.

Dr. La Paz, the foremost expert on the green fireballs, confirmed the queer radio and TV interference.

"This was no ordinary meteorite," he said. "It was something unusual."

Like all the other green fireballs, the strange missile had silently exploded without leaving a trace.

Two nights later at Knoxville, Tennessee, a large disc and two smaller ones were sighted as they flew overhead in formation.

The same night another three-disc formation was seen at Ionia, Michigan, by two amateur astronomers, William R. McLaughlin and Clark Burgeon. Both believed the unknown machines were under intelligent control. Identical sightings at Caledonia and Grand Rapids were also reported to Air Defense.

At approximately the same hour an oval-shaped saucer was sighted near Ramore, Ontario, by Constable Florian Giabowski of the Ontario Provincial Police. As he watched from his patrol car, the saucer seemed to disintegrate in a shower of brilliant particles. The constable's report was confirmed by a pilot flying in the same area. Immediately after the incident an odd blue rain began to fall. Samples tested later by the Defense Research Board proved to be moderately radioactive.

Six hours after the "blue rain" fell a "noiseless blue-white ball" was reported by police in Minneapolis and at Fargo and Sioux Falls, South Dakota. Estimating its speed to be about 1000 miles per hour, police said the UFO's brilliant light illuminated the ground for several seconds.

But even these published cases gave little hint of the scores of reports clattering in on Intelligence teletypes. One of these undisclosed sightings, on the night of September 27, alerted all Air Defense Commands east of the Mississippi. At 9:24 P.M. an enormous glowing disc flashed low over Pennsylvania. Flying at tremendous speed, the UFO was seen by the crews of three airliners, one of them Eastern Airlines Flight 694. When the Eastern plane landed at Baltimore's Friendship Airport, the crew was questioned for two hours by Air Force Intelligence officers.

Next morning, tipped off by Lou Corbin, I asked the CAA for the names of this Eastern flight crew. The senior pilot, I learned, was Captain William Call. When I phoned him, he said he could not discuss the sighting, which had been reported under JANAP 146.

"But there's one case I can talk about," he said. "A short time ago, on a flight from Boston, we were circling over Hartford Airport at 8000 feet. We were on instruments in the overcast, waiting our turn to land. All of a sudden there was a tremendous flash—apparently from some terrific explosion. For a second I thought an A-bomb had gone off."

"The Hartford tower called that they had had a bad scare. An American airliner was 'holding' underneath us and the tower thought we'd collided. I never found out what the explosion was, but I can tell you this: none of us ever saw anything like it before."

"Those queer blasts have been going on for over two years," I said. "At first the Air Force blamed them on pilots going through the sound barrier——"

"How could that light up the sky?" said Captain Call.

"This Hartford thing was no sonic boom. Whatever it was, it lit up a 100-mile area."

After he hung up, I thought back over the mysterious explosion reports. Some, but not all, had been definitely connected with UFO's.

These mysterious "sky quakes" had alarmed thousands of people. Shortly after midnight on May 11, 1952, several strange blasts shook Seattle, and a blinding white flash lighted the sky. Within seconds police and newspaper switchboards were swamped with calls from alarmed citizens. At the same time two Northwest Airline pilots, Captain B. C. Carlson and First Officer Earl Perry, reported that a strange brilliant object had shot in front of them, then broken into two pieces which shot out "like Roman candles."

Five months later, on October 18, 1952, the town of Glen Cove, Long Island, was jarred by two mysterious explosions. The blasts broke windows, cracked sidewalks, and knocked children off their feet. A quick check showed that no jets had gone through the sound barrier. The explosions remained a mystery.

Another sky quake, which shook the town of Guilford, Connecticut, occurred on January 1, 1953. Prior to the blast, a strange light had been seen ascending southwest of the village.

Throughout 1953 the reports continued, coming from Fort Francis, Ontario, and from Grand Isle, Hauppauge, and Farmingdale, New York.

Then on January 7, 1954, one of the mystery blasts was definitely linked to the saucers. That night, at Dieppe, France, a disc was sighted above the city moving at high speed. Immediately afterward a typical sky quake shook many Dieppe houses, frightening hundreds of residents.

Though perhaps only by coincidence, several blasts had occurred when Mars and the earth neared each other. On June 29, just before the BOAC sighting, an aerial explosion shook Nyack and other cities in Rockland County, New York. Again telephone calls poured into police stations, newspaper offices, and radio stations. At Palisades Seismograph Observatory in New Jersey, officials confirmed that the blast had not been an earthquake. It was also determined that no jets had gone through the sound barrier.

Eight days later, Torquay, England, was shaken by a double explosion. Thousands of people, said the London *News Chronicle,* were startled by the blasts.

"An elderly woman collapsed with fright. Dogs bolted, terrified. Slates were dislodged from the roofs of the Torre Abbey. Plaster fell from walls, and ceilings and doors were blown open."

The double explosion was first blamed on a mysterious delta-wing jet plane. But after a full investigation the Air Ministry denied this explanation. The strange machine remained unidentified.

Then, on September 18, for the second time a UFO was linked with a sky quake. Just before a strange explosion was heard over Oakland, California, two deputy sheriffs and a retired Air Force officer reported seeing a green object in the sky.

There were several other cases, but none of them gave me a clue to the explanation. It was possible the explosions had been caused by accidents aboard the space ships, but this did not seem likely. For any major accident would certainly send wreckage crashing to earth—or so I thought then.

The quakes were proof of some powerful force, apparently sound waves. Though we were only on the threshold of ultrasonics, it had already been proved that sound waves, both silent and audible, could be dangerous when focused. But why would the UFO beings focus sound waves in such a manner?

I was still puzzling over it when Bob Stirling called to give me a report from France. The French Air Ministry, he told me, had just announced an official investigation after receiving 267 saucer reports during the past month.

"There have been sightings all over Europe," he added. "The Swedish Defense Ministry just announced they were checking saucer reports too. So are the Italians. They began just after that Rome sighting on September 18. Remember that report of a cigar-shaped saucer I sent you?"

"Yes, that was the one that scared a lot of people when it came down over Rome."

"There's one bad angle to all this," said Stirling. "Did you see Robert S. Allen's column a little while back?"

"Which column?" I asked. "First he said that UFO's were interplanetary and then that they were secret U. S. weapons."

"I mean the last one. I just hope nobody reprints that story abroad. Of course we know it's not true. But imagine what would happen if foreign newspapers played it up."

"Bob, that would be dynamite. We'd be accused of spying on everybody, even our allies. And the Reds would probably accuse us of planning to capture the world."

"Most governments would know that wasn't true," Stirling said.

"They all should know it," I replied. "Besides that, they should know we couldn't possibly be far enough advanced to build the saucers."

"Yes, but a few newspapers could stampede the people."

"You're right," I said. "We might end up with everyone suspecting us."

From the day Allen's story appeared, it worried the silence group because of this very danger. But an official denial would only draw more attention to the story.

Yet each day new foreign sightings were increasing the danger Stirling had mentioned. Hundreds of saucers had been reported in Ceylon, Canada, Brazil, Argentina, Australia, New Zealand, Africa, and all parts of Europe. In many of these countries the witnesses were expert observers: pilots, meteorologists, astronomers, and weather-bureau observers. In one typical French case it was the government weather station that had reported sighting an oval-shaped craft moving with tremendous speed.

"It left a trail of sparks," said the senior weather observer, "and no known heavenly body could be confused with it."

What made the problem worse, from the silence group's viewpoint, were the scores of *less* authentic reports, some of them wild tales of saucer landings and contacts with weird creatures.

On September 10, in south France, M. Antoine Mazoud reported he had been approached by a small creature wearing a "crash helmet." After kissing him in true French style, the strange being climbed into a cigar-shaped machine and soared away.

Two weeks later, in the Guardunha Mountains in Portugal, three Portuguese peasants reported that a saucer had landed in a field nearby. According to the report, two small creatures in shiny metallic outfits climbed out and began to collect grass and stones. Seeing the three Portuguese, these space creatures motioned them to come closer. When the three men backed away, the metal-clad creatures boarded their saucer and rapidly took off.

Then on September 30 a small saucer was reported to have landed near Maisancelles, France. Later, French police claimed to have discovered imprints in the ground where the machine presumably had landed.

These cases were typical of scores of reports, most of them obviously inspired by excitement or hysteria. Within a short time all sorts of weird creatures had been reported. One such report described a zebra-striped space man who changed color like a chameleon to match his background; another, a being with brilliant eyes and a huge mustache, who wore rubbers and spoke Latin; and still another, a gigantic figure wearing what looked like a diver's suit.

Ordinarily the Pentagon censors would have welcomed such tales which, oddly enough, reached this country when serious reports did not. But the danger from Allen's story robbed them of any humor, for the censors feared the saucers would be called American secret weapons.

One night at Walschied, a report suddenly spread that Martians had landed in a villager's garden. While the women fled into the church, dozens of Frenchmen seized guns and clubs and bravely closed in on the garden. There in the dusk they could see the "invaders"—small figures with glowing heads. The Frenchmen started to charge, when suddenly they realized the truth. The "Martians" were huge chrysanthemums, each one covered with white cloth for protection in case of an early frost.

Clearly, the seeds of panic had been sown in most of the world. It was grimly clear to the UFO censors that something had to be done, not only to offset the secret-weapon story abroad, but also to divert attention here from the new wave of sightings.

The first step was taken on October 9 when an Air Force statement was released through the Chicago *Tribune* press service at Washington. Under the headlines "Finds Saucers Exist Solely in Imagination," the *Tribune* story declared:

"The Air Force said today that after seven years of exhaustive investigation by its Air Technical Intelligence Center at Dayton, Ohio, it has failed to uncover any proof that flying saucers exist except in the imagination of observers. . . .

"The Air Force also noted it has been unable to find any observatory or professionally recognized astronomer who has observed or photographed any flying object in space that could be authenticated as a vehicle from another planet or another nation.

"The Air Force said the only reason it is keeping its investigation reports under wraps is to protect the privacy of the observers and to avoid provocation of further outbreaks of saucer sightings."

In conclusion the story gave the Air Force's usual explanations: weather balloons, light reflections, stars and planets, electrical particles in clouds, aircraft, meteors, and hoaxes.

The Air Force statement on astronomers was typical of the silence group's double talk. Several top astronomers had observed strange ships which, they insisted, could not be earth-made aircraft. Among them were Dr. Clyde Tombaugh and Dr. Seymour Hess. But by using the phrase, "could be authenticated," the silence group evaded this issue.

The planted *Tribune* story was immediately followed, on October 10, by an Air Force statement released at Fort Worth, Texas:

"Any mysterious white balls or flashing lights seen moving across the United States from now to December 15 will have no connection with flying saucers. They will be 37-foot plastic balloons released near Tracy, California, where winds from 28 to 110 miles an hour will float them east. Timing devices will explode helium-filled bags after two or three days' travel, and 300 pounds of experimental equipment will parachute to the ground."

Although some of the California balloons might be mistaken for flying saucers, this attempt to explain *all* saucer sightings for a two-month period seemed to me a plain cover-up.

As if to compound the confusion, International News Service immediately published a "roundup" story from abroad.

Flying saucer reports, said INS, had just come in from Germany, Belgium, Egypt, Argentina, Lebanon, and the French Cameroons.

At a glider school in Frankfort, Germany, several pilots including former Luftwaffe flyers watched a silvery disc move silently over their field.

In Münster, Germany, a movie projectionist named Franz Hoge reported watching a saucer land in a field. Hoge, said INS, discovered a cigar-shaped machine hovering six feet above the ground, giving off a brilliant blue radiance which nearly blinded him. Just after this, he sighted four small, peculiarly-shaped creatures with "thick-set bodies, oversized heads, and delicate legs."

Because of Hoge's story some UFO censors found it easy to ridicule the entire INS account. But a report, flashed to them from London on October 14, hit with a harder impact. For this was an officially confirmed Royal Air Force report.

Shortly after 4:00 P.M., Flight Lieutenant J. R. Salandin had taken off from North Weald, Essex, in a Meteor jet fighter. It was a bright, clear day, and as Salandin climbed above the Thames Estuary he sighted two other Meteor jets flying high above him.

As his plane reached 16,000 feet, Salandin suddenly saw two round objects racing between the other Meteors. Within seconds the two UFO's vanished. As he turned back, looking through his canopy windshield, Salandin froze.

Coming at him, head on, was another flying saucer! In the last split second the saucer flipped to one side and streaked past the fighter.

But in that taut moment Salandin got a clear view of the mystery ship. The main body was like two saucers pressed together. It had a dome-shaped top and a similar round projection beneath. It glowed with a silver metallic gleam.

"The object was traveling at a tremendous speed," Flight Lieutenant Salandin later told the British *Flying Saucer Review*. "I was so shaken I had to fly around quietly for about 10 minutes to recover."

After the Pentagon's frantic attempts to label all sightings as mistakes or illusions, Salandin's officially confirmed report gave UFO censors the jitters. It would not take many news stories like these to expose the cover-up policy.

To their relief there was no sign of Salandin's story in the next morning's papers. But a Reuters dispatch from Nairobi, Kenya, quickly filled the gap. As if timed to answer the Chicago *Tribune* story, the Nairobi dispatch reported that a flying saucer had been sighted by G. Duncan Fletcher, vice-president of the Kenya Astronomical Association. Moreover, after analyzing hundreds of reports, including sightings over East Africa, Fletcher calmly made public his conviction that the saucers came from outer space.

"From all the information available they are steadily mapping every part of our earth," he told the Reuters agency. "Reports have been made by observers who have seen these unidentified flying objects over atomic plants, dock yards, airfields, naval bases, and some of the larger cities of the world. Their approach to us is, I suggest, similar to what our own approach would be if the boot were on the other foot. Suppose we were to visit Venus. I do not think that we would land until we had made every possible investigation.

"The obvious thing is that we should map, photograph, and if possible carry out a thorough investigation before we wantonly risked life by hasty landing. It is not unreasonable therefore that whatever controls the UFO's is doing exactly that."

A few hours after I read this statement, which amounted to a rebuttal of the Air Force slam against astronomers, Frank Edwards phoned.

After he left Mutual, Frank had built up an independent weekly program, which he taped for distribution to radio stations all over the country. This was his day to record the next week's broadcast.

"Can you come over here?" Frank asked quickly.

"Why, what's happened?"

"It's about the clamp on the Mars discoveries. Dr. Slipher's back from South Africa, and I've just heard he wants to break the news about Mars. There's a fight on about it.

If you can help me get the dope, I'd like to use it on this program I'm about to tape."

"I'll be right over," I said.

During the last few eventful weeks I had half forgotten about the Mars Committee. As I drove in to Washington, I recalled what Dr. Slipher had said before he left for South Africa—that he would instantly announce any discovery of life on Mars.

From April to September he and his staff had constantly watched Mars. But he had made just one statement—that photographs of Mars showed new and interesting changes. After that, silence.

By now, however, hints of startling Mars discoveries had begun to trickle out in various astronomer's journals. Even by the 1st of June the existence of more than 40 canals had been definitely confirmed by the Mars Committee. In addition, the existence of 15 large oases also had been confirmed. But very few of the general public had any idea of this.

When I met Frank, his round, good-humored face showed unusual excitement.

"Here's the dope," he said quickly. "Dr. Slipher got back here a few days ago with thousands of photographs taken at Blomfontein. I was told that they have proof the canals are real. And that they connect with all the oases. I think Dr. Slipher is still in Washington. Do you know anybody who could locate him for me?"

"Yes, Mr. Booth up at *National Geographic* would know. I'll see what I can find out."

Before calling Booth, I jotted down a few questions. One point—the key to the canal riddle—had already been stated publicly by Dr. Robert S. Richardson, the Mars expert at Palomar Observatory. Writing in *This Week* magazine, Dr. Richardson had said:

"Astronomers hope to obtain photographs which will show markings on Mars so clearly that we can determine whether the canals are natural or artificial. On a planet as smooth as Mars it seems reasonable to suppose that real canals would be built along what are called "great circle" paths—the name sailors give to the shortest distance between points on the surface of a sphere.

"If the photographs show that the canals always lie along great circle paths it would be an indication they are the work of intelligent beings."

In conclusion Dr. Richardson said:

"It is conceivable that some form of life, quite different from ours, might have developed on Mars. . . ."

When I got Booth on the phone he told me that Dr. Slipher had left Washington.

"Do you have his final report on the canals?" I said.

"We have part of it," Booth said guardedly. "Also a report on photographs taken in June at Lowell Observatory. The Lowell pictures show at least one new canal. It runs from the south polar cap and could then be seen quite easily since that side of Mars was tilted toward the earth. The north polar cap was tilted away."

"Has Palomar reported yet?" I said.

"No. They got some pictures with the 200-inch telescope," replied Booth, "but they're still analyzing them."

"Mr. Booth," I said, "remember you told me there would be frequent news stories about what the Mars Committee sighted. What happened?"

Booth hesitated.

"Well, they were all very busy. There were difficulties of communication, coordination, and so on."

"Then is everything going to be held up?" I asked.

"No. Dr. Slipher will make a statement in the very near future."

"Did any of the pictures"—I tried to make it sound casual —"show that the canals followed great circle courses?"

For a moment I thought Booth was not going to answer.

"Yes, they did," he said slowly. "After analyzing the first group of pictures, Dr. Slipher said positively that the canals followed great-circle lines."

So Redell had had it straight, back in June.

"Is he going to make that public?" I asked quickly.

"I don't know." Booth paused again. "There's some disagreement as to what was seen."

"Then there won't be an official Mars Committee report?"

"No. Perhaps in 1956—they're planning another close watch for then."

I hung up and told Frank what Booth had said.

"So they're great circles!" Frank said. "That proves it. The canals are artificial waterways, just as Lowell said."

"Are you going to use it?" I asked.

"I'll try to get hold of Dr. Slipher first."

For two or three days Frank tried to locate the astronomer, but before he could succeed, Dr. Slipher's statement was on the press wires.

Though he evidently had been persuaded not to mention the great-circle discovery, he had come close to breaking the news.

"Mars is alive. It has to be," he told the press. After revealing the discovery of new canals, he disclosed significant changes in the Martian geography. The oases of Mars, Dr. Slipher said, changed color, grew, and shrank with the seasons. In 1954 these were broader and more intense in color than any he had seen in 50 years of observation.

"This last year," he added, "must have been a very good and fertile year on Mars."

When the story came out, I called Frank Edwards.

"Yes, I just saw it," he said. "They must have really put the pressure on Dr. Slipher."

"It looks bad," I said. "If they can stop a man like that, the blackout must really be tightening."

15 The Invisible Saucers

But the censors had little time to rejoice. In rapid succession foreign reports appeared in the headlines day after day.

On October 23 a Buenos Aires report described a disc that had maneuvered over the city.

Next day a formation of "circular silver-colored" objects was sighted by Brazilian Air Force pilots at Pôrto Alegre, Brazil. In an official statement the Air Force Base Command said the objects were moving at tremendous speed over the base:

"It was impossible to calculate the altitude or velocity at which the objects moved, but the speed was greater than that of any of which the base has knowledge. Their general shape was circular, they were silver-colored and shimmering. The objects were not celestial because their movements appeared to be mechanical and intermittent."

The Air Base Command said the saucers were observed by officers and enlisted men, by personnel of the Vargas Airline, and by civilians in Pôrto Alegre. The Air Ministry in Rio de Janeiro, it added, was officially investigating.

The day after the official Brazilian announcement Yugoslavian Air Force officers were startled by a flight of saucers just after sunrise. Within 48 hours the government announced at Belgrade that the mystery was "being taken very seriously."

According to official reports scores of glowing objects had streaked over Yugoslavia, giving off a bluish glow. One of the flights, moving between Zagreb and Belgrade at fantastic speed, was clocked by two weather-station observatories. It was found they had covered the 250 miles in five minutes at a rate of 3000 miles an hour. Several of the Yugoslavian astronomers stated the UFO's could not have been meteors and probably were not any form of "heavenly body."

The official Yugoslavian investigation had been announced only 24 hours when a new flying-saucer report was flashed to the United States from Rome. On October 28 a flying disc was sighted over Rome by many observers, including U. S. Ambassador Clare Boothe Luce.

"I saw something, but I don't know what it was," Ambassador Luce admitted.

As the saucer raced over the fashionable Boulevard Via Veneto, it was sighted by Maurizio Andreolo, an AP reporter.

"It looked," he said, "like a moon dashing across the sky at fantastic speed. It flew silently."

On this same night flying saucers returned to Washington, D. C. Once again, as in 1952 and during the two tense nights of June, 1954, Control Center radarmen tracked the mysterious formations as they maneuvered over the capital. Again a hasty alert sent interceptors skyward, streaking up after the UFO's. Before they could reach the saucers' altitude, the strange machines had raced off into the night. But by this time they had been seen by hundreds of people in Washington and its suburbs.

Quickly the silence group went into action to avoid a repetition of the 1952 hysteria. An explanation was hurriedly given to the newspapers, tagged as a CAA report to avoid any Air Force connection.

Admitting the flying-saucer reports, CAA tower operators at the National Airport were quoted as saying that witnesses were misled by airplane landing lights.

"It was one of those clear nights," the statement read, "when the ceiling was so high—some 30,000 feet—that it wasn't considered a ceiling at all. Besides, for some unexplained reason, air traffic was unusually heavy. To guard against collisions, aircraft turned on their lights with the result that the metropolitan area was full of 'flying saucers.'"

This incredible explanation was a clear indication of the UFO censors' desperation. Every night dozens of airliners fly over Washington, and the sight of landing lights is so common as to be ignored by most of the population. Moreover, all aircraft approaching Washington are contacted by the Control Center when they are still miles from the field. After the Center guides them into the proper approach lanes, the tower takes over with final landing instructions. Under such precise control it is impossible for any sudden "unexplained" increase of normal traffic to occur.

Was there perhaps a new order to explain away immediately all saucer sightings?

To see if I had missed any recent clue I checked back through the October reports. There was one aerial mystery, but so far as I knew it was not linked to the flying saucers. On October 12 an F-100, one of our latest type jets, had disintegrated over California. Investigators found there had been no explosion, as first reported. Since the pilot had been killed, no one knew what had happened. But there was evidence that the jet fighter had been torn apart by a powerful force.

Two days after this Lou Corbin called me to report another development.

"Do you know anything about a 'crashed-object' program?" he asked me.

"No. Whose project is it?"

"It's an Air Force deal, unless somebody's trying to trick me. You've heard of the 4602nd Air Intelligence Service Squadron, of course?"

"Yes. It's a hush-hush unit. They have investigators in all Air Defense Squadrons."

"Well, I've been contacted by one of them. First I thought it might be some kind of hoax. But I've double-checked. He actually is with the 4602nd."

"Sounds queer, Lou. They're not supposed to talk to anyone outside of Intelligence."

"I know. But he may be under special orders. Anyway, he's against the secrecy policy. He told me the 4602nd had a special program called the 'investigation of unidentified crashed objects.'"

"If it's true, that *is* big," I said. "It could mean they've actually got their hands on some flying saucers."

"He wouldn't admit that," said Corbin. "But I got the impression they'd recovered some kind of 'objects'—probably something dropped from a saucer."

Before he hung up, Corbin told me of an odd incident on one of his recent programs.

"I was interviewing two Air Force officers about their tie-in with the Civil Air Patrol. One of them was a captain who had just returned from Alaska. I happened to know he'd worked on the UFO investigation up there. When we finished with the CAP, I asked him why the Air Force was so secretive about flying saucers."

"For a second I thought he'd blow up. Then he got hold of himself and said he didn't know anything about the subject. After we were off the air, back in my office, he jumped me for springing the question on him. We had quite a hassle and then, all of a sudden, he blurted this out.

"'What good would it do you if you did know the truth?'"

"Did anybody else hear it?" I asked him.

"Yes. Helen Brooks—she's another WFBR announcer. That's all I could get out of him. He knew he'd said too much and he clammed up."

Immediately after I talked with Corbin, I learned that three unexplained aircraft accidents had occurred on the night of the 28th, just before the saucers raced over Washington. Any one of them would have been enough to upset the most stoic observer.

Early in the evening a Navy jet fighter made an emergency landing five miles at sea near Norfolk, Virginia. Though the pilot was rescued, no explanation of the accident was made public. A few hours after this, two twin-engined antisub patrol planes vanished offshore, also in the Norfolk area. At their base in Norfolk, officers said neither crew had reported trouble in their last radio messages. Though both planes were equipped with life rafts, no survivors were found.

Then came the most dramatic development of all. On Saturday night, October 31, a giant Navy transport carrying 42 persons also disappeared somewhere over the Atlantic. In a routine flight the four-engined Super Constellation had taken off from Patuxent, Maryland, carrying Navy personnel and two or three Navy families to a base in the Azores. As in the other cases, there had been no SOS, no indication of trouble—only an ominous silence after the last routine radio report.

For four days the aircraft carrier *Leyte* and 29 other vessels combed a wide area. At the same time aircraft crews scanned an expanse 200 miles on each side of the missing transport's course.

But not a trace was found—no wreckage, no bodies, nothing.

Though I knew of no link with the flying saucers, this case reminded me inevitably of the F-89 disappearance over Lake Superior. It was almost a year since that fateful night in '53 when the Kimross jet had been lost.

I was still thinking about the Kimross mystery when an air-mail letter from London brought me a baffling new report.

One day in late September, as UFO sightings were increasing all over Europe, the British War Office received an incredible radar report. At noon on the preceding day a strange U-formation had appeared on a civilian radarscope. Counting the blips, the operator found the formation consisted of 40 or 50 UFO's, covering an area 12 miles long and eight miles wide. Flying west at 12,000 feet, the saucers changed with a precise movement from a U-formation to two parallel lines. A few moments later these lines broke and the UFO's reformed in a perfect Z.

Incredulous at first, the War Office and the Air Ministry started a routine investigation. It had hardly begun when the mysterious UFO's returned. As before, they arrived at noon over the same area. Like a well-trained aircraft squadron, they changed precisely from the first U-formation to parallel lines, then to the final Z before they disappeared.

At a score of War Office and Air Ministry radar stations, astonished operators fully confirmed the first report. Though the Air Ministry was sure these were no British aircraft, a quick check was made. In addition, British Intelligence agents on the continent searched for a clue to the mystery formation. But no one in Europe had seen the strange machines.

Up to then, each time radar had caught the objects over England, cloudy skies had hidden them from the ground. But the third appearance came on a bright, clear day. By now not only radar stations but RAF bases and jet patrols had been put on the alert.

As before, the familiar formation appeared at noon. Again the unknown craft separated into two parallel lines and then formed the huge Z. But this time the War Office made a startling discovery.

Though tracked perfectly on all radarscopes, the UFO formation was invisible to the human eye.

Even with all the official evidence, some members of the

Air Ministry refused to believe the reports. All radar stations were ordered to recheck their equipment. When the equipment was found to be in order, Civil Defense plane-spotters and the RAF were ordered to maintain special alerts.

Four more times the mystery formation returned at noon, performing its strange maneuvers over the area. Each time ground observers trained binoculars on the area indicated by radar. Each time RAF pilots flying above 12,000 feet stared down from their jets, looking for the unknown machines.

But all they could see was an empty sky.

For over a month this story was kept from the public. Then some of the details confirmed by the British War Office appeared in the London *Sunday Dispatch* under a six-column double-banner headline, "Strange Sights in Sky Baffle War Office."

Though the headlines mentioned "sights," this dramatic new story explained that the mysterious formation had never been actually seen.

"They are invisible to the human eye," a War Office spokesman told the *Dispatch*. "Every time, they have followed the same pattern, always around mid-day. All our radar sets in the area have picked them up."

Neither the War Office nor the Air Ministry could explain what the radar blips meant. But a careful check had shown they were not caused by any identifiable aircraft.

When the *Dispatch* asked what the objects could be, the War Office spokesman said he had been given top-level orders to "maintain the utmost secrecy."

Then he added, "Even if I did know what they are, I am too worried to say anything."

Of all the saucer reports this was one of the most baffling. Flying-saucer formations—usually V's—had been sighted several times. And in a few cases formations had actually changed—as at Hamilton Air Force Base in California, on August 3. On that occasion several discs which had flown in a circle were seen by Air Force pilots to take up a diamond-shaped formation.

But *invisible* UFO's—that was hard to believe. Had the story not been backed by the staid British War Office and reported by the highly reputable London *Dispatch,* I would have thought it a hoax.

Listing the key points, I tried to reach Senior Radar Controller Harry Barnes. But the Control Center told me he had just gone off duty. When I phoned Paul Redell, I found that he was getting ready to return to the Coast for an indefinite stay.

"I'm tied up with office conferences all day," he told me. "If you want to meet me at the airport this evening we might have a few minutes——"

"Let me come in and drive you out," I suggested. "We can talk on the way."

"Okay, I'll call you back about the time."

That evening I picked him up at his F Street hotel. As we swung south on 14th Street, I started to tell about the report from London.

But he interrupted.

"Yes, I know about it, and I'm pretty sure it's happened here too."

"Paul, this floors me. I've always thought of the saucers as solid objects, probably metallic——"

"So have I," said Redell. "I still do."

I stared across at him as we stopped for traffic at Pennsylvania Avenue.

"Don't tell me you believe in this 'dematerialization' business!"

"The fourth dimension? That hasn't anything to do with it," he said.

"Then how can the things make themselves invisible?"

Redell did not answer until we crossed the avenue and were passing the Commerce Building.

"Look," he said, "I'm not trying to be mysterious. But I believe that the answer is tied in with some highly classified research I've heard about. Even though our company isn't working on it, I can't say a thing."

"Can you tell me this?" I asked him. "This secret research —I know we're trying to duplicate the saucers as fast as possible—do you mean we already know about the invisibility angle and are trying to achieve that too?"

Redell considered for a moment and then shook his head. "I'm sorry, Don, I can't answer that either. There's one lead I can give you, because it's on the record. Do you remember some strange radar reports in World War II about phantom objects—they later called it the 'ghost of Nansei-shoto'?"

"I ought to know it," I answered. "It just happens I know the Combat Intelligence Center officer who made that first report. His name is James Dawson and he lives in Washington. In fact he gave me a report on the incident."

Redell made a quick gesture.

"All right. Check it over. The Nansei-shoto thing is exactly the same as what happened over England. Some day when the lid is lifted, I'll explain it."

We rode along in silence for a few minutes. I tried to puzzle out Redell's meaning. Then, as we started across the highway bridge, I remembered another question I had meant to ask him some time ago.

"Paul, do you remember I told you about that F-89 incident, the plane that was lost over Lake Superior?"

When Redell did not answer after a moment, I took a quick look at him. He was eying me curiously.

"What made you bring that up?" he said.

"I'd meant to ask you several times. I just remembered."

"The reason I asked," said Redell, "was that it might . . . Don, I'm not trying to be coy, but this also could be tied in with the same deal. That is, it may be hooked to one basic fact and that's the thing I can't talk about."

"Then you know what happened to the F-89?"

Redell hesitated, looking out thoughtfully over the Potomac. As we reached the end of the bridge and circled down toward the Mount Vernon Boulevard, he glanced back.

"I don't *know* what happened, but there's one theoretical possibility."

That was all he would say. As I let him out at the airport, I asked one final question.

"Paul, this possibility you mentioned. If it's right, would it mean good or bad news?"

"God only knows," he replied.

The discovery of *visible* saucers had been serious enough, since normal aircraft were helpless against them. But at least they could be seen and, if necessary, attacked with guided missiles. The discovery now of invisible flying saucers would be enough to frighten anyone.

When I got home I looked up the report Dawson had given me on the Nansei-shoto riddle. During World War II Dawson had been a Combat Information Center officer aboard an aircraft carrier. His job, like that of other CIC officers, was to direct fighter aircraft on task-force missions and to supply combat information to the task-force commanders. In the last year of the war he had taken part in the main Okinawa attack and helped direct numerous air strikes and antisub patrols in the last bloody struggle to crush Japan.

At the time covered by this report, Dawson's task force was patrolling the Nansei-shoto Archipelago, a group of rocky little islands south of Okinawa. Working with other task forces, their planes pounded the air bases on the Nansei-shoto Islands (Ryu Kyu Islands) to prevent their attacking our landing forces at Okinawa.

It was during this time that Dawson and the CIC men met the "ghost of Nansei-shoto."

It was a bright day with clouds scattered at 5000 feet. Down in the Combat Information Center of Dawson's carrier, he and two intercept officers sat before a huge round radarscope, its greenish-white glow reflecting on their faces. Watching the glass screen, Dawson could see all the task-force ships—the two carriers, with their escort cruisers and destroyers—and also all aircraft within a radius of 100 miles.

In front of the three officers was a large transparent plotting board. Two plotters with headphones stood ready to mark the position of any enemy aircraft.

To the rear, in a darkened cubicle, a Navy radar operator kept a constant watch on his scope. He reported every change at 30-second intervals.

On this particular day most of the task-force planes were absent on a support mission. Only 12 remained to protect the ship—four in the air and four on each of the two carriers' flight decks.

Dawson was checking the latest weather reports when one of the intercept officers gave an exclamation. Quickly Dawson looked toward the huge plexiglass plotting board. Marking down a new radar report, one plotter had just drawn a huge circled X at a point 120 miles from the carrier. Moments later he marked VL beside it—the symbol for a very large blip.

Dawson grabbed a handphone connected with the radar operator.

"What's that large plot you just sent?" he demanded.

"Looks like 200 or 300 bogeys," the answer came back.

Seconds later a plotter penciled the ominous words on the board: 200 to 300 aircraft, unidentified.

Almost unable to believe the report, Dawson looked down at the scope before him. But there it was: a huge greenish-white blob now on the verge of the 100-mile circle.

He turned swiftly to one intercept officer.

"Try to get the speed estimate," he said. The officer made a quick check.

"I don't believe it," he muttered.

"What is it?" said Dawson.

"It's 650 knots," the intercept officer told him.

For a moment intense quiet fell over the Combat Information Center. There was no plane on earth that could make 650 knots—almost 700 miles an hour. Or was it possible the Japs had somehow pulled a miracle and secretly built a huge force of supersonic planes?

It couldn't be—and Dawson knew it.

But no matter what it was, this was a mass raid coming in rapidly from the northeast. And all they had to oppose them were 12 inferior fighters. Quickly the CIC men flashed word to the bridge. A second later the "General Quarters" alarm clanged through the loud-speaker system. Up on the flight deck four engines roared into life.

Twelve propeller-driven fighters against that horde of fast mystery machines! It was pitifully small, Dawson thought grimly. Yet it was all they could do. As the eight remaining planes of the task force roared off toward the mystery raiders, Dawson looked again at the plotting board.

The unknown raiders, flying at 12,000 feet, were 80 miles away. Then, as Dawson watched, two "arms" began to extend like curving tentacles from the main body of the approaching mass. Dawson groaned. They were spreading out as if to cover the entire task force of Navy vessels.

At Dawson's direction the Navy planes—now 45 miles away —were flying at 15,000 feet. Tautly the CIC men watched the blips of the fighters as they neared the massed unknowns.

"Bogeys now 20 miles," rapped one of the intercept officers, calling off the distance from the objects to the planes. And abruptly all three officers stared at one another. The visibility at that height was 50 miles. Long before now the mystery formation should have been sighted by the pilots.

"Bogeys now only 10 miles . . . five miles . . . three miles . . . look down, *look down!*"

For five or ten seconds the loud-speakers were silent. Then came the senior pilot's reply.

"Nothing in sight . . . no bogeys . . . nothing!"

Dumfounded, Dawson and the others sat still for a moment. The blips of the unknown craft were still racing toward the carriers and their escort ships. Hurriedly recalling the fighters, Dawson seized his phone and warned the bridge of the impending attack.

"You're crazy!" the captain shouted. "There's nothing in sight. What the hell's going on down there?"

Dawson stared back at the scope. The raiders, closing at terrific speed, were now only five miles away. Dropping his phone, he ran out to the catwalk beside the flight deck.

But there was only empty blue sky above . . .

Later Dawson learned that the fighter director on the flagship also had seen the phantom machines on a radarscope. In the weeks that followed, other Navy CIC men tracked similar invisible craft.

After the war the Navy officially confirmed the "ghost of Nansei-shoto." But even six years later, when I first met James Dawson, no explanation had ever been found—or at least made public.

"Whatever the answer," Dawson told me, "I hope they'll continue to be neutral. It's not a pleasant thing to sit there helplessly and watch those 'invisible' aircraft close in on you."

16 "Angel's Hair"

The day after I checked the Nansei-shoto report, I managed to reach Harry Barnes at the airport Control Center. During my investigation of the mysterious Washington sighting in 1952 we had become good friends. I had intended to ask him about the invisible UFO's, but as soon as I mentioned "flying saucers," Barnes stopped me.

"I'm sorry, but I couldn't answer any questions on UFO's unless you first submitted them to the CAA."

"All right. Maybe I'll try it—but I don't think it'll do any good."

Before I could draw up the questions for the CAA, I was interrupted by an old Air Force feud.

Some months before, a Cincinnati businessman, Thomas D. Eickhoff, had determined to get to the bottom of the flying-saucer mystery. On June 8 he had driven to Dayton. With his wife as a witness, he had a three-hour conversation with Colonel John O'Mara, Deputy Commander of ATIC. This was just before O'Mara's surprising revelation of "700 sightings a week."

Later, in a statement notarized at my request, Eickhoff told me that Colonel O'Mara had denied the existence of the Utah pictures. When Eickhoff referred to my other claims, Colonel O'Mara denied I had received any official material from the Air Force. In effect, said Eickhoff, Colonel O'Mara had labeled me a liar and a fraud.

When he returned to Cincinnati, Eickhoff relayed this information to Leonard Stringfield, publisher of CRIFO. Calling Colonel O'Mara at Dayton, Stringfield told me, he was given similar statements by the colonel.

When I first heard of this from Eickhoff and Stringfield, I called Captain White at the Pentagon.

"I'll relay it to the Directorate of Intelligence," he said. "But I can't believe Colonel O'Mara really would say anything like that."

A month later he told me that Colonel O'Mara had denied making any such comment.

"I want that in writing," I said. "Will you ask the Directorate to get it for me?"

White promised he would pass on my request.

Afterward I learned that O'Mara had been called to Washington. But by November I still had no answer.

On November 10, I wrote the Air Force and asked that O'Mara be ordered to retract any charges he had made. Next day White told me that Intelligence was still investigating.

"It will probably take another week or so," White said.

While I was waiting, I checked over a number of strange UFO developments, beginning with the "angel's-hair" case at Marysville, Ohio.

On November 1, two teachers and about 60 students reported sighting a cigar-shaped flying saucer which had hovered over Jerome Elementary School. According to Principal Rodney Warrick, one of the witnesses, the strange machine appeared to have windows. Its luminosity was so brilliant that he had to shield his eyes.

Suddenly the object, moving silently, accelerated to a terrific speed. As it raced westward it left a three-mile trail of milky-white asbestos-like strands which settled over trees, bushes, and telephone lines.

Both Warrick and the other teacher, Mrs. George Dittmar,

recovered some of the "angel's hair"—the name which had been applied in similar cases.

When they pulled one strand into a thread, they found it so tough that it could hardly be broken. But a few moments after they had touched it, the substance disappeared.

Warrick, however, managed to preserve one specimen in a glass jar, though he reported that his hands temporarily turned green from handling it.

Though in 1952 I had been skeptical of angel's-hair reports, there was now convincing evidence of its link with the flying saucers. The '52 report had stated that hundreds of citizens in northern France had watched a huge cigar-shaped machine escorted by a squadron of flying discs. As the formation speeded up, a trail of angel's hair was seen to come from the tail of the mother ship.

In one incredible news story from France frightened citizens insisted they had seen some of the weblike substance trap a doctor like an insect caught in a web. As he struggled, the witnesses said, the angel's hair released him, regathered, and rose into the air.

It was this unbelievable detail which had made me reject the angel's-hair story. But since then the phenomenon had been fully confirmed. One report had come from Pierre Clostermann, a French air ace. While flying near Marseilles, Clostermann sighted a fast-moving saucer from which, he said, "little white flakes were escaping."

Then, on April 15, 1953, a news report from Auckland, New Zealand, added new evidence. On that day a mass of the strange white substance had drifted down from the sky over Ongaonga. For a while, before it evaporated, it covered fields, buildings, wires, trees, and fences for hundreds of yards around. As in the other cases the substance quickly disintegrated when handled.

On November 16, 1953, a new familiar trail of angel's hair was seen in the San Fernando Valley, just after a saucer passed over the area. Later the discovery was revealed in a four-column story with the headline, "Valley Mystery Craft Spins Web." Under the by-line of Gordon Grant, the story said:

"A fluffy blanket, dead-white, almost ephemeral in its delicacy and apparently electrically charged, may be the San Fernando Valley's first physical contact with visitors from outer space. It is reported to have streamed like a lacy ribbon from a mysterious craft that sped over the valley."

Within 24 hours aviation engineers from three companies —Lockheed, North American, and Douglas—appeared on the scene to examine the mysterious filaments. There was a rumor that the Air Force had asked them to make the investigation.

Then, on February 1, 1954, there had been a second angel's-hair case in the San Fernando Valley. After this there had been a long lull in such reports until mid-October, when the Fort Wayne *News Sentinel* reported that strange "white cocoons" had been drifting down over the city for several days.

Despite the evidence there was no clear explanation. Apparently the angel's hair was some kind of a fuel exhaust confined specifically to the cigar-shaped saucers. In some news stories, witnesses had expressed fear it might be radioactive. But up until now, as far as I knew, there was no proof of this.

Though few important UFO sightings made headlines in early November, a dramatic case on the 11th broke through the blackout. At 3:00 P.M. a huge, round, glowing object appeared over Louisville, Kentucky. Sighted by thousands, it caused a rush of calls to newspapers and police. Confirmed by the 784th Ground Control radar unit, the saucer was tracked as it passed near Godman Field, where in 1952 Captain Thomas Mantell had begun his fatal chase of another saucer.

After checking the radar reports, Lieutenant Colonel Lee Merkel, Base Commander of the Kentucky Air National Guard, notified Wright-Patterson Field.

Then a strange sequence of events began.

According to Wright-Patterson an F-86 was immediately sent to investigate. But its pilot, they said, could not even sight the object. Just after this, Colonel Merkel and another Air Guard pilot tried to close in on the object, which, to them, was now quite visible.

After he landed, Colonel Merkel said the UFO was traveling against the wind, which would have been impossible for a balloon.

"I don't believe in flying saucers," he told reporters, "but I'm definitely getting curious."

In Louisville, Ground Observer Corps officials sent pictures taken by the *Courier-Journal* to "higher-ups" in the Air Force.

Four days later, in spite of the evidence, the UFO was explained away as a large research balloon "believed to have been released near Minneapolis."

When I called White to check on the Louisville incident, he told me the latest on O'Mara. The investigation was now being handled by Lieutenant Colonel Joseph Bloomer in the Directorate of Air Force Intelligence.

"Why don't you see Colonel Bloomer personally?" asked White. "You'll find him quite fair."

"All right, I'll call him. But there's one thing I'd like to ask you first. I hear that Colonel O'Mara also denied there was ever a secret Intelligence analysis drawn up in '52. I happen to know it was drawn up by Major Dewey Fournet. And since Ruppelt has confirmed that Fournet believed the saucers were interplanetary, it's pretty obvious his report said so too."

"Yes, I know about that report," White answered, "but I

don't know O'Mara's angle. You'd better ask Colonel Bloomer about it."

I made a date to see Colonel Bloomer on November 25. Before going into the Pentagon I assembled my evidence— the ATIC list, the official clearance letter, the statement by Captain Ed Ruppelt, and the canceled Utah press release. In addition, I listed all the Air Force statements and contradictions on the Utah pictures. These included one point known to few of the public:

Early in 1954 the Cleveland *Press,* a Scripps-Howard paper, had asked to see the Utah film. After some delay the Pentagon agreed to let a Cleveland *Press* writer view the film at Dayton. But by the time he was ready to make the trip he was told by ATIC that their only copy had just burned up.

However, said ATIC, there was probably a master film at the Pentagon. Following up, the Cleveland *Press* rechecked.

"We have no copy here," said an Air Force spokesman. "But we believe there is one at Dayton."

But the *Press,* tired of this run-around, gave up the struggle.

When I saw Colonel Bloomer he told me that O'Mara had already corrected his error in regard to the Utah pictures.

"That is, he admitted to Stringfield that there is no question of the Utah pictures' existence or the analysis."

"No one told Eickhoff that," I said.

"Judging from this evidence, I think Colonel O'Mara will be instructed to put Mr. Eickhoff straight."

Before I left I asked the colonel about Fournet's secret report. Like Captain White, he admitted that my published statement about this Intelligence analysis was correct.

"The report did conclude that the UFO's were extraterrestrial," he said. "Major Fournet urged General Samford to release it, but the general did not agree. The report is filed as an unfinished Air Force document."

What Bloomer himself believed I could not tell. But he

made no attempt to alter my own convictions or to laugh off the saucer problem.

Within 24 hours Colonel O'Mara was summoned to the Pentagon by General Samford and directed to erase any false impression he had given regarding my book.

On December 1, I received a copy of O'Mara's letter to Thomas B. Eickhoff, insisting that Eickhoff had misunderstood him. Colonel O'Mara admitted that *Flying Saucers from Outer Space* contained officially released Air Force reports.

"I did express to you," he wrote Eickhoff, "that I might differ with Major Keyhoe's opinions but never that he was a liar and a fraud."

From the start I had believed the sworn statements by Eickhoff and Stringfield. But even though O'Mara denied any attempted smear, his letter was a complete vindication for me. Important as this was, however, a new UFO development quickly overshadowed it.

At 2:00 P.M. on November 30 a mysterious bright flash in the sky was reported simultaneously in Atlanta, Newman, and Columbus, Georgia; in Sylacauga and Birmingham, Alabama; and as far away as Greenville, Mississippi. This brilliant light was immediately followed by a series of strange explosions, apparently centered high in the sky above Sylacauga.

Moments later a black object, six inches in diameter, crashed into the home of Mrs. Hewlett Hodges.

Smashing a three-foot-wide hole in the roof, the shining black object tore through the living-room ceiling. Striking the radio, it bounced off and gashed Mrs. Hodges' arm.

Meanwhile, the mysterious explosions had caused a hurried Air Defense alert. A three-state search for fallen objects was immediately begun by squadrons of Air Force planes.

When word of the "Sylacauga object" reached the Air Force, Intelligence officers flew to the scene from Maxwell

Air Force Base at Montgomery. Explaining that "the Air Force is required to examine such strange objects," they whisked it away to Maxwell Field, from which it was flown immediately to ATIC.

An hour or two later the object was labeled a meteorite.

As soon as this appeared in the papers, I received a call from Lou Corbin. "It's plain that this is part of the Air Force 'unidentified crashed-objects' investigation. They must believe the thing is linked with the saucers."

"It doesn't look like a coincidence," I said, "that this object fell just after those explosions. If it had been a meteor exploding, it wouldn't have made such a bright flash in the daytime."

"In the first news story," Corbin told me, "it was called an unidentified flying object. At least that's the way the Maxwell Field officers explained why they had started the search."

"This reminds me of that East New Haven signboard case," I commented. "On that occasion the object wasn't recovered. Judging from the size of the hole it made, however, it was probably about the same size."

"It's a queer business," said Corbin, "and apparently they're worried more than ever about things leaking out. I found that out four nights ago after a sighting at Millville, New Jersey."

On the night of November 26, Corbin said, an object with four reddish-yellow lights forming a rectangle had circled over Millville. Shortly afterward a searchlight had caught the object, revealing it to be a huge disc. As soon as the light touched it, the UFO speeded up and swiftly disappeared.

One of the witnesses, Mrs. Lois Barbour, called the nearest CAA office. Minutes later she received a call from Captain W. J. Thompson at Olmstead Air Force Base. From his questions it was obvious that jets were attempting an interception.

"I got the dope from a reporter I know at Millville,"

Corbin told me. "When I phoned Captain Thompson he said Air Defense had been alerted by CAA's Air Traffic Control in New York. He refused to say anything about the Millville sighting—told me it was classified. But right on top of that he admitted knowing about the investigation of 'unidentified crashed objects.' And here's the payoff. He told me they had orders to report all press and radio queries to high authorities. From the way he talked, I think that includes the CAA too."

"That doesn't surprise me," I said.

After talking with Corbin I checked back on the East New Haven signboard incident. Fortunately I had a complete report from Mrs. Coral Lorenzen, one of the first private UFO investigators. A competent private astronomer, Mrs. Lorenzen, aided by her husband, an electronics expert, had organized a UFO investigation group known as APRO (Aerial Phenomena Research Organization). Unlike some later UFO investigation groups, Mrs. Lorenzen and APRO had blasted at the unsupported claims of contacts with space men and other extravagant saucer stories. As a result, APRO's membership now included a large number of pilots, aeronautical engineers, astronomers, and other scientists, as well as the general public.*

Just after the East New Haven incident an investigation was made by Mr. Joseph Barbieri and Mr. August C. Roberts, representing another inquiry group known as SPACE.

In a report later relayed to Mrs. Lorenzen, Barbieri added dramatic details to the first news story.

On the night of August 19, 1953, hundreds of East New Haven residents had heard a whistling and a thunderous roar, followed by a blast which shook doors and windows and momentarily dimmed house lights.

Out-of-door witnesses told Barbieri and Roberts that a red

* APRO address: 519 New York Street, Alamagordo, New Mexico.

ball of fire, trailing sparks, had smashed through the steel signboard as if it were tissue paper. Then, angling upward, it streaked on, barely missing a passing automobile.

Barbieri secured a section of the signboard and attempted to get an analysis of the strange yellow deposits around the edge of the hole. Balked in his attempt, he turned the problem over to Mrs. Lorenzen and APRO. An analysis was then made by the Anderson Laboratories at Milwaukee and the Chicago Spectrographic Service Laboratory. Both confirmed that the gold-colored metal found in pits around the hole was definitely copper.

"It is my opinion," Mrs. Lorenzen wrote in sending me the analyses, "that the object was a missile of some type which had gone out of control and come too close to the ground."

Along with the analyses, Mrs. Lorenzen had sent me a section of the signboard metal and two photographs of the hole made in the billboard. The heavy-gauge steel had been torn. The edges were twisted back, curled, in proof of the terrific impact from the unknown object. Had it struck anywhere but the billboard, the results might have been disastrous.

The analyses proved that the object could not have been a meteor. It was a disquieting thought that it might have been a missile from outer space.

On December 1 a flying-saucer photograph taken in Sicily appeared in papers all over the United States. In New York the *Herald Tribune* ran it on the front page, accompanied by a story describing the careful United Press investigation which had proved this photograph was not a fake. Unexpectedly, the Air Force admitted it was investigating this important foreign sighting.

In another foreign story the following day the government of Iran reported a rush of saucer reports and added:

"If these are from other governments, please keep them at home. We already have enough trouble."

Then from Caracas came a wire service story reporting a mass sighting by most of the population. Like other reports, this showed there was an increase in foreign sightings.

That same day a puzzling report on Mars was released by the Carnegie Institution in Washington. For almost six months, the Institution revealed, it had known of a mysterious marking on Mars showing as the letter W.

Seen in motion pictures, taken in blue light, the gigantic W was found to measure 1100 miles from tip to tip. Round knobs at its apexes proved to be more than 300 miles in diameter. These huge knobs, said the Carnegie Institution, were extremely bright, almost as brilliant as Mars' white polar caps.

This enormous W was explained as "presumably a cloud formation in the upper atmosphere of the planet," which rotated at the same speed as Mars.

I was looking up the reports of strange Martian clouds when Frank Edwards phoned me.

"Have you seen that Mars W story?" he inquired.

"Yes, I was just starting to check on it."

"How the devil could any cloud form a shape like that— let alone hold it for days?" Frank demanded.

"It's no ordinary cloud, that's plain. In fact I don't believe that any kind of cloud could hold its shape and rotate at the same speed as the planet. I was just checking a statement by Walter H. Haas, Director of the Association of Lunar and Planetary Observers. He had an article on Mars in the June, '54, issue of *Sky and Telescope*. Here's what he says about Martian clouds:

" 'It is difficult to distinguish between true cloud projections and apparent projections caused by the irradiation of bright areas close to the edge of the disc.' "

Frank was silent for a moment.

"I get it," he said. "You think this W may have been laid out on the ground with some kind of material that would radiate light?"

"Well, at least it's possible. Maybe there is some natural answer, but it's curious that the W never showed up before. It could be an artificial construction. It could even be some kind of signal, though I suppose most people would think that was silly."

"Sure. But it's not any sillier than the idea of a rigidly shaped cloud, 1100 miles long, rotating around Mars."

At 1:40 A.M. the day after the W announcement the town of East Lansing, Michigan, was shaken by a mysterious sky blast. The detonation woke most of the town and brought hundreds running out-of-doors. At first it was rumored that a sonic boom from a jet had caused the explosive effect. But Selfridge Air Force Base denied that this was the answer. According to Major Maxwell Gruman, no jets were in central Michigan at that hour. He added that pilots had strict orders not to break the sound barrier.

A few days later at a press conference President Eisenhower was asked about the flying saucers.

"Recent news reports," said Garnett D. Horner of the Washington *Star,* "indicate that some European governments are seriously investigating the flying-saucer problem."

Then he asked the President if the Air Force believed some of these flying objects were of extraterrestrial origin.

President Eisenhower's answer, paraphrased under press-conference rules, was as follows: The last time he had talked on this subject, a man whom he trusted from the Air Force had said that it was, as far as he knew, inaccurate to believe that the objects were coming from another planet.

Apparently the question had taken the President by surprise. He treated the subject solemnly and made no attempt to explain what the saucers might be.

As soon as I heard this was on the press wires, I phoned Captain White.

"On May 15," I said, "General Twining implied that the saucers may be coming from Mars. Does the President's statement mean that General Twining and the Air Force now deny this possibility?"

"Not at all," answered White. "President Eisenhower was speaking entirely for himself. What he said is not to be construed as an official Air Force statement. The situation is exactly as it was before."

"Let's clear that up," I suggested. "Three or four times—once in a statement given to *See* magazine—the Air Force has said it is quite possible we could be visited by beings from other worlds. Also, the Air Force has said that they never denied this possibility."

"That's true," agreed White, "but our official stand is this: We still have no authentic physical evidence that we're being visited by space ships."

"Meaning you don't have any captured or crashed saucers, or bodies of space creatures?"

"Right," said White. He added that the UFO investigation was continuing just as General Twining had reported on May 15.

Knowing the seriousness of the problem, I could understand President Eisenhower's public statement. Many times high government officials, from the President on down, had been forced to evade questions bearing on the national interest, as in the H-bomb situation. Moreover, the President's curiously worded answer was not a flat denial of the interplanetary explanation. If he had wished to kill off the spaceship answer once and for all, it would have been an easy matter to have said:

"As Commander-in-Chief of the Armed Forces I have been

given all the evidence. On this basis I hereby announce that the flying saucers absolutely are not interplanetary machines."

Instead, soon after this press conference, President Eisenhower asked the Air Force for a full briefing on all the latest UFO developments. This was admitted by Air Force Secretary Harold Talbott in a talk at the Press Club. Afterward Talbott tried to offset the admission by quoting a crackpot letter from a man who claimed to have come from Venus. But the ridicule policy was now wearing thin, as additional foreign sightings became public.

The very day after the President's remarks the Australian Navy released a top-secret UFO report they had withheld since September. During a routine flight a Royal Australian Navy pilot had encountered two glowing objects while flying at 15,000 feet. As the two saucers flashed past his "Sea Fury" —a propeller-driven fighter—he hastily radioed Nowra Naval Air Station. When the station radar-control officers checked their scopes, three moving objects were visible. Calling the pilot, they directed him to make a sharp turn. When he complied, one blip was identified as that of his plane. The other objects, continuing ahead at high speed, were then officially confirmed as "unidentified flying objects."

As a result of this and other sightings, a special radar watch was established. All Australian Air Force and Navy pilots were ordered to be on the alert for flying saucers.

When this Navy report was released, it was announced as the "first authenticated information" that flying saucers existed.

Meantime a series of far more disturbing stories had startled South America. Though none of these stories appeared in the United States press, they were headlined in Venezuelan newspapers. In addition, a representative of

APRO made a personal investigation, reporting his findings to the director.

When the first story was relayed to me, I took it to be just another imaginary "creature" tale. And there is still no proof that the stories are true. But even if they are groundless, they have played a large part in building up fear of the saucers in South American countries.

The first encounter is supposed to have been at Petare, a suburb of Caracas. At 2:00 A.M. on November 28, two Venezuelans, Gustavo Gonzales and José Ponce, were driving their truck to Caracas markets to purchase food stuffs for delivery.

Suddenly, they said, they were startled to see a luminous sphere about ten feet in diameter blocking a side street. It appeared to be suspended about six feet above the ground. As the two men climbed out of their truck they reported a dwarfish figure came toward them. According to Gonzales, when he seized the creature he found its body was oddly unyielding and covered with stiff hair.

To his amazement, the Venezuelan story ran, the little creature gave him a violent push, knocking him 15 feet. On seeing this, Ponce took to his heels and ran to a nearby traffic inspector's office.

Gonzales, drawing a knife, lunged at the creature which was approaching him with extended claws. But the blade glanced off the dwarf's shoulder, as if it had struck a hard surface.

By this time two or three more of the strange creatures had appeared. One of them, Gonzales reported, focused a blinding light on him for a moment. Then they all jumped into the sphere, which rose swiftly out of sight.

When Gonzales and Ponce told traffic inspectors this fantastic story, the police—not unreasonably—assumed they were either drunk or out of their minds. But an examination by doctors proved they were sane and sober, though in a highly nervous state. In addition, Gonzales' torn clothing and scratched arms indicated some kind of struggle.

This was the first actual report of hostility, though there had been other recent "creature" tales from abroad.

According to one Italian report, a flying disc had landed on a sports field one night in early November. By the bright glow the disc cast over the ground, villagers could see three or four small creatures wearing transparent helmets. Several of the Italians said they could see one creature's face, which looked to them like a "little elephant." When the villagers charged the saucer, the strange creatures quickly entered the machine and took off.

Since there had already been one publicized saucer hoax in Italy, I put this down as another wild account. But by mid-November other "space-creature" stories were beginning to spread in Paraguay and Brazil. And from Ethiopia came a report that people in scores of villages had been frightened by the "sky dragons."

Though Venezuelan police and most of the public discounted the Petare incident, new sightings, followed by more creature reports, caused this bizarre story to be re-examined.

On December 1 a Catholic priest, Father Jésus Hernandez Chapellin, reported sighting a luminous disc over Coro, Falcon State. A few hours after this, another glowing UFO was seen hovering just above the ground at Borburata, Venezuela. Next day a third saucer shot directly across the path of a plane piloted by Saul Paez Paredes. So close was the UFO that its violent passage threw the plane almost out of control. Badly frightened, Paredes hurriedly returned to his take-off point at Maracaibo.

Then the "hairy dwarfs" story broke into print again with an even more sensational report. Here is the story that was given to the Venezuelan public:

On December 9, two young Venezuelan peasants, Lorenzo Flores and Jésus Gomez, were hunting in an area near the

Trans-Andean Highway, between Chico and Corro de las Torros. Suddenly they spied a bright light, which they thought at first came from a car on the nearby road. As they approached, they saw a round object "like two washbowls placed on top of each other." Hovering a few feet from the ground, the machine appeared to be about nine feet in diameter. The brilliant glow came from the underside.

"Then we saw four little men coming out of it," Flores said later. "They were about three feet tall. When they realized we were there, they got Gomez and tried to drag him toward the object."

During the struggle Gomez dropped his machete. Flores, swinging his unloaded shotgun, struck at one dwarf with the butt. As though it had hit solid rock, the shotgun broke in two.

At this moment the lights of a car came in sight from the highway. The dwarfs quickly released Gomez and all four of the creatures raced toward the saucer.

Without waiting to see what happened, the two youngsters fled. Scratched and bruised, their shirts torn to shreds, they hurried into Carora and told police their story.

A few minutes later a truck driver also came in to report sighting a glowing disc-shaped object. From his report it appeared the UFO had risen from the spot where the dwarfs had been seen.

When an armed police squad hurried to the scene, they found signs of a struggle. Nearby lay the machete and the broken shotgun.

When the story quickly spread, causing near-panic in Carora, the two boys were jailed. Then a commission of doctors and psychiatrists was sent from Caracas to examine them. Afterward, during prolonged questioning by the police, Flores and Gomez were said to have retracted part of the story. But later, when reporters requestioned them, they insisted they had told the truth.

When an APRO representative queried one of the psychiatrists, the doctor told him the commission had found Gomez and Flores perfectly sane and healthy. On further investigation he learned of a point that carried weight with many Venezuelans. To peasants, he was told, a shotgun is a treasured object.

"No peasant in his right senses would ever think of deliberately breaking his shotgun to fake a saucer sighting—especially two boys who would gain nothing by it."

If the boys had been crazy, the APRO representative wrote, they would have been promptly interned in a mental hospital or asylum. If they had been lying, they would have been jailed for months or fined for creating public disorder. But instead they were soon released by the police.

Other reports quickly increased the hysteria. On December 10 a Caracas physician and his father reported seeing two dwarfish creatures running toward a glowing UFO in the vicinity of La Floresta. Two other bizarre reports added fuel to the flames.

At Barquisimeto a Venezuelan professor told police that a gleaming disc had chased his car on the highway to Guanaro. As he was approaching Guanaro, the professor said, a round white object swept down over the road. Panic-stricken, he took out his gun and fired at the object as it circled around his car.

Then, pushing the accelerator to the floor, he raced toward the town. When he returned with the sheriff and a policeman, the disc was flying southward, leaving a bluish trail.

Another hairy-dwarf attack story was made public on December 16. As reported to police, this latest encounter occurred in the Exposition Park at San Carlos, Venezuela.

It was about mid-evening when Jésus Paz and two friends drove to the park. A little later, when Paz had momentarily separated from his friends, they heard him scream. Rushing toward the spot, they found Paz unconscious on the ground.

Nearby, they said, a hairy dwarf was running toward a flat, shiny craft which hovered close to the ground. One of the men, Luis Mejia, hurled a stone at the saucer as it rose swiftly into the air.

When Paz was taken to a hospital, doctors found several long, deep scratches in his right side and back, as if he had been savagely clawed. Next day when he recovered from a severe state of shock, Paz told police he had been set upon too quickly to see the strange creature closely. But his comrades, under intensive grilling by the police, stubbornly stuck to their story.

Though they still seemed incredible, these "creature" stories gained credence with additional Venezuelans when, on December 19, another report came in:

At Valencia an 18-year-old jockey, José Parra, told police he had seen six small hairy creatures near a saucer which floated silently near the ground. According to Parra, one of the creatures transfixed him with a bright violet-colored light. Then the dwarfs ran to the mysterious craft, which quickly rose into the sky.

After detectives from Valencia examined the spot, they reported finding tracks which they were unable to identify.

Before the Venezuelan dwarf reports there had been very little similarity between any of the "creature" stories. Most of them were such obvious fakes they were not even worth considering. Some of the Venezuelan reports also had a suspicious sound. Yet APRO's on-the-scene investigator was convinced that the story told by Gomez and Flores, at least, was true.

The existence of these hairy dwarfs was hard for me to accept, even though the Ituri pygmies of Africa come close to fitting their description. This pygmy race, existing in East Africa's Ituri forest, was almost unknown until it was studied by the Reverend Dr. Martin Guisinde, professor of anthropology at the Catholic University of America. Father

Guisinde, who for years has studied small-sized beings in many parts of the world, found that the Ituri pygmies had clay-yellow bodies covered with thick, dark brown hair. Small creatures—less than five feet high and weighing less than 90 pounds—these pygmies maneuver through the forest as expertly as monkeys, swinging from branch to branch.

Since the towering jungle trees completely hide the sky at all times, the Ituri pygmies live out their lives in a dimly lighted world. So accustomed are they to this semi-darkness that they actually fear the sunlight. Even if they dared venture outside the forest, their strange eyes, conditioned to darkness, would be almost blinded by the sun's glare.

As I examined the curious evidence, something inside me fought against acceptance of the hairy-dwarf idea. My feeling was, I realized, a subconscious longing—the same thing which John Du Barry and I had discussed that night at Larchmont. I knew now that I hoped the UFO race would *not* be unlike our own.

In the light of evolution, however, the chances seemed to be against such a similarity. These odds, I remembered, had been summed up in *McLean's* magazine by a Canadian zoologist, Professor Norman J. Berrill, of McGill University. Answering the question, "Are We Alone in the Universe?" Professor Berrill had agreed with Dr. Harlow Shapley that a huge number of planets must be inhabited.

"Well-placed planets," said Professor Berrill, "will evolve life, and life sooner or later evolves mind."

But each life-bearing planet, he had said, must be unique. Some would be larger, some smaller, than the earth. There would be different atmospheres and many varying factors.

"Human beings with our shape and size are to be found only upon this earth . . . never on any other planet, from here to Eternity. Almost certainly there will be beings of kinds unaccountable that possess intelligence and power, deep emotion, beauty in essence, and wisdom grown perhaps far beyond our own. In all that really matters we are almost certainly not alone."

Never on another planet, from here to Eternity . . .

If Berrill were right, it meant an end to all hope of someday meeting beings like ourselves. But even the greatest of scientists sometimes were wrong.

And even if the hairy-dwarf stories were true, I realized it still need not drop the curtain upon our dreams. There might be more than one race involved in the long world-wide surveillance by the flying saucers.

The various South American reports, many of them accompanied by front-page newspaper stories, did make one point clear. In Venezuela and Brazil, at least, officials were not ridiculing the actual saucer reports. On the contrary, the Brazilian Air Force in a public statement had requested the aid of all nations in solving the UFO problem. Following this, Brazilian Air Force officers had been briefed on saucers by Colonel Jao Adil Oliveiera. Factual observations and photographs of saucers, said Colonel Oliveiera, proved that this problem merited serious attention and study.

But even though there was no blackout in South America, few of their sightings were published in this country.

When I saw Bob Stirling at the end of '54, I told him about the Venezuelan reports.

"Why hasn't the UP carried those stories?" I asked him.

Stirling shook his head.

"They weren't stopped by the UP. I haven't seen a word about any 'dwarf' stories from Venezuela."

"They're not censored in Venezuela—I can show you the front-page stories. Would it be possible for the silence group to block them down there?"

"I don't know," replied Stirling. Then he paused. "But this hairy-dwarf business—I've got something to tell you. I got it from a Navy man I've known personally for years."

He gave me the name in confidence, a source I couldn't question.

"You may think it's silly," Stirling went on, "but this man swears that a Navy pilot got a close look at a saucer one night, so close he could see a strange creature inside it."

I stared at him for a second.

"All right, I told you it might sound silly," said Stirling.

"It's not exactly that." Then I told him about the Pearl Harbor "creature" report.

"Don, it sounds as if it might be true. Do you know what the thing looked like?"

"No," I said. "Only that it evidently scared the pilot."

"Do you think this hairy-dwarf business could be the answer?" asked Stirling.

"I suppose it could be, Bob," I said slowly, "but I hope to heaven those stories turn out to be hoaxes."

17 Oberth and the G-Field

After talking with Bob Stirling I remembered my plan to draw up a master chart for a final analysis of all the UFO riddles. But before I could start, there was a series of new developments that changed the picture.

As the 1955 New Year began, foreign reports continued to hold the spotlight. On January 1 a five-saucer formation was sighted at Lima, Peru. For five minutes, seen by many witnesses, the discs hovered over the city, giving off an intense silvery light.

The next day two Venezuelan airline crews encountered a luminous disc while en route to Maracaibo. During the next week similar reports came from a dozen other countries.

Then, toward mid-January, the Directorate of Air Force Intelligence was badly jolted by a collision report from California. At approximately 5:30 P.M., on January 14, a large fiery object was seen dropping from the sky near Idyllwild. Immediately afterward, a radio flash from a B-47 jet bomber electrified Intelligence officers at March Field.

"An unknown object just hit our wing!" the bomber captain reported.

Fortunately the damaged wing did not crumple, and the pilot carefully nursed the plane down to an emergency landing. For several hours Intelligence officers and Air Force special investigators searched the area in a hunt for the

247

fallen object. At the same time witnesses who had seen the fireball drop from the sky were questioned by other Intelligence officers. But the Air Force men refused to explain what had happened.

Nine days later another mysterious fireball streaked down from the sky into Darby, Pennsylvania. About the size of a grapefruit, the flaming missile crashed through a second-floor window of William C. Cunningham's house. When Cunningham, a 50-year-old widower, attempted to scoop up the blazing object and hurl it out of the window, his right hand was burned to the bone. Within a few seconds flames from the object had set fire to the house, wrecking the upper floor.

Afterward, pieces of the fireball were tested by firemen. Whatever the object was, it had none of the characteristics of ordinary metal.

"It's the most unusual thing I've seen in my 25 years' experience," Fire Marshal Joseph X. Francis told the United Press. "We subjected the pieces we found to a 1700-degree heat, and they didn't melt. They only glowed to a cherry red, cooled off rapidly, and retained their shape. We also tested them with a magnet but got no reaction. Their resistance to electricity is almost zero."

When the pieces cooled, the fire marshal said, the metal was found to be a dull silver on the outside. But when they were broken open, the interior shone brightly.

At first Darby police believed that the mysterious object might be a meteorite. But this answer was rejected after statements by Dr. I. M. Levitt, Director of Fels Planetarium in Philadelphia, and Dr. C. P. Oliver, Emeritus Professor of Astronomy at the University of Pennsylvania. Meteorites, Dr. Levitt declared, usually burn themselves out before hitting the ground. Dr. Oliver, also refuting the meteorite explanation, suggested that the fireball might have been a homemade bomb.

But Fire Marshal Francis' report showed that this was impossible. In the first place, it was obvious that the missile was made of some metal unknown on earth. In addition, no human hand could have thrown it. A powerful catapult device would have been required to hurl the object from the ground so that it would arc upward, and then slant down steeply into Cunningham's bedroom.

There was only one other explanation. The mysterious fireball was some type of aerial missile, apparently identical with the one which had crashed through the East New Haven signboard in 1953.

Next day, by an ironic coincidence, the Navy wrote me as follows on the flying-saucer problem: "There is no indication whatsoever that any danger may be involved."

The official statement was signed by Captain L. D. Coates, USN, Deputy and Assistant Chief of Naval Research.

Regardless of the "no-danger" answer, UFO sightings continued to increase.

In South America a published report by veteran airline pilots convinced thousands of people that the sighting reports were true. The encounter occurred on February 2, 1955, over the route from Maiquetía to Mérida. Piloted by Captain Dario Celis, a famous Venezuelan flyer, an Aeropost airliner was flying at 7500 feet between Barquisimeto and Valera. It was a clear day, with visibility unlimited. Until 11:15 A.M. the flight was normal.

Suddenly Captain Celis and his copilot, B. J. Cortes, spotted a strange round "apparatus" flying swiftly toward the plane. Rotating counterclockwise, the mysterious machine shone with a greenish light. Around its center was a red ring or band which emitted flashes of brilliant light. Above and below this band were lighted portholes.

Hurriedly Captain Celis cut in his mike to call the Barquisimeto radio station. After reporting the saucer, he waited for an answer. But the receiver had gone dead. (Later the Barquisimeto radio operators stated that just as Captain Celis had begun his report, communication was cut off.)

As Captain Celis went back to alert the passengers, Cortes banked toward the rotating UFO. Instantly the saucer whirled downward. Then, leveling off, it raced away at tremendous speed.

When the plane landed, the pilots learned of the sudden break in radio communication—not only at Barquisimeto but at Valera, which was also receiving the information. Not until the airliner was a few miles from Valera airport had the radio resumed normal operation.

Both flyers told reporters they had never believed in flying saucers.

"But now," said Captain Celis, "not only are we convinced of their existence, but also that they are controlled." Then he added, "This was the most sensational experience of my career as a pilot, and I will remember the incident forever."

The pilots' detailed report, which made front-page headlines, was fully confirmed by the passengers.

Just three nights later the commanding officer of the ocean liner *Vera Cruz* reported that a "huge, luminous craft, cruising at fantastic speed," had passed above his ship. Sighted off the eastern Venezuelan coast, the mystery craft was observed by the captain himself as well as by several members of the crew and passengers.

The growing conviction in South America that the flying saucers were space ships was suddenly given a tremendous boost by a noted aviation authority from the United States. On February 2, while visiting Bogotá, Colombia, William P. Lear, manufacturer of aircraft and electronic equipment, told a news conference that the flying saucers were real.

"I believe that the flying saucers come from outer space and are piloted by beings of superior intelligence," Lear told Bogotá reporters. He added that the saucers probably came from planets outside the range of our observation.

Because of his prominence, Lear's statement carried unusual weight. In 1950 President Truman had presented him with the famous Collier Aviation Trophy after Lear developed an electronic pilot for jet aircraft.

Known as an outspoken fighter for his beliefs, Lear had recently urged the United States government to rush a space-ship program. He had also predicted that the United States would soon begin work on an artificial satellite, to circle the earth at an altitude of 500 miles. It was obvious to most observers that Lear knew the inside story of the flying saucers.

When Lear's story was flashed to the United States by the AP, it was a hard blow for the UFO censors. But this was only the beginning. Within 24 hours Lear amplified his first statement:

"I feel the flying saucers are real," he said, "because of four points."

First, he said, there have been numerous manifestations over long periods of time.

Second, many observations have been made simultaneously by reliable observers.

Third, there are great possibilities linked with the theory of gravitational fields.

Fourth, there are now serious efforts in progress to prove the existence of antigravitational forces and to convert atomic energy directly to electricity.

This new AP story dismayed the Pentagon, for it could easily disclose our top-secret research to duplicate the UFO's propulsion. There had already been one hint, despite Pentagon precautions. During a meeting of aviation leaders in New York on January 25 G. S. Trimble, vice-president of advanced design for the Glenn L. Martin Aircraft Company, had made an amazing disclosure.

"Unlimited power, freedom from gravitational attraction, and infinitely short travel time are now becoming feasible," he told the press. Then he added that eventually all commercial air transportation would be in vehicles operating on these fantastic principles.

And it did seem fantastic that machines could float in the air, completely free from the pull of the earth's gravity.

At the same meeting Dr. Walter R. Dornberger, guided-missile consultant for the Bell Aircraft Corporation, predicted that airliners would eventually travel at speeds of 10,000 miles an hour. Though he did not mention gravitational-field propulsion, the implication was clear.

Two days after these statements were made, I received an air-mail letter from Redell containing a clipping of the AP's interview with Lear. Circling the gravitational-field item with red crayon, Redell had attached a one-line memo which read:

"Now you know."

For several minutes I puzzled over the words. It was plain, of course, that the "anti-G" research was the subject Redell had previously refused to discuss. But his cryptic words hinted at far more than that—perhaps a missing link in the Kimross mystery or a key to the "invisible saucers" riddle.

Until this time I had not dug deeply into the antigravitational field theory. But the idea itself was not new, it had been used by science-fiction writers for many years. For that very reason, perhaps, the "antigravity" suggestion had been widely ridiculed.

As a pilot, I myself had once scoffed at the suggestion. Until Einstein published his famous Unified Field Theory, there had been little scientific backing for this idea.

Even after Einstein's announcement that electricity, magnetism, and gravity were all manifestations of one force, few people had fully accepted the thought that we might someday neutralize gravity. But as W. B. Smith had told me, there were important scientists who did believe it.

Only a few days before Lear's startling announcement

I had received a letter from Professor Hermann Oberth in answer to several questions I had asked him. After giving me permission to quote his stated belief that the saucers were space ships manned by superior beings, Professor Oberth mentioned the electromagnetic-propulsion theory. In his opinion, he said, this was not the true explanation for the flying saucers' operation. Instead, he told me, the saucers probably created their own gravitational fields, which would allow them to hover motionless above the earth, accelerate at tremendous speed, and make violent turns that would cause ordinary aircraft to disintegrate.

Along with his letter, Professor Oberth sent me a copy of a lecture he had recently given in Germany. As soon as possible I had the lecture translated. It was a concise and revealing statement. In his talk, given to both German scientists and the general public, Professor Oberth had confirmed authentic reports of flying discs and elliptical or cigar-shaped machines. In agreement with our Air Force Intelligence reports, he stated that in sunlight the discs had a metallic glow and that at night their colors changed from dark orange to red, then to yellow, and then to a dazzling white as they reached top speeds.

With ordinary methods of propulsion, he said, their accelerations would be so great that any creatures aboard would be crushed against the sides or rear of the machine. But there was one method which would eliminate this problem and also explain all UFO reports. This, Professor Oberth declared, would be the creation of artificial G-fields.

First, he explained, even the most dangerous acceleration would not harm any beings aboard, for the propulsion force would apply simultaneously to them as well as to the space ship. Even when a saucer made swift changes of speed and direction, passengers would feel no effect.

Second, the G-field would enable space ships to reach

extremely high velocities, even approaching the speed of light.

Third, the G-field would also explain the silence of the UFO's. Because of the saucer's own gravitational pull, the surrounding air would be dragged along with it. As a result there would be no air eddies, no turbulence, and no sound.

Fourth, Professor Oberth declared, the variation in saucers' glow could be accounted for by the transformation of what he called "obstructive rays" into rays made up of longer waves, which would release light and electricity.

In addition to these points, there were several others which Professor Oberth's analysis explained. One was the lack of frictional heat during the UFO's swift passage through our atmosphere. Even at much lower speeds ordinary metal alloys would melt, and therefore it had been believed that the saucers were constructed of some unknown metal capable of withstanding the tremendously high temperatures.

But with a G-field this would not be required. For the same principle which accounted for the UFOs' silence also explained why they did not burn up when traveling at thousands of miles an hour. Since the gravitational field would draw the surrounding air along with the saucer, there would be no friction against the machine itself to cause overheating.

If artificial gravitational fields were the key to the saucers' operation, this would alter one commonly held belief: that most of the "saucers" were under remote control. For, as Professor Oberth had pointed out, even the most violent maneuvers would not disturb passengers or crews aboard. And, undoubtedly, beings who could create artificial G-fields would be able to vary and control them, so that even if the UFO creatures came from a planet with a gravity far different than the earth's they could probably create, inside their space ships, the identical gravitational conditions which existed on their planet.

But I still had no idea how such G-fields could be created.

From Redell's hint, and from the statements by Trimbell and Lear, it was evident that our own scientists had found the key—and almost certainly by analyzing the UFOs' operations.

Thinking back to my earlier talk with Redell, I suddenly remembered how W. B. Smith also had evaded my questions on the Kimross mystery. Because of Smith's official position, I did not feel free to query him again, but I dashed off a note to Redell asking him two questions:

"Would light rays be bent by a G-field? Could such a G-field be instantly reversed?"

I had intended, while waiting for Redell's answer, to dig up what I could on this unusual subject. But a new outbreak of sightings and several mysterious accidents interrupted my plans. For two weeks developments came thick and fast.

The action began on February 6 when a strange machine was sighted over New Zealand's South Island. Moments later it was seen flying at 200 feet, by farmers at Inchbonnie, 30 miles inland. Hundreds of observers at widely separated points reported seeing the strange silver shape as it flashed overhead. Described as cigar-shaped, and traveling at tremendous speed, the object cast a dazzling light as it sped toward the Southern Alps.

Suddenly the object appeared to explode, so violently that the force of the blast was felt over several hundred square miles. Shortly afterward a tall column of smoke was seen to rise above the mountains, but no wreckage was found.

On the night of February 7 a similar fiery object startled hundreds of people from central Florida to Cuba. Reported by ship and airline crews, the brilliant UFO caused one pilot to zoom his plane 1000 feet.

"I thought it was coming in the window," said Captain Francis Black, an Eastern Airlines pilot. "It looked like a ball of fire, ten or 15 feet in diameter."

When he landed at Miami, Captain Black was told that

what he had seen was a meteor. But another airline pilot, Captain William B. Nash of Pan-American Airways, quickly exposed this apparent cover-up. In a letter to CRIFO Captain Nash reported:

"It was a very odd meteor. I found that a PAA crew with Captain Charles Elmore in command saw three bright white lights south of their DC-6 as they crossed Biscayne Bay. The lights, much brighter than aircraft flares, also were seen by the Miami airport tower, but could not be identified.

"Between 7:55 and 8:35 P.M.," concluded Captain Nash, "there were three separate sightings, completely disproving the 'meteor' explanation."

Just after noon the following day a brand-new B-57 jet bomber mysteriously exploded over Bel Air, Maryland, killing the pilot. The plane, in perfect condition, had just taken off from the Glenn L. Martin plant at Baltimore. After the unexplained blast, the body of the pilot, still strapped in his ejection seat, was found about 1500 feet from the wreckage. A second airman, who had managed to bail out, was found with one leg severed and the other badly mangled.

A few hours later Lou Corbin phoned and told me he had privately checked on the crash with an Air Force officer.

"He told me," said Corbin, "they had absolutely no explanation for it."

At approximately the same hour two Canadian Air Force Sabrejets crashed near Chatham, New Brunswick, killing both pilots. Here, too, no explanation could be found for the disasters.

Next morning, as Canadian and U. S. Air Forces were investigating these strange accidents, newspapers revealed the inside story of another baffling disaster which had happened four months before.

On October 12, 1954, an F-100 Super Sabrejet had disintegrated over California, killing test pilot George Welsh. For three months the North American Aviation Corporation had investigated the case. Now, on February 9, it was revealed that the plane had encountered a mysterious force, throwing it violently to one side.

"Aerodynamic phenomena never before experienced by man caused the F-100 disaster," the company told the AP.

The ink was hardly dry on this puzzling admission when news of still another strange disaster reached the Pentagon.

Just before noon, on the 9th of February, 1955, two F-94 Starfire jet fighters had crashed near Goose Bay Air Force Base in Labrador. No explanation had been found, Intelligence officers reported.

That night papers in the United States carried this story on the crashes:

"4 Crewmen Die as 2 Jets Crash"

"St. John's, Newfoundland, February 9th. AP.—Two United States Air Force F-94 Starfire jet fighters crashed today 16 miles from Goose Bay Airport in Labrador, and the four crew members were killed.

"United States Northeast Air Command Headquarters here said the jets were on routine flights. They did not make clear whether they crashed independently or tangled in the air."

Early next day I phoned Captain White at the Pentagon.

"What happened to those two F-94's at Goose Bay?" I asked.

"They collided," he told me.

"What was the cause, bad weather?"

"I don't know," answered White. "That's all we were told."

That very afternoon another AP story appeared which completely contradicted what White had said.

"St. John's, Newfoundland, February 10th.—Four United States airmen died yesterday in two American Air Force F-94 Starfire jet fighters which crashed into the bush and burned near Goose Bay, Labrador.

"United States Northeast Air Command Headquarters

here said the planes went down within five minutes of each other and almost seven miles apart."

Carefully I reread the second report. If this was the true story, why had Captain White told me the jets had collided? Had he been given orders to put out this explanation? If so, why had the Northeast Air Command given out the facts? But for the contradictory stories, the accidents would have been taken for an actual collision.

It was on this same day, February 10, that William P. Lear once again focused attention upon the flying saucers. In an interview at Grand Rapids, where one of his plants is located, Lear revealed that he had seen a saucer while flying near Palm Springs, California, two months before.

Lear told the Grand Rapids *Herald* that he and his pilot, Hal Herman of Los Angeles, both sighted the object from Lear's private plane at an altitude of 12,000 feet. In shape, he said, it fitted the familiar descriptions of flying discs. Giving off a greenish glow, it hovered motionless for a few seconds, then disappeared from sight.

When he reported the sighting to an airway radio station, two other pilots in the vicinity immediately radioed that they also had seen the saucer.

In the *Herald* interview, Lear again stated his belief that the saucers come from outer space and are directed by an intelligence beyond that of humans.

The saucers, Lear went on, evidently come from a planet with beings who have overcome the law of gravity. He then predicted that we were close to mastering this secret, which he called the "missing link" in the revised Einstein theory.

"The day is approaching," Lear said, "when man will build vehicles that travel on the ground or fly with equal facility, overcoming the law of gravity."

Concluding, he revealed that an American aviation company, which he would not identify, was already conducting gravitational-field research.

Then on February 11, as the silence group was fuming over Lear's newest disclosures, word of a peculiar sighting by a Pan-American Airlines crew came in on the Pentagon teletypes. Though the Intelligence report was kept secret, the incident was confirmed later by Captain James King in a news story printed at Maiquetía, Venezuela.

"We were flying between Miami and New York," Captain King told Maiquetía reporters, "when suddenly, close to the plane and under the wings, two strange reddish-green objects passed by. They were also seen by some of the passengers."

Captain King, the newspaper added, had never before believed in the existence of flying saucers. But after this sighting his opinion had quickly changed.

Less than 24 hours later Canada was again the scene of a mysterious aerial tragedy. On February 12, while on an Arctic training flight, a U. S. Air Force Stratojet bomber exploded at 35,000 feet, killing two of the four crew members. The other two, Lieutenant Colonel K. G. McGrew and Captain L. E. Epton, were hurled unconscious from the plane as it disintegrated. Both revived in time to open their parachutes.

Neither of the survivors could explain what had happened. There had not been an instant's warning before the explosion. But there was no actual proof that the blast was linked with the saucers.

But the next day, when a Belgian airliner vanished near Rome, there was clear evidence that a UFO might have been involved.

Carrying 29 persons, including four Americans, the four-engine DC-6 was approaching Rome's Ciampino Airport, cleared for a routine landing. A few minutes before it was due at the field, the Belgian captain radioed that he had seen a fireball in the sky. Before he could finish his report, the radio went dead. Airport tower operators anxiously scanned the sky, but the plane did not appear.

During the search for the missing airliner a mysterious "orange spot in the sky" was reported near Rome.

Then, after a six-day search, the lost plane was found wrecked in the mountains, with all aboard dead.

This accident was later blamed on bad weather conditions, although the Belgian captain was experienced in instrument landings.

Meanwhile, several new developments had made headlines in this country.

On the night of February 14 another of the weird green fireballs flashed across Texas. Its fiery glow was seen as far east as Jackson, Mississippi.

Streaking silently through the sky, the mysterious object was observed by thousands, including three control-tower operators at Pound's Field, Tyler, Texas.

"It was about midnight," said J. N. Aber, one of the control-tower operators. "This light seemed to pop out of the sky directly over us—like a huge electric arc. It was greenish, like the tip of a welder's torch. It was a blinding light, the brightest I ever saw. The whole room lit up for a second."

All three operators agreed that the fireball was moving so swiftly that it crossed the horizon in little more than a second.

Four days after this an announcement at Adler Planetarium in Chicago stirred new speculation about satellites orbiting the earth.

In a report endorsed by the planetarium, Mr. John P. Bagby, an experienced astronomer and electronic engineer, disclosed the discovery of "tiny moons" orbiting the earth at a distance of 475 miles. Bagby, a member of the American Meteor Society and the Royal Astronomical Society of Canada, had previously recruited a team of skilled amateur astronomers to help him track the unknown objects.

These "moonlets," as Bagby termed them, appeared to be traveling about 18,000 miles an hour. Though Bagby, like

Dr. Clyde Tombaugh, avoided any hint that these satellites actually were artificial space platforms, it was one more link in the chain of evidence confirming the space-base operations.

By coincidence another astronomer simultaneously drew attention to the question of inhabited planets. In the February issue of *Sky and Telescope* Dr. Otto Struve of Leuschner Observatory, University of California, drew this conclusion:

"The total number of planets with some form of life could be in the billions."

Strangely enough, Dr. Struve had been one of the most vehement skeptics, denouncing all saucer reports as nonsense. Though his new announcement did not mention UFO's, his sudden belief in countless inhabited worlds seemed a curious change from his previous stand.

For a few days after the green fireball flashed over Texas there was a lull in sighting reports. Then, on the night of February 21, there came evidence that one of the cigar-shaped mother ships had passed over New York State.

Out of the sky that night, over the town of Horseheads, there suddenly appeared a mass of the gray, cobwebby substance known as angel's hair. Within a few minutes the strands had spread over houses, trees, and bushes.

The following day a sample of angel's hair was analyzed by Dr. Charles B. Rutenber, Professor of Chemistry at Elmira College. The strange fiber, he found, was radioactive, though not dangerously so. Describing it as "white, fibrous, and heavily impregnated with soot and dirt," he said it was apparently some kind of waste material which had been damaged in an explosion.

When February came to an end I reviewed the series of crashes from the 8th to the 13th of the month. In that short period seven airplanes had suffered mysterious accidents. Possibly this was only coincidence, but the apparent cover-up on the Starfire crashes at Goose Bay, together with what

Lou Corbin had told me about the bomber crash in Maryland, revived my fears.

Once again I found myself thinking back to the Kimross disaster, to all the other sobering aspects of the flying-saucer mystery. Though I had not yet admitted it, even to myself, the chances that the UFO's were hostile seemed to have increased. But the crashes, the strange explosions, were only one small part of the flying-saucer picture, and even that part was blurred.

There was only one thing to do: sum up all the new evidence and try to find a clue to the final answer. Perhaps it was impossible. Perhaps we could not know the explanation until the UFO beings were ready to act.

18 Redell Explains a Riddle

Though I had begun to work on the master chart in March, it was not until July that I was ready to make a final analysis.

Since the end of February, there had been a steady influx of sighting reports, but few of them added new information. However, there had been other developments—aside from actual sightings—which helped to fill some gaps in the UFO jigsaw puzzle.

The first of these was the surprising report about the moon by Dr. Gerard P. Kuiper, of the University of Chicago. Dr. Kuiper was famous, I knew, as an authority on "planetary atmospheres." Several times in recent years he had been under contract to the Office of Naval Research for special celestial investigations. His opinions as to the possibility of life on other planets were highly respected by his brother scientists.

Normally even amateur astronomers seldom spend more than a few hours at a time observing the moon. And few professionals watch the moon at all. But in this special study, through the 82-inch McDonald telescope at Fort Davis, Texas, Dr. Kuiper spent many 12-hour periods watching the lunar sphere. As a result his vision was sharpened to an unusual degree, enabling him to see far more details than are usually observable.

When the moon was full, Dr. Kuiper stated, he had seen thousands of glistening white spots, apparently the tops of inverted cones.

"These cones looked," he declared, "as if they had been turned out on a lathe from blocks of white chalk."

In his report to the National Academy of Sciences Dr. Kuiper stated that these white objects—which British astronomers previously had called "domes"—could be seen all over the surface of the moon, though they were clustered most thickly near the moon's equator. He added, significantly, that though the strange cones were relatively recent features, their nature and origin were a mystery.

Within a few days after this report became public, I learned of another moon study—this one supposed to be secret. For months astronomers at Mount Palomar had been observing the moon, making long observations whenever conditions permitted. Not only had their photographs confirmed the existence of the mysterious bridge, reported by Wilkins, but a spectrographic analysis had proved it was constructed of metal. . . .

As I was compiling this material for the chart, I saw that another aviation executive had followed in Lear's footsteps and publicly hinted at our secret G-field research.

On March 9 Stanley Hiller, Jr., famous helicopter inventor, told the San Francisco Advertising Club the following:

"Don't scoff at the possibility of anti-gravitational devices, though they may sound as Buck Rogerish as rotorless helicopters." He added that military security prevented him from revealing further details.

Approximately one month later, on April 6, I saw that three green fireballs had streaked across New Mexico. One of the objects, according to Civil Air Patrol Lieutenant Paul Mallott, had plunged from the sky and exploded near the mountains.

"Suddenly," Mallott said, "there was a white, blinding flash with no color to it at all. There was no smoke, but a huge cloud of dust arose above the mountain when the object struck and apparently exploded."

At Hobbs, New Mexico, other observers had reported that a fireball approximately 12 inches in diameter had plunged into the earth a few miles east of the town. Searchers could find no fragments.

Meanwhile, Dr. Lincoln La Paz, head of the New Mexico Meteoritics Institute, disclosed that there had been heavy radio short-wave and TV disturbances as the fireballs passed over the state, and that Air Force officers at nearby bases were concerned. La Paz said these could not be normal meteorites, since it was incredible for more than one meteorite to fall in any one day.

"I don't know what they are," he added, "but they are all of the same family. Also, and very important, when a meteor hits the upper atmosphere and shatters, it may spread fragments from ten to 15 miles. Here, however, we have sightings from about 250 miles across the state.

"The important thing," said Dr. La Paz, "is that the fireball was a brilliant Kelly green as opposed to the blue or blue-green color seen in ordinary meteor falls."

Then La Paz quoted an Albuquerque attorney, Quincy Adams, who had seen one of the green fireballs from his eighth-floor office window.

"It was so bright it looked like an explosion half a mile away," Adams told La Paz.

"Actually it was 200 miles away," La Paz revealed. "That's how bright it was."

Only two days after the sighting of these fireballs, there came the first public hint that Air Force jets might now be firing on the saucers. At 9:30 A.M. on April 8, a round, bright object was sighted between Rockford and Cherry Valley, Illinois. A few minutes later three Air Force jets streaked across the sky. With guns blazing, one of the jets whirled in for a quick pass at the UFO.

A few seconds before this, the sound of the racing jets had been heard by John C. Gregory, executive secretary of the Winnebago County Civil Defense Council. Hurrying to the top of the City Hall building, he saw the jets converge on their target.

Suddenly a second object, brilliant white, streaked past the jets.

A second later there was a flaming explosion as the larger object blew up. The jets circled for a few moments, then climbed up and raced away.

In addition to John Gregory, dozens of witnesses had seen the strange attack, including several GOC observers. Immediately afterward, the GOC spotters were told not to discuss the incident, but by this time the story had spread all over town.

At the Rockford *Register* a quick call was made to the jets' base, O'Hare Field at Park Ridge. The editor was told that the pilots had fired on a weather balloon which had been launched at Minneapolis. There was no mention of the mysterious object which had streaked past the fighters, nor was there any explanation for this amazing attack on a weather balloon over a populated area.

Whether or not the *Register* editors suspected the truth is not clear, but there was a strong hint of doubt in their headline story that evening:

JETS BLAST BALLOON NEAR CHERRY VALLEY

FLAME NOTED AS 3 PLANES RIP TARGET

"Three Air Force jets, a weather balloon, and an interloper from out of nowhere added up to an aerial display between Rockford and Cherry Valley about 9:30 A.M. today.

"John C. Gregory, Executive Secretary of the Winnebago

County Civil Defense Council, said he witnessed the weather balloon blowing up between here and Cherry Valley after the jets made a pass at it.

" 'Just prior to the explosion,' Gregory said, 'another flat, spherical object described as "brilliant white" shot by the jets at a high speed, going from southeast to northwest.'

"The jets were from O'Hare Field in Park Ridge. Air Force officials at the field said the weather balloon was sent up from Minneapolis."

From the phrase, "another flat, spherical object" it was apparent that Gregory knew the pilots' target had not been a balloon. But no other details could be secured either at O'Hare Field or at the Pentagon.

Later Captain White insisted that the Air Force had no knowledge of such an incident and that its jets would never endanger lives by firing on weather balloons. When I heard this answer, I was positive that White had been ordered to deny attacks on saucers, for the evidence in the Rockford case was impossible to dismiss.

This still-unexplained attack at Rockford was quickly followed by a sighting at Plattsburg, New York. At 1:31 A.M. a UFO was seen maneuvering over the city by two GOC observers, Jim Roddy and Allen R. Roberts. From then until dawn the two observers watched the saucer through high-powered binoculars, reporting regularly to the Albany Air Filter Center.

Then at sunrise the UFO began a vertical ascent. As it rose into the sky, the two observers witnessed a strange sight.

"From underneath the object," said Roddy, "a stream of eight green lights shot to the ground. Then a blast of white flame also shot out, and the UFO began climbing straight upward. Finally it disappeared at an altitude of about 60,000 feet."

But though the Albany Filter Center had been in touch

with developments, Air Defense denied that any strange object had been reported at Plattsburg.

Nine days later, on April 18, Dr. Harold C. Urey, head of the University of Chicago's Institute for Nuclear Studies, publicly disclosed his belief in the existence of inhabited planets.

"It is exceedingly probable," said Dr. Urey, "that there is other life in the universe more intelligent than ours.

"So far as we know," he added, "the earth is unique in having a great free oxygen supply on which our life depends. But the absence of oxygen would not mean the absence of life. There are animals and plants on this earth which live without oxygen."

Since Dr. Urey was one of the top members of the international Mars Committee, it seemed probable that the Mars discoveries had led him to make this statement. For in March, 1954, he had asserted that proof of life on Mars would mean that life could exist anywhere in the universe.

In the following month the silence group had had another jolt in the shape of a news report from London written by Dorothy Kilgallen.

In this syndicated UP story the New York *Journal-American* reporter made a startling announcement:

"British scientists and airmen, after examining the wreckage of one mysterious flying ship, are convinced these strange aerial objects are not optical illusions or Soviet inventions, but are actually flying saucers which originate on another planet.

"The source of my information is a British official of Cabinet rank who prefers to remain unidentified.

" 'We believe, on the basis of our inquiries thus far, that the saucers were staffed by small men—probably under four feet tall,' my informant told me. 'It's frightening, but there's no denying the flying saucers come from another planet.' "

At the Pentagon, in a hasty attempt to offset this revelation, the Air Force told newsmen it was "highly skeptical" of the report.

Three days after the Kilgallen story appeared in American papers, an article on artificial satellites by columnist Stewart Alsop caused another angry outburst at both the Pentagon and the National Security Council. For Alsop had learned what the UFO censors believed a well-hidden secret —that emergency satellite-detection projects had been set up at White Sands and Mount Wilson, California. So furious was NSC Secretary Cutler, Alsop later reported, that even Alsop's old friends at NSC were afraid to be seen with the columnist.

That the censorship on UFO's was constantly tightening was plain from other developments.

On June 13, 1955, Frank Edwards and a TV film producer had gone to the Navy Department and asked for a few unclassified Navy pictures of rockets. At first they were told that pictures would be available within a few hours, since copies had already been released to the press.

"Everything was lovely," Frank told me that evening. "That is, until they found out we wanted to show the pictures on TV during a panel discussion of saucers. About an hour later one of the Navy men called me back. He said they had strict orders not to cooperate on any publicity connected with flying saucers."

Another proof of the censors' fight to block all UFO publicity was the complete absence of news stories based on pilots' reports. Since the "balloon" attack incident at Rockford, Illinois, reports of dramatic encounters by military and airline pilots had continued to pour into Air Force Intelligence. But not one of these stories appeared in the papers, though time and again jets were scrambled to chase saucers maneuvering near cities.

Despite the increased blackout, however, some pilots' reports continued to reach me through long-established contacts. Those which were fully confirmed I added to the chart. In several cases reports from three or four areas, all covering the same period, suggested that the UFO's were operating en masse over the United States.

In one of these officially hidden cases, on the night of June 16, scores of UFO's reconnoitered the area from the Mississippi to the Atlantic.

At 11 o'clock, CST, a Flying Tiger Airlines plane was on a routine flight, 40 miles northeast of Springfield, Missouri. Suddenly a blue-white disc, moving at tremendous speed, shot in toward the plane. After circling around it in a tight turn, the saucer tilted up steeply and streaked out of sight.

Hurriedly the captain of the plane radioed the nearest CAA tower. Unknown to him, his was only one of dozens of sightings reported by pilots within the last few minutes. Before midnight Air Force Intelligence was swamped, with CAA and GOC messages pouring into Air Filter Centers from Chicago to Baltimore.

By midnight all Air Defense Commands east of the Mississippi were on a full alert, as scores of armed jet night-fighters pursued the low-flying objects.

Though I had learned of this important sighting early the next morning, my first hint of the widespread alert did not come until the day after that, when Lou Corbin called me from Baltimore.

"Did you hear about the uproar over here?" he asked. "It was on the night of the 16th."

"No," I answered. "But I heard of one report."

Then I told him about the Flying Tiger Airlines case.

"The Air Force was almost wild that night," said Corbin. "At the Baltimore Filter Center reports came in from GOC posts all over Maryland and up and down the coast. They said the saucers were over Washington too."

"The Pentagon certainly put a clamp on it," I told him. "Usually I get a tip on any sightings around this area."

"Yes," Corbin replied. "They've tightened up so much that I don't know how much longer I can get information."

By the end of June my master chart was almost completed. But on rechecking all the material, I discovered several points I had previously overlooked—or which at the time I had not connected with the flying-saucer problem.

One of these items was the mysterious death of thousands of birds during September and October of 1954. At dawn on September 11 thousands of dead birds had been found around Friendship Airport at Baltimore. When examined by Game Warden Fielding Crawford, they proved to be oven birds, yellow-throats, red-eyed veros, black and white warblers, magnolia warblers, Connecticut warblers, and redstarts.

Baffled at first, Crawford suggested that the birds might have flown into the beam of the two-million-candlepower ceiling light over the airport. Apparently, he said, this had blinded them, causing them to fly into the ground. However, Crawford added, autopsies would be performed to rule out the chance that the birds might have eaten bugs sprayed by some powerful insecticide.

That all these varied types of birds could have been poisoned and then have flown to the airport to die seemed incredible. But so did the ceiling-beam answer. For airport ceiling lights had been shining into the sky for years all over the country. And no mass bird deaths had ever been reported before.

Then, a month later, the mystery had deepened. On the morning of October 9 birds by tens of thousands were found dead in Alabama, Georgia, South Carolina, Kansas, Tennessee, and Pennsylvania.

At the Allentown, Pennsylvania, Airport, where the situation was typical, hundreds of dead and dying birds were carted away by the truckload. Wildlife authorities admitted they had no idea as to what had caused the incident. Dr. John E. Trainer, an ornithologist at Muhlenberg College, told reporters that atmospheric conditions might have killed the birds. But neither he nor other ornithologists could suggest what kind of conditions might lead to such widespread disaster.

The next item added to the analysis list was labeled "Runaway rockets." For more than two years I had heard rumors that one or two rockets fired at White Sands had failed to return to earth. But even the powerful two-stage V-2 Wac-Corporal rocket had a vertical range of only 250 miles. Without a great increase in power, it seemed impossible for any of our rockets to have escaped from the earth's gravitational pull.

Yet within recent weeks I had received new confirmation of the rumor from a source I believed reliable. Not only had a V-2 disappeared, he said, but also a Nike rocket fired in a routine test. This last seemed to me almost unbelievable, since a Nike's range is far less than that of a V-2. But my informant swore it had occurred.

The third item involved a French Air Force pilot. As in the Walesville case, the pilot was pursuing a flying saucer. Suddenly a mysterious heat filled the cockpit. Though half-dazed, he managed to make a violent turn away from the object. He was sure the UFO had caused the strange heat, though he could offer no explanation as to how it had been accomplished.

I also listed a recent report given me by Lieutenant Commander Frank Thomas. According to Thomas, a peculiar object had fallen near Washington during the mass saucer sightings in 1952. Retrieved by a naval officer, it was later analyzed by the Bureau of Standards.

From the description Thomas gave me, I realized it was similar to the object which had crashed through the house at Sylacauga, Alabama. However, one side of it was flat with odd markings, as if it had been milled. During tests the unknown substance proved to be fire-resistant. But the analysis, Thomas said, had failed to determine whether it was an artificially constructed object or a fragment of some unknown type of meteorite. Afterward the object had been sent to W. B. Smith at Ottawa for further analysis by Project Magnet engineers.

Though I had scores of flying-saucer pictures from all over the world, many were obviously false. But there were three which seemed authentic enough to list on my master chart. One of these, taken on July 10, 1950, by two well-known and reputable pilots, showed two saucers flying below their plane, with a dark background of trees below.

After a careful check, the Seattle *Post-Intelligencer* had printed the photograph, which was taken by pilots J. K. Rockman and A. L. Meakin. The newspaper stated that the photograph had also been examined by Army Intelligence officers.

The second picture, showing an "unexplained aerial object," had been photographed on August 31, 1953, by G. P. Drury, Deputy Regional Director of Civil Aviation for Port Moresby. The UFO, sighted over New Guinea, was moving at high speed. By chance Drury had with him a movie camera equipped with a telephoto lens. After filming the saucer, he submitted the pictures to the Australian Ministry for Air, to be analyzed and identified. Later this picture was flown to the United States for detailed analysis at ATIC. (The U. S. Air Force analysis has never been released.)

A third picture, verified by U. S. Navy and Marine Corps officers, was taken by Marine Corporal Ralph Mayher at the height of the saucer sightings in July, 1952.

Mayher had told me the picture was still being kept under wraps by the Air Force.

"Except for a small section I retained," he said, "the film

was turned over to an Air Force Intelligence major who flew from Washington to Miami. I have asked the Air Force at least three times, twice in writing, to return the film, or at least to tell me what they found on analysis. I wanted to see if it confirmed the findings of the University of Miami—an acceleration to 7550 miles per hour—but I have never received a word."

The sixth new item for my chart concerned the false "Soviet weapon" stories. During the spring of 1955 an old rumor that the saucers were secret Russian weapons had begun to circulate again in two or three countries—mainly Germany and the United States. According to one published report the Russians had seized a Nazi aerial device known as the V-7 and spirited it to the USSR. By now, the story ran, the Russians had improved the device with the aid of Horst Pinkell, a German scientist.

But now Professor Hermann Oberth had thoroughly squelched those wild tales. It was true, he said, that he and German engineers had developed the V-7, a machine which possibly could be mistaken for a UFO.

"But it was only a helicopter," Professor Oberth stated. "The propeller had two wings, each 25 metres long with Staurohre jet tubes at the end."

It would be possible, Oberth said, for the rotating wings to look like a glowing disc at night.

"But," he added, "the V-7 makes an infernal noise, whereas most of the UFO's are reported to be silent. In addition," he said, "this V-7 always causes heavy vapor trails—seldom created by saucers."

Oberth added that the velocity of the V-7 could not even remotely approach that of the saucers, nor could it approach the accelerations and maneuvers of the mysterious UFO's.

Besides this, all of the facts which nullified the false "American secret weapon" answer applied equally to such claims for a Soviet device. Though these explanations had

been debunked, I put them down on the analysis list as part
of the UFO story.

Earlier in June I had written Paul Redell and told him of
my analysis plans. Then I had asked if he would help me by
answering a series of questions, if I mailed them to the Coast.
In answer, he had suggested that I hold off, since he expected to be in Washington within two weeks. Then later
he wrote that he would be delayed until some time in July.
Now he was almost due.

While I was waiting for Redell's arrival, I studied the
chart looking for clues. One explanation had occurred to me
several times since 1953. But it seemed so preposterous that
I had never mentioned it to anyone. I was thinking over this
puzzle one day when I had a call from Frank Edwards. Later
that afternoon we met in Washington.

"I just got back from New York," he said. "Do you know
anything new?"

I told him about the recent developments.

"There's one sighting you don't have," said Frank. "I just
received the report from London, Ontario. Two or three
days ago—it was on July 12—nine UFO's were sighted near
Innerkip. The London, Ontario, *Evening Free Press* says
eight of them were oval and chrome-colored and the other
—apparently it was larger—seemed to be round and silver.

"The next day several witnesses at London, Ontario,
sighted a disc nearly 200 feet in diameter. It flew south over
the lake and then suddenly shot up and disappeared. According to an Ottawa dispatch, which I just saw, the RCAF
has alerted all its pilots to be on the watch for flying saucers."

"That's very interesting—the RCAF's admitting it," I said.
"Here the Air Force is clamping down tighter than ever."

"Yes, and the Navy too, except for that queer one they
pulled when they released that photo on July 1. I saw it in
the New York *Times*—it shows what they call an 'unusual

cloud formation over the city of Marseilles, France.' Did you see it?"

"No, it wasn't printed here."

"Well, here's what the *Times* caption said:

" 'FLYING SAUCERS? The U. S. Navy released this photo on Friday, which they say shows an "unusual cloud formation over the city of Marseilles, France." The picture was made on November 4th, 1954. The Navy gave no indication as to why they released the photograph, nor any information as to why they considered its release pertinent.' "

"That's certainly odd," I commented.

"Yes," said Frank, "particularly when you compare it with the deal we got when we asked for pictures of those rockets. Then, the policy was *not* to give out pictures that would publicize saucers in any way. Now they hand this out to the papers and set off the very thing they said they were trying to keep quiet."

A few minutes later he asked me about a strange double explosion that had occurred over London, England, early on July 5.

I had read the UP story in a Washington paper:

2 MYSTERY BLASTS JOLT
50 MILE AREA AT LONDON

"London, July 5th. Mysterious twin explosions jolted a 50-square mile area here early today, sending thousands of Londoners rushing into the streets in alarm.

"The two 'booms' in quick succession jolted London buildings with such force that burglar alarms were touched off. Britons in remote suburbs rushed into the streets and their gardens because of the blast that shattered the early morning silence.

"U. S. Air Force officials, the British Air Ministry, and Scotland Yard said they were unable to explain the explosions, after day-long investigations.

"Officials classed the double boom with another mysterious explosion that rumbled over London at 1:30 A.M. on March 16th.

"Like this morning's twin explosions the March blast was heard for miles around London. It never has been explained officially.

"This morning's jolting booms set telephone switchboards aglow in the Air Ministry and Scotland Yard. 'It's a mystery,' Scotland Yard said. 'The London Control Center has no reports of any aircraft flying at the time that could have crashed through the sound barrier.'

"The U. S. Air Force said, 'No American aircraft were involved.' "

"That must have been a real blast," I said to Frank. "Do you know whether there were any UFO reports connected with it?"

"If there were, the Air Ministry hid them. Didn't you see the follow-up story?"

"No, what was it?" I asked.

"Well, for two days they kept trying to find the answer. Now keep that in mind—two days to check every air base and every manufacturer that had any jet supersonic planes. London was really getting stirred up about it. Evidently the Air Ministry and the War Office could see they were in for real trouble. So what happened? Read this—it's the AP story that appeared two days afterward."

I read the clipping:

"London, July 7th. The test pilot who startled Londoners out of their sleep early this week with an unscheduled burst through the sound barrier apologized last night for the mystery stir he caused.

"The fuss began early Tuesday when Dickie Martin, pilot for the Gloucester Aircraft Company, was test-flying a twin-jet delta-wing Javelin over London at a routine 700 miles an hour.

"Suddenly Mr. Martin's oxygen tube got tangled in his parachute harness. When he tried to free it, the plane swerved, gathered speed, and rocketed through the sound barrier.

"Frightened Londoners phoned police that a bomb had gone off. Sailors on the Thames prepared to abandon their ships, convinced that the boilers had burst. Scotland Yard made extensive inquiries but could find no explanation.

"The Gloucester Company finally got in touch with the Air Ministry to explain what had happened."

I was astonished. "Frank, that's the craziest cover-up I've seen yet."

"Isn't it?" Frank agreed. "The British are getting almost as bad as the hush-hush boys here. You know damned well if that had really happened, the Air Ministry would have had the dope from the Gloucester Company within an hour. The company would have never dared sit on it for two days while all that hysteria was building up."

"Not only that," I replied, "this idea of the pilot's oxygen tube getting tangled in his 'chute harness is ridiculous. The way they're constructed—to guard against such things—the odds against it are a thousand to one."

"What do you think really caused those blasts?" Frank asked me.

"I don't know, but I'm going to be talking with an aeronautical engineer in the next few days. I'll see if he has any ideas."

But it was almost a week before Redell finally arrived from California. For three days he was too busy for any long conversation, and I knew the analysis itself would take time. Finally, one evening, he came out to my home. When I showed him the master chart, he studied it silently for several minutes.

"It's an amazing picture, isn't it, when you get it all together?"

"Yes, it certainly proves that something tremendous is going on," I replied.

Redell sat down in a chair near my study window.

"Before we start," he said, "I'd like to make one thing clear. What I've learned didn't come from classified sources, so I'm not violating security in discussing this."

"I wouldn't ask you to break security, Paul. But I need help on some of these technical angles, especially the gravitational field. I have a lot of questions about that."

Redell nodded. "I can discuss that now, since Trimble and Lear broke the ice. But let's start at the top of your list."

I had also drawn up a witness list, naming hundreds of pilots, radar experts, and other reliable witnesses here and abroad. Most of the sightings shown on the chart had been double-checked and confirmed.

"There are a few incidents," I told Redell, "with only one source. Like the strange explosion report I got from Captain William Call of Eastern Air Lines—this one here." I pointed out the Hartford sky-quake item. "A man of Captain Call's reputation certainly wouldn't make that up. Also, from the way the CAA acted when I asked about it, it's obvious the Hartford tower had reported the blast too."

Redell glanced over the list of incidents and the statements the witnesses had made.

"There's no arguing with all that evidence," he said. "In my opinion these reports prove the existence of mother ships and saucers. The machines are certainly under intelligent control, and they're capable of fantastic speeds and maneuvers. Also, these reports prove the saucers could not possibly be made here on earth. And from the older records it appears that they have been observing the earth for centuries."

When we came to the Mars mystery, the first item to be

analyzed, Redell agreed with me that Mars seemed to be inhabited.

"And I also believe," he said, "from the increase in sightings when Mars is near us, that some of the saucers are operating from there. From the canal evidence, it looks as if Mars has been inhabited by an intelligent race for a long, long time."

"Back in June," I reminded him, "you said that the race might have died out and that the canals might be filling automatically when the polar caps melted."

"That was before I saw the astronomers' 1954 reports. From the way the areas beside the canals and all those oases turned green, the entire canal network must have been operating perfectly. Without workers to keep the system in order, some canals would be blocked by banks caving in or by silting.

"Also, another engineer and I studied the problem last winter, and we concluded it would require a large number of pumping stations to keep the water flowing over such long distances. When you add the canal evidence to all the other reports, I think it shows that Mars is inhabited."

Next we examined the moon reports.

"Even with no other evidence," Redell said, "the bridge that Wilkins and O'Neill discovered indicates there's an intelligent race on the moon."

"From the old reports," I added, "it looks as if they may have been there during the last two centuries."

Redell picked up a picture of the moon I'd clipped to the report, a photograph taken with the 100-inch telescope at Mount Wilson.

"It still gives me a queer feeling," he said, "to think that there's probably an unknown race that close to us."

"I know," I said. "I have the same feeling. And I suppose if Dr. Wilkins is right about the network of caves, then the moon could even be a world with hundreds of underground cities, though somehow I still can't believe it."

I looked at the next item. "Do you have anything new on orbiting space bases?"

Redell shook his head.

"After that *Aviation Week* story, quoting La Paz, the Pentagon raised hell, and the people I know are afraid to breathe a word. But I'm certain that we're being orbited by two space bases, and maybe more—the satellite-detection people at White Sands and Mt. Wilson have been searching the sky 24 hours a day."

"I'm certain too, Paul; all the circumstantial evidence bears it out. But we've no solid proof."

The next subject listed was labeled "Green fireballs and other missiles." Redell looked over the first few lines, then glanced at the master chart.

"I see you're including the Portola Road incident along with the fireball that crashed into a house in Darby, Pennsylvania."

"I realize the green fireballs are a separate problem," I answered. "But they all seem to have been some kind of missile, so I put them together."

Redell swung around and looked thoughtfully down at the Potomac.

"I think you've been right about the green fireballs all along. They seem to be some kind of missile under intelligent guidance. That case in New Mexico where three appeared in one day clinches it for me."

"I think they're ranging devices," I replied. "I wonder if they're being sent as some kind of warning to us. The UFO beings certainly aren't trying to harm anyone—the green fireballs always explode over uninhabited areas."

"I won't argue it with you," said Redell. "There may be some entirely different purpose, though I'll admit I can't figure it out."

Then he motioned to the chart.

"But I believe these other items belong in a separate group. The windshield pitting might have been an answer to our 'artificial meteor' experiments, as I suggested before. How it was done, I don't know."

"Do you know what the Air Force found out about that?" I inquired.

"No, the Air Matériel Command report is classified," Redell replied.

"What about the Portola Road pellets and the Darby fireball and that object at New Haven?"

Redell hesitated.

"In the Portola Road case," he said, "I think those pellets were deliberately aimed. Their falling in a precise rectangle makes it almost conclusive. It may have been a test or a warning—I don't pretend to know the answer.

"But the Darby fireball and the one at New Haven"—he turned back to look at the chart—"I believe they were accidents. After all, no matter how far advanced, even a super space race would sometimes make mistakes. Our own pilots have accidentally dropped bombs and rockets, even tools out of open-cockpit planes. It's quite possible that these fireballs were unintentionally released."

I eyed him curiously a moment.

"When I last saw you, Paul, you didn't talk like this. You seemed to think there might be a real chance of danger."

"Yes, I know, but I've done a lot of thinking since then. There have been some new angles . . . " he broke off. "I see the next item is marked 'Bird deaths.' Now that's one I never heard of."

I brought out the files and showed him the reports.

"There's no *proof* of any tie-in with the saucers," I explained. "But there were UFO reports in the Maryland area on the night that the birds fell at Friendship Airport. However, that may have been pure coincidence."

Redell read the news reports.

"There's one possible explanation," he said thoughtfully. "On each of those nights, one or more saucers may have passed over the area. If even one disc flew close enough to any birds, the saucer's gravitational field would pull them in against the ship hard enough to kill or injure them.

"A single UFO could pick up a large number of birds, a few at a time, while flying over a wide area. Later, whoever was in control could have momentarily reduced the G-field, dropping all the birds in one spot."

"If the saucers do operate by G-fields," I said, "I think you've hit it."

Redell reached into a pocket for his tobacco pouch. After he lighted his pipe, he ran his eye down the other items to be analyzed. As I'd expected, he immediately linked two of them with gravitational-field effects. One was the "angel's-hair" phenomenon. The other was the radio and television interference frequently linked with the flying saucers.

"That interference is fairly easy to understand," said Redell. "A powerful electromagnetic field certainly can interfere with radio and television reception. And the creation of such a field by the saucers is consistent with Einstein's Unified Field Theory.

"The 'angel's-hair' phenomenon is also explainable," Redell continued.

"It seems fairly clear that the 'angel's hair' is caused by ionization from the saucers' discharge and the action of the G-field upon it. That's not original with me," he added. "I think it was first suggested by a Frenchman named Plantier. You'll find it discussed more fully in a book called *Lueurs sur les soucoupes volantes* by Aimé Michel."

Even before this I had read Michel's discussion of the Plantier theory.

In most respects Plantier's analysis agreed closely with that of Professor Hermann Oberth. But whereas Oberth had not explained how a G-field could be achieved, Plantier suggested that the saucers' G-fields were created by means of cosmic radiation.*

For several years cosmic forces in outer space had been known to be tremendous. On July 8, 1954, Dr. Marcel Schein, an authority on nuclear physics at the University of Chicago, reported his discovery of a tiny cosmic particle with a force of ten million billion volts. With such colossal power available in space, it was only a question of how it could be harnessed for propulsion.

Through the use of cosmic rays, Plantier said, a space ship could be surrounded by a powerful gravitational-force field, which could be varied and directed at will. It would be possible, by orienting the G-field, not only to attract but to repulse any approaching object.

Also, according to Plantier, the ionization of the atmosphere in the wake of the craft would, as a result of the intensity of the G-field, be sufficient to produce ultra-heavy particles. These, in contact with the elements in the surrounding air, would cause novel chemical reactions—in other words, "angel's hair." As the ionization decreased, the "angel's hair" would disintegrate.

"This 'angel's-hair' answer might also explain that blue rain in Canada," I said to Redell.

Redell read the "blue rain" report.

"Yes," he said. "Some of the rain drops would absorb the 'angel's-hair' radioactivity, and the chemical effect would cause the rain to change color.

"Plantier also has an explanation for the strange sky quakes. If the force field broke down while the UFO was flying at tremendous speed, the surrounding air would cease to be carried along with the machine. According to Plantier,

* Translated for me by Isabel L. Davis and Ted Bloecher of Civilian Saucer Intelligence.

the UFO would collide with motionless air, causing it to disintegrate with a bright flash and a thunderous roar.

"That certainly fits the Dieppe report," I said. "Also, that case in New Zealand where a cigar-shaped object was seen to explode over the Southern Alps."

"And it would also fit the saucer explosion over New Mexico last April," said Redell. "It looks as if Plantier may have the right explanation."

"One point we haven't covered, Paul—those invisible saucers over England. I think I know the answer—remember I wrote to you and asked if a G-field would bend light rays?"

Redell gave me an apologetic grin.

"I'm sorry, I meant to answer you. I think you're right. I think that *is* the answer. You remember Einstein proved that rays from stars are deflected by the gravitational field of the sun?"

"Yes, that's what put me on to the idea."

"Well, it's now fully accepted that *all* light rays are deflected by a strong gravitational field. Apparently the G-field around a single saucer isn't enough to cause this effect; but with a large number of saucers in formation, the G-fields would be strong enough to deflect the light rays at such an angle that the saucers would be invisible."

"I think that's the answer in the English case. It would also explain the ghost of Nansei-shoto. Apparently Dawson and the other CIC men were right—they were actually tracking a huge saucer formation."

Next I laid out the London *Despatch* story describing the curious Z and U formations tracked by English radar operators. Redell glanced at the headlines.

"I saw that," Redell said. "I can't help but think that the UFO's were trying to signal our planet, forming the same letters every day."

"Yes, but signaling like that doesn't make sense. If the saucer beings wanted to communicate with us——"

"They may not be able to communicate," Redell pointed out. "In the first place, they'd have to unscramble at least 20 languages, not to mention the dialects, to get an accurate picture of life in our world. Now, here on earth, if you meet a foreigner, you can point to some familiar object, like a loaf of bread, or a bus, or maybe a girl coming down the street. Then you say your word for it and he says his. That's how the first linguists got started. But the space creatures can't do that——"

"Then how would they know our alphabet to form those Z and U letters?"

"Perhaps from seeing big signs on tops of buildings, for one thing," said Redell. "You know the ones that name a city with an arrow pointing to the airport. And there are thousands of other signs that could be photographed from miles up with long-range cameras, or picked up by a TV-type of scanner."

Redell reached for an ashtray, emptied the ashes from his pipe.

"Why do you think they formed those letters?" I said.

Redell hesitated. "Maybe they had a meaning, but I think it was probably just to get attention—to show our world they are intelligent beings. They probably expected some answer that would show we understood. Unfortunately there's been no organized program to signal the saucers. Or if there was, it's been kept strictly secret."

"This certainly upsets a lot of my ideas," I confessed. "But it could explain one thing—that huge W on Mars, which the Carnegie Institution reported."

Redell started to reply, then he looked at the clock on the mantel.

"I've got to run," he said. "I have an early appointment."

"But we're not half through," I protested. "We haven't even mentioned the strange accidents."

"Let's hold that until tomorrow night. I can make it then if you're free."

"All right," I said. "But before you go, tell me this. You seem convinced the UFO beings aren't hostile. Why?"

Redell had started toward the study door. He turned, with an expression I couldn't fathom.

"It was the Kimross case," he said. "I think that's the key to the whole thing."

19 The Vanishing Planes

All the next day Redell's parting words kept running through my mind.

Since November of '53 the Kimross mystery had haunted me. I too had felt it might be the key to the flying-saucer riddle.

But through the following months my fear that it had been a hostile act increased. Redell's quiet conviction that it proved a *lack* of hostility brought me up against a blank wall.

Wondering if I had overlooked some reason for his belief, I went back over all the possible motives which had been suggested for the saucers' surveillance of the earth. Since the UFOs' mass appearance in '47, the motives suggested had ranged from "attempts at friendly contacts" to "plans for complete annihilation of everyone on earth."

One idea, suggested by Air Chief Marshal Lord Dowding, was that the UFO beings, if not planning a friendly contact, might merely be making a scientific survey of a newly discovered inhabited planet. In contrast, Colonel W. C. Odell, U. S. Air Force Intelligence, had said that an unknown race might be planning to migrate here from some dying planet.

The most common theory, and a logical one, was that any planet race about to begin space travel would be of serious concern to races already traveling in space, especially those in our own or nearby solar systems. In self-protection, they would undoubtedly be disturbed by our space-rocket tests and A-bomb blasts. To make sure we would not be a menace when we finally achieved space travel, they might set up a constant saucer patrol to watch our every step.

Their failure to land for direct contact might be explained in several ways. If their planet's gravity varied greatly from that of the earth's, they might fear some dangerous effect if they landed.

To the unknown UFO creatures our atmosphere might be poisonous. Or at least incapable of supporting their kind of life. They might fear many things—earth diseases, or even that we would try to capture the saucers and them. They might fear, and with reason, that their landing here would start a panic unless the earth races had been fully prepared.

Now, however, there was an explanation for the UFOs' silence—provided Redell was right. But a block to communication didn't prove the UFO beings were friendly. And though I still hoped they were, the fateful Kimross F-89 chase kept coming back into my mind.

Just a month before, on June 17, I had again asked the Air Force about this disaster. The next day I had had an answer from Captain Perry E. Hudson, the PIO assigned to handle inquiries on crashes.

"I rechecked that Kimross report," Captain Hudson told me. "No bodies were ever found, nor any wreckage."

"Has the Air Force ever made the cause public?"

"We assume," Captain Hudson replied, "that the plane went into the lake."

I was thinking back to the Truax Field report on that disaster when Redell arrived. I showed him a list of the accidents which had been linked with the saucers.

"There are dozens of unsolved cases," I told him. "But most of them probably had ordinary causes. I've used only the ones that have been definitely linked to the saucers—the Kimross, Walesville, and Idyllwild accidents."

"Idyllwild?" said Redell. "What happened there?"

"An unknown object hit the wing of a B-47, and the plane had to make an emergency landing." I gave him the details. "It looks just like the Comet jet-airliner case at Calcutta in '52, except that the Comet crashed."

"The British now say that it exploded from metal fatigue," interposed Redell.

"I know that. But a different story came out at the inquiry. The British Civil Aviation Ministry had one of its top investigators, J. H. Lett, working on the case. At a public hearing Lett reported that the Comet evidently had been hit in flight by a 'fairly heavy body' of some kind. He said there was no sign of ordinary structural failure.

"When I quoted Lett in '53, the Civil Aviation Ministry told London papers no such statement had ever been made. But when I wrote them, they finally wrote back and confirmed Lett's statement. They insisted, though, that Lett meant a piece of the Comet's wing might have broken off and hit the fuselage. But from the way Lett worded his statement it seemed obvious that he considered the 'heavy body' an unidentified object."

"Even so, the collision could have been accidental," said Redell. "So could this other case, at Idyllwild."

"I'd like to think they were all unintentional," I returned, "but you've got to admit the Walesville and Kimross cases look bad."

Redell looked at me for a moment.

"Let's face it," he said quietly. "Any advanced space race could undoubtedly destroy us if they wished. We could even destroy ourselves, with the H-bomb—and the way we're heading maybe we will. But a race advanced enough for space travel would certainly have means and weapons far beyond ours."

"All right, Paul," I said. "I agree that we're in their power——"

Redell held up his hand.

"Wait a minute. I just want to show how *completely* we're in their power. You remember what Oberth and our own Defense Department said about the satellites—how they could use sun mirrors and burn all the cities to ashes? Oberth also said they could melt glaciers. It's been calculated that if the Greenland glacier were melted it would raise the ocean level enough to cover most cities along the Atlantic coast. If they melted *all* the Arctic and Antarctic ice, there'd be damned little left of the human race.

"The point is," he continued, "they haven't attacked us yet."

"What about the Kimross case?"

Redell hesitated. "What do you think happened that night?" His face had the odd expression I'd noted the night before.

"At first I thought they'd collided," I answered, "though with the F-89's radar and Ground Control to warn the pilot, I couldn't see how that could happen. But when they didn't find any wreckage, I knew it was no ordinary collision.

"Then, when I heard of the G-field theory, I thought that perhaps the jet had gotten too close to the saucer and that the saucer had used a reversed G-field beam. If I understand the G-field theory correctly, it would have been as if the plane had hit a stone wall."

"Yes," said Redell. "The violent vibration alone could tear the plane apart. But there still would be wreckage."

"Couldn't the plane have disintegrated?"

"A force capable of doing that—when the plane was so close that their blips merged—would have destroyed the saucer too. Then there would have been no blip at all, and Ground Control saw one move off the scope."

"But somehow they completely did away with the jet, Paul. There's no other possible explanation."

Redell hesitated.

"Well, there could be another one, though it's so incredible I find it hard to believe. Do you remember the Air Force Intelligence colonel who said ATIC would consider even the most extravagant ideas in the hope of solving the saucer mystery?"

"Yes. *Look* magazine quoted him in 1952."

"One idea they must have considered is that the plane wasn't destroyed at all."

"Do you mean that the saucer carried it off?"

"Don't tell me you never thought of it."

"Yes," I said slowly. "I did, when I heard that the two blips merged. But I never really believed it. Paul, that would be too fantastic."

"Certainly, it's fantastic. So are the flying saucers. So was the idea of airplanes and space rockets—when they were first suggested."

"But for a saucer to make off with a plane!"

"Look. We ourselves have 'mother ships' that launch and retrieve small machines. Twenty years ago, if anybody had told you we'd have B-36 bombers taking Sabrejet fighters aboard, you'd have thought he was crazy."

"How could the saucer creatures manage it?"

"There'd be a few problems, of course," Redell replied. "They'd have to cut off the jet's engine, but they could probably do that with an electromagnetic beam. And by gradually increasing the G-field, they could draw the F-89 to the saucer."

"Even if it were true—and I don't believe it either—how could it prove they're *not* hostile? It looks to me like the opposite."

"If hostility were the key, Don, why wouldn't they simply destroy the plane? Since they didn't, I can think of only one explanation: they're trying to prepare for a peaceful contact with the earth—that is, assuming for the moment that the plane was captured.

"We know they've been observing us for years. Perhaps they can't see any other way to make us realize the truth. After all, when they come down here our jets chase them. So this might seem the best way to solve the problem: by making off with human beings and keeping them until they had established communication."

"You mean until they had learned each other's language?"

"I suppose so. Maybe they'd use sign language at first. Finally they'd understand each other. It would be the first step toward the meeting of two worlds."

I turned to the window and looked up at the far-off stars.

"It's a frightening thought, Paul."

"I know it's shocking, but it's better than an attack. And if it's the answer in the Kimross case, then it could explain some of the other cases as well. Do you remember when a flight of Navy torpedo-bombers disappeared after they took off from Fort Lauderdale, Florida?"

"Yes, but that was almost ten years ago. I didn't have any reason to check into it. Weren't those accidents blamed on bad weather?"

"They weren't accidents. The planes just vanished. And it never was explained."

Redell unzipped his brief case and took out a bulky folder.

"Here's the summary, based on the Navy's reports . . ."

The case of the vanishing Navy planes had begun as a routine flight.

On the afternoon of December 5, 1945, five TBM "Avengers" stood on the ramp at Fort Lauderdale Naval Air Station.

The Avengers, torpedo-bombers, normally carried three men—a pilot, a gunner, and a radio operator. On this day, however, one crewman had failed to report. The five pilots, a Marine, and four Navy men, warmed up their engines and checked their instruments for the flight. Climbing in behind them, their crews closed the canopies and fastened their safety belts.

Each man was equipped with a life jacket, and all five Avengers carried self-inflating life rafts. The planes had been carefully checked—compasses, controls, and engines were all in perfect condition.

At 2:10 P.M. the flight leader gunned his engine, and the first Avenger roared down the runway. In rapid succession the others followed, climbing into a clear blue sky. Cruising at 215 mph, the planes flew out over the Atlantic.

According to their navigation plan, the formation was to fly 160 miles eastward toward the Bahamas, then north for 40 miles, and finally, completing the triangle, back to the Naval Air Station. It was to be a relatively short flight, requiring less than two hours.

But at 3:45 P.M. the Fort Lauderdale station received a strange radio message. In a worried voice the flight leader reported:

"We seem to be off course. I'm not sure of our position."

During the next hour more calls came in, each a little more tense. It seemed impossible for all five compasses to have failed. Yet how else could the pilots have become so utterly lost?

At about four o'clock the anxious listeners ashore overheard a brief conversation. Apparently in a panic, the flight leader had turned over command to another pilot.

Then, at four-twenty-five, another message came through from the overdue formation:

"Our position still not certain. Believe we are about 225 miles northeast of base."

In response to this message a huge Martin Mariner flying boat was hurriedly dispatched to the scene. Built to withstand rough landings at sea, the Mariner was a powerful plane, 77 feet long, with a wing span of 124 feet. Equipped with full rescue and survival equipment, and manned by a crew of 13, the Mariner roared off to guide the Avengers home.

Afterward, Operations at Fort Lauderdale called the Avengers to tell them that help was on the way. But not a word came back from the five torpedo-planes.

Several minutes later Operations called the Mariner to check its position.

There was no answer. For five taut minutes the base radio operator anxiously repeated the call. But the Mariner's radio, like all the Avengers', was ominously silent.

Now thoroughly alarmed, Operations flashed word to the Coast Guard at Miami. As swiftly as possible, a Coast Guard rescue plane took off. Following the Mariner's course, it reached the Avengers' last estimated position. There was not a sign of the six missing planes.

As the sea grew dark, Navy and Coast Guard vessels began a hurried search, watching vainly for signal flares from life rafts. At dawn the escort carrier *Solomons* put out to sea with 30 planes to begin an aerial hunt.

By now over 20 vessels were methodically combing the sea. Within two hours 240 planes were crisscrossing the sky from Florida to the Bahamas.

For two days the massed searchers covered the sea area surrounding Florida—300 miles into the Atlantic, and 200 miles into the Gulf of Mexico.

Still there was not a trace of the six lost planes.

But the Navy stubbornly refused to give up. The planes had to be somewhere. Perhaps they had crashed at some desolate spot ashore.

For two more days low-flying planes and ground crews carefully searched the Everglades. The area at sea was widened until finally the planes and ships had covered 280,000 square miles—the greatest air-sea search ever made.

At last, convinced they would never find the lost planes,

the Navy ended the hunt. But even then, search teams continued to scour the Florida beaches, even the distant Bahama Islands, hoping to find a clue. Every bit of debris cast up by the tides was carefully examined. For weeks this painstaking search went on, until the Navy's last hope died.

Months later a Naval Board of Inquiry formally stated that no trace had been found of the missing men or their planes.

"The Board members," the report concluded, "were not able to make even a good guess as to what happened."

Later an AP reporter at Fort Lauderdale asked the Navy if the mystery had ever been solved.

There was still no clue, one station officer told him, as to the fate of the missing men and their planes.

"They vanished as completely," he said, "as if they had flown to Mars."

"That's an amazing report," I told Redell. He had been pacing the room as I read the summary.

"I think this analysis makes the facts even more astonishing," said Redell.

He sat by the window as I checked the main points.

If the Avengers had flown too far east, the analysis showed, the crews would have seen the Bahama Islands. Great Bahama, almost 25 miles long, would have been easily visible, especially in such clear weather. Had they flown southeast, the pilots would have seen both Andros and Great Abaca Islands. Flying west or southwest, they would have crossed either the Florida Keys or the mainland itself. The only open areas were directly north and south. Even there, islands, Keys, or the mainland would have been visible to one side or the other on such a clear day.

Redell leaned over as I finished the first section.

"Since they didn't sight land," he said, "there's only one explanation. They were circling constantly midway between Florida and the Bahamas. That means something had thrown off all five compasses, apparently to the same degree. Radio-station tape recordings of the pilots' conversations show they were all badly confused. Possibly the compass error was deliberately varied during those three hours to keep them circling. If it had been a constant error they'd have flown straight and seen land in some direction."

Next, the analysis had covered the forced-landing or "ditching" angle. If by some incredible coincidence, the engines of all the Avengers had failed, the pilots would have had to ditch at sea. But even this would not normally mean tragedy, for all torpedo-plane pilots are specially trained in ditching procedure.

Moreover, all five of the Avengers' engines would not have failed at once. When the first engine stopped, the plane's pilot would have swiftly radioed a "Mayday" alarm—signaling he was in trouble. As the other planes' engines cut out, more "Mayday" calls would have filled the air to bring rescue planes and ships.

Even if the planes had ditched, most, if not all, of the 14 men should have escaped. The sea was fairly calm, and the pilots should have stalled their planes in without any serious damage. Normally, all of the crews would have gotten into their rubber life rafts. The crewmen's pneumatic jackets would have kept them afloat while the rafts were inflating.

If the crews had bailed out, after some strange mid-air accident, they would still have had their rafts and Mae West life jackets to keep them afloat. In scores of cases Navy pilots and crews had existed for days, even weeks, in open sea, after similar bail-outs or ditchings.

Even if they had all crashed, which was almost inconceivable, wreckage and bodies would have been found strewed over several square miles.

The same thing held true in the case of the Martin Mariner. Under ordinary conditions the Mariner flying boat could fly on one of its two Cyclone engines. In case of a forced landing or in any emergency, the crew would have radioed their base. And should the Mariner's radio have failed, the operator could have used a hand-cranked generator for emergency transmissions.

Like the Avengers, the huge plane was fully equipped with life jackets and rafts.

"It's absolutely impossible," Redell declared, "for any of those six planes to have ditched or crashed. The searchers would have found wreckage and some of the crew—dead or alive. Do you agree?"

"Yes, I think you're right. Those planes must have been completely destroyed——"

"Unless the saucers took them," Redell replied. "If that theory is correct, an electromagnetic beam could have thrown off the compasses and also silenced the radios. The same thing could have happened to the Mariner."

"But to make off with all those planes!" I said. "The saucer would have to have been enormous."

"Well, we've had proof they use giant mother ships," Redell responded. "In that Gulf of Mexico case, the one-half-inch blip on the scope shows the mother ship was over 1000 feet long—probably nearer 1500. Also, there may have been more than one saucer in the Florida case. Again, I'm just temporarily assuming the capture explanation."

"It's still unbelievable," I muttered. I sat there, my mind half-numbed by the picture Redell had painted.

Redell gave me a serious glance.

"If it's true—and I've been fighting the idea the way you're doing now—it might also explain the Navy Super-Constellation's disappearance over the Atlantic in October of '54. You probably saw the story; there were 42 people aboard, some of them Navy wives and their children."

"Yes, I looked into that," I said. "It occurred to me that it might have been destroyed by a saucer. It happened soon after those UFO's were flying over Virginia."

"The Navy Constellation vanished exactly like the six planes from Fort Lauderdale. Radio silence—even though they had two transmitters. Not a trace of wreckage or bodies, though hundreds of planes and ships searched for days."

"I got one statement from Commander Andy Bright, head of the Navy's Aviation Safety Section. He said they could offer no explanation."

Redell spread his hands. "They certainly wouldn't make this answer public."

"No, even if they knew it was true. And there may be some strange explanation we haven't even considered. But I believe this accounts for the blackout—even if the censors don't have the complete answer."

"Yes, you can see why they'd fight to keep it secret."

"Even so, they're wrong to hide what they've learned. No matter what the explanation is, the world should be prepared."

Redell did not answer. I turned and saw him stare up into the night.

"Paul, what do you honestly believe?"

He looked back.

"I really don't know," he said gravely. "It's haunted me for weeks. Logic provides one answer, instinct another. What do *you* believe?"

Slowly I shook my head.

"I don't know either, Paul. I can only wonder."

APPENDIX I

JANAP 146(B)   Nonregistered

DECLASSIFIED per
DA MESSAGE 473987 dated
12 December 1953

COMMUNICATION INSTRUCTIONS FOR
REPORTING VITAL INTELLIGENCE
SIGHTINGS FROM AIRCRAFT
(CIRVIS)

JANAP 146(B)

THE JOINT CHIEFS OF STAFF
JOINT COMMUNICATIONS-ELECTRONICS COMMITTEE
WASHINGTON 25, D.C.
September 1951

6 September 1951

LETTER OF PROMULGATION

• • •   • • •   • • •

7. THIS DOCUMENT CONTAINS INFORMATION AFFECT-
ING THE NATIONAL DEFENSE OF THE UNITED STATES
WITHIN THE MEANING OF THE ESPIONAGE LAWS,
TITLE 18, U.S.C., SECTIONS 793 and 794. THE TRANSMIS-
SION OR THE REVELATION OF ITS CONTENTS IN ANY
MANNER TO AN UNAUTHORIZED PERSON IS PRO-
HIBITED BY LAW.

CHAPTER I

102. *SCOPE.*

a. This publication is limited to the reporting of information of
vital importance to the security of the United States of America, its
territories and possessions, which, in the opinion of the observer, re-
quires prompt defensive and/or investigative action by the U. S. Armed
Forces.

CHAPTER II

CIRVIS REPORTS

SECTION I – GENERAL

201. *INFORMATION TO BE REPORTED AND WHEN TO RE-
PORT.*

(1) Immediately (except over foreign territory—See Art. 215).
(b) Unidentified flying objects.

• • •   • • •   • • •

205. *PRECEDENCE (PRIORITY OF TRANSMISSION).*
Transmission of CIRVIS reports will be preceded by or include
the international "Urgency Signal," military precedence of "Emergency," or "Emergency U. S. Government," as appropriate for the
communications means, system of service employed.

206. *ADDRESSING.*

a. ALL CIRVIS messages will be multiple addressed to:

(1) CG, AIR DEFENSE COMMAND, ENT AFB, COLORADO
SPRINGS, COLORADO. (Commanding General, Air Defense Command, Ent Air Force Base, Colorado Springs, Colorado).

(2) SECDEF WASHINGTON DC (Secretary of Defense, Washington, D.C.) who will transmit copies of the reports to the Central Intelligence Agency and other appropriate agencies.

(3) Nearest U. S. Military Command with which communication may be effected.

・ ・ ・   ・ ・ ・   ・ ・ ・

208. ACCEPTANCE OF AND RESPONSIBILITY FOR CIRVIS REPORTS.

a. All military communications activities, as described in paragraph 206, when receiving or being asked to relay or deliver CIRVIS reports, shall accept, forward and/or deliver immediately without question, the contents of such reports *EXACTLY AS RECEIVED* by the most expeditious means available, in strict accordance with the instructions contained herein. All civilian communications activities will be urged to follow the same procedure. Insofar as is practicable, military facilities of the United States of America or those under United States control will be utilized.

・ ・ ・   ・ ・ ・   ・ ・ ・

e. Fixed and mobile military communications facilities, and military personnel having occasion to handle CIRVIS reports are responsible, and all civilian facilities and personnel are urged, to lend assistance in all cases required in expediting CIRVIS reports. Maximum care must be taken by all persons handling CIRVIS reports to insure positive immediate delivery.

SECTION III — SECURITY

209. MILITARY AND CIVILIAN.

a. All persons aware of the contents or existence of a CIRVIS report are governed by the Communications Act of 1934 and amendments thereto, and Espionage Laws.

・ ・ ・   ・ ・ ・   ・ ・ ・

(2) CIRVIS reports contain information affecting the National Defense of the United States within the meaning of the Espionage Laws, 18 U. S. Code, 793 and 794. The unauthorized transmission or revelation of the contents of CIRVIS reports in any manner is prohibited.

・ ・ ・   ・ ・ ・   ・ ・ ・

APPENDIX II

FOR THE PRESS

The color movie film footage which you are about to see was taken seven miles north of Tremonton, Utah, on U.S. Highway 30, at 11:10 A.M. (MST), July 2, 1952.

The photographs were taken by Warrant Officer Delbert C. Newhouse, Aviation Supply Depot, Naval Supply Center, Oakland, California, and were forwarded to the Air Technical Intelligence Center, Wright-Patterson Air Force Base, Dayton, Ohio, for evaluation purposes.

The camera used by Warrant Officer Newhouse was a Bell & Howell Auto Master with a three inch telephoto lens. The camera was held by hand. The first few feet of film were taken at F-8; the balance at F-16, at sixteen frames per second.

This film is the property of Warrant Officer Newhouse, the Air Force thus cannot make the film available to the Press or other media for publication purposes. Any such request should be directed to W. O. Newhouse.

The account given by W. O. Newhouse and his wife was nerally as follows: On July 2, 1952, Newhouse was driving from Washington, D.C. to Portland, Oregon, when his wife noticed a group of objects in the sky which she could not identify. She asked Newhouse to stop the car and look.

Newhouse saw the group of 12-14 objects, which bore no resemblance to anything he had seen before, milling about in a rough formation and proceeding in an apparent westerly direction.

He opened the luggage compartment of his car, got his movie camera out of a suitcase, and proceeded to take the pictures. There was no reference point above the horizon so he was unable to make any estimates as to size, speed, or distance. Toward the end of his observation one of the objects reversed course and proceeded away from the rest of the group. Newhouse held the camera still and allowed this single object to pass across the field of view of the camera, picking it up again later in its course. He repeated this for two or three passes. By this time all the objects had disappeared.

The pictures obtained by Newhouse have been studied by the Photo Reconnaissance Laboratory, Wright-Air Development Center, Wright-Patterson AFB, Dayton, Ohio, and by the U. S. Navy Photo Interpretation Center, Washington, D.C. The Laboratories are of the opinion that these photographs would be extremely difficult to produce under simulated conditions.

Since there was no known object, such as a cloud, tree, or mountain in the film, it has been impossible to determine accurately distance, speed or size of the objects.

It has been impossible also to determine what the objects are, because of their being beyond the resolution power of the lens used. However, certain observations can be made based on analysis by the photographic laboratories:

1. They appear to be a light source rather than reflected light. It is felt that if they were reflected light some blinking would have occurred as they passed through the flight movements observed on the film.

2. The size of the objects could not be determined as they appear merely as points of light, however they all seem to be of the same size.

3. The shape of the objects could not be determined for the same reason, but they appear circular.

4. The general color of the objects seems to be bluish-white, the other colors noted apparently being due to color aberration in the lens and to processing defects.

5. Speed of the objects can be calculated only on the basis of the distance from, and their movement relative to, the observer. It is felt that if the objects were balloons or aircraft of known dimensions, they could have been identified if within a distance of 5 miles. The resolution power of the lens is insufficient to identify objects of such dimensions if in excess of five miles. If the distance is assumed to be five miles and the movement perpendicular to the line of sight, the average velocity would be 653.3 mph; likewise, at 2½ miles distance the average speed would be 326.75 mph, and at 7½ miles 980.25 mph.

6. Generally, the movement of the individual object in flight appears to follow an elliptical or circular pattern within the group.

As was stated, it cannot be determined what the objects are. However, there are a few things which it is believed they are not:

1. Balloons—with the telephoto lens used, weather balloons within five miles distance could have been identified. The speeds calculated for the objects if only 2½ miles away of 326.75 mph is in excess of any wind blown balloons.

2. Aircraft—within a five miles range an aircraft of 40 foot wing span could be identified clearly. At the time the photographs were taken, there was no group flying by aircraft capable of the assumed speeds, and certainly not capable of such maneuvers at those speeds.

3. Birds—these objects appear to be a light source rather than reflecting light, but should they be only reflecting light no bird is sufficiently reflective to cause the film to react as strongly as it has done.

Lack of detail in the images caused by the objects and a corresponding lack of accurate data as to size, speed, distance, etc., makes it impossible to explain the sighting. In view of this lack of data the Air Force therefore will not speculate concerning the nature of the objects.

APPENDIX III

Long Beach 15, Calif.
April 11, 1954

Major Donald E. Keyhoe
Alexandria, Virginia

Dear Major Keyhoe,

In regard to your letter of April 8, 1954, I would be glad to clarify the following points:

1. During the period of July 1951 to August 1953, while I was in charge of the Air Force's investigation of unidentified flying objects, certain reports were declassified and sent to you at the request of the Office of Public Information of the Department of Defense. As per policy at the time, declassification consisted of removing the names of people involved in the sighting and any reference to classified military equipment (i.e. radars, aircraft performance, etc.). The procedure in sending you such information was that I would receive a request for the data either direct from OPI/DD or the Director of Intelligence, by wire or telephone. It would go back by wire, cleared by my superiors. In many instances I was informed that the data were for you.

2. I have read your book, "Flying Saucers From Outer Space" and to the best of my knowledge the sightings that you credit to the Air Force and the Air Force conclusions on each are those that I sent to you through the OPI/DD.

3. Movies do exist, or I should say did exist as I have not seen them recently, that were taken in July 1952 by a Navy Chief Petty Officer near Trementon, Utah. To the best of my knowledge the movie itself was never classified, but a classified analysis was made. Sometime in the late winter or early spring of 1953 I wrote a press release about this movie and wired it to the Pentagon. This was my last contact with the "Tremonton Movies." I heard via the grapevine that the release was not given out due to a dispute over the wording, but I cannot confirm this fact as I was out of the picture as far as press releases were concerned.

4. Regarding my comments on the letter on the jacket on the back of your book, from Al Chop to Henry Holt and Company, I agree that it is correct in all respects. *If* the reported speeds and maneuvers of the reported objects are correct I also agree that they must be from another planet as our level of technical "know-how" is not high enough to build such craft. Many people in high military circles agree on this point, the only question was were the reports correct in their descriptions of speed and maneuvers. The Air Force did not believe they were.

5. Regarding a theory by Dr. Menzel that all UFOs were sundogs, halos, light refraction, etc., I was told by advisors to our organization (ATIC) that this theory was not valid except for a few cases that we had already written off as such. This was communicated to you through the OPI/DD, again cleared by my superiors.

I hope that the above explanations will be of value to you in better understanding what took place in my office during my tenure as chief of Project Blue Book.

Yours truly,
Edward J. Ruppelt

APPENDIX IV

PRNC 3820.1
Code 03
23 July 1954

HEADQUARTERS
POTOMAC RIVER NAVAL COMMAND
WASHINGTON 25, D.C.

PRNC INSTRUCTION 3820.1
From: Commandant, Potomac River Naval Command
To: Distribution List II
Subj: Unidentified flying objects; reporting of
Ref: (a) OPNAV NOTICE 3820 of 26 Sep 1952
          (b) JANAP 146(C)
          (c) Air Force Letter 200-5 of 29 Apr 1952 (enclosure (1) to ref (a))
          (d) COMEASTSEAFRON INSTRUCTION 3820.2

1. **Purpose.** To provide guidance for procedures to be followed for reporting unidentified flying objects.

2. **Definition.** Unidentified flying objects as used in this Instruction relate to any airborne object which by performance, aerodynamic characteristics, or unusual features does not conform to any presently known aircraft or missile type.

3. **Background.** Reference (a) states that the U. S. Air Force has the primary responsibility for collection of subject information and has requested the cooperation of all naval activities in reporting such information.

4. **Action.**

   a. Addressees are requested to report any data on unidentified flying objects without delay by message in multiple address to:

   ACTION: (a) Director of Intelligence, Headquarters USAF, Washington 25, D.C.

(b) Air Technical Intelligence Center, Wright-Patterson AFB, Ohio—ATTN: ATLAA-2C.

(c) Commander, Air Defense Command, Ent AFB, Colorado Springs, Colorado

(d) Commander, Eastern Air Defense Force, Stewart AFB, Newburgh, N.Y.

INFO: (e) Director of Naval Intelligence, Navy Department, Washington 25, D.C.

(f) Commander Eastern Sea Frontier, 90 Church Street, New York 7, N.Y.

(g) Commandant, Potomac River Naval Command, U. S. Naval Gun Factory, Washington 25, D.C.

b. The symbol FLYOBRPT [Flying Objects Report] will appear at the beginning of the text of messages to facilitate identification.

c. Reports will include, insofar as possible:

(1) A brief description of the object(s); shape, size, color, number, formation if more than one, aerodynamic features, trail or exhaust, propulsion system, speed, sound, maneuvers, manner of disappearance, and other pertinent or unusual features.

(2) Time of sighting in 24-hour clock zonal time, and length of time observed.

(3) Manner of observation; visual or electronic, from air (give speed, altitude, and type of aircraft), or surface. Any type of optical or electronic equipment used should be described.

(4) Location of observer during sighting, giving exact latitude and longitude as closely as feasible, and/or reference to a known landmark. Location of object(s) with respect to observer, giving distance, direction, and altitude.

(5) Identifying information of observer(s) and witness(s), estimate of reliability and experience, and any factors bearing on estimated reliability of the sighting.

(6) Weather and winds aloft conditions at time and place of sighting(s).

(7) Any activity or condition, meteorological or otherwise, which might account for the sighting.

(8) Existence of any physical evidence such as fragments, photographs and the like, of the sighting.

(9) Interception or identification action taken. (Such action may be taken whenever feasible, complying with existing air defense directives).

(10) Location of any air traffic in the general area at the time of the sighting.

d. It should be noted that the above instructions are separate from those required for reporting normal surface and air sightings prescribed by reference (b) and CINCLANTFLT instructions concerning same.

e. Addressees are requested to give these instructions wide dissemination within their commands.

T. B. HILL [Rear Admiral, USN]
V. HAVARD, JR. [Captain, USN]
Chief of Staff

APPENDIX V

*AFR 200-2

* This Regulation supersedes AFR 200-2, 26 August 1953, including Change
200-2A, 2 November 1953.

DEPARTMENT OF THE AIR FORCE
WASHINGTON, 12 AUGUST 1954

INTELLIGENCE

Unidentified Flying Objects Reporting (Short Title: UFOB)

1. **Purpose and Scope.** This Regulation establishes procedures for reporting information and evidence pertaining to unidentified flying
objects and sets forth the responsibility of Air Force activities in
this regard. It applies to all Air Force activities.

2. **Definitions:**
   a. *Unidentified Flying Objects (UFOB)*—Relates to any airborne object which by performance, aerodynamic characteristics, or unusual features does not conform to any presently known aircraft
   or missile type, or which cannot be positively identified as a
   familiar object.
   b. *Familiar Objects*—Include balloons, astronomical bodies, birds,
   and so forth.

3. **Objectives.** Air Force interest in unidentified flying objects is two-
fold: First as a possible threat to the security of the United States
and its forces, and secondly, to determine technical aspects involved.

· · ·   · · ·   · · ·

4. **Responsibility:**
   a. *Reporting.* Commanders of Air Force activities will report all information and evidence that may come to their attention, including that received from adjacent commands of the other
   services and from civilians.

b. *Investigation.* Air Defense Command will conduct all field investigations within the ZI, to determine the identity of any UFOB. [ZI (Zone of the Interior) includes continental area of the United States.]

c. *Analysis.* The Air Technical Intelligence Center (ATIC), Wright-Patterson Air Force Base, Ohio will analyze and evaluate: All information and evidence reported within the ZI after the Air Defense Command has exhausted all efforts to identify the UFOB; and all information and evidence collected in oversea areas.

d. *Cooperation.* All activities will cooperate with Air Defense Command representatives to insure the economical and prompt success of an investigation, including the furnishing of air and ground transportation, when feasible.

. . .　　. . .　　. . .

6. **ZI Collection.**

a. All Air Force activities are authorized to conduct such preliminary investigation as may be required for reporting purposes; however, investigations should not be carried beyond this point, unless such action is requested by the 4602d AISS.

. . .　　. . .　　. . .

7. **Reporting.** All information relating to UFOB's will be reported promptly. . . .

a. (1) *Electrical Reports.* All electrical reports will be multiple addressed to:

(a) Commander, Air Defense Command, Ent Air Force Base, Colorado Springs, Colorado.

(b) Nearest Air Division (Defense). (For ZI only.)

(c) Commander, Air Technical Intelligence Center, Wright-Patterson Air Force Base, Ohio.

(d) Director of Intelligence, Headquarters USAF, Washington 25, D. C.

. . .　　. . .　　. . .

d. *Report Format.* Reports will include the following numbered items:

(1) Description of the object(s):

(a) Shape.

(b) Size compared to a known object (use one of the following terms: Head of a pin, pea, dime, nickel, quarter, half dollar, silver dollar, baseball, grapefruit, or basketball) held in the hand at about arms length.

(c) Color.

(d) Number.

    (e) Formation, if more than one.
    (f) Any discernible features or details.
    (g) Tail, trail, or exhaust, including size of same compared to size of object(s).
    (h) Sound. If heard, describe sound.
    (i) Other pertinent or unusual features.

(2) Description of course of object(s):
    (a) What first called the attention of observer(s) to the object(s)?
    (b) Angle of elevation and azimuth of the object(s) when first observed.
    (c) Angle of elevation and azimuth of object(s) upon disappearance.
    (d) Description of flight path and maneuvers of object(s).
    (e) Manner of disappearance of object(s).
    (f) Length of time in sight.

(3) Manner of observation:
    (a) Use one or any combination of the following items: Ground-visual, ground-electronic, air-electronic. (If electronic, specify type of radar.)
    (b) Statement as to optical aids (telescopes, binoculars, and so forth) used and description thereof.
    (c) If the sighting is made while airborne, give type aircraft, identification number, altitude, heading, speed, and home station.

(4) Time and date of sighting:
    (a) Zulu time-date group of sighting.
    (b) Light conditions (use one of the following terms): Night, day, dawn, dusk.

(5) Locations of observer(s). Exact latitude and longitude of each observer, or Georef position, or position with reference to a known landmark.

(6) Identifying information of all observer(s):
    (a) Civilian—Name, age, mailing address, occupation.
    (b) Military—Name, grade, organization, duty, and estimate of reliability.

(7) Weather and winds-aloft conditions at time and place of sightings.
    (a) Observer(s) account of weather conditions.
    (b) Report from nearest AWS or U. S. Weather Bureau Office of wind direction and velocity in degrees and knots at surface, 6,000′, 10,000′, 16,000′, 20,000′, 30,000′, 50,000′, and 80,000′, if available.
    (c) Ceiling.
    (d) Visibility.

 (e) Amount of cloud cover.

 (f) Thunderstorms in area and quadrant in which located.

 (8) Any other unusual activity or condition, meteorological, astronomical, or otherwise, which might account for the sighting.

 (9) Interception or identification action taken (such action may be taken whenever feasible, complying with existing air defense directives).

 (10) Location of any air traffic in the area at time of sighting.

 (11) Position title and comments of the preparing officer, including his preliminary analysis of the possible cause of the sighting(s).

 (12) Existence of physical evidence, such as materials and photographs.

8. **Evidence.** The existence of physical evidence (photographs or materiel) will be promptly reported.

 a. Photographic:

  (1) *Visual.* The negative and two prints will be forwarded; all original film, including wherever possible both prints and negatives, will be titled or otherwise properly identified as to place, time, and date of the incident (see "Intelligence Collection Instructions" (ICI), June 1954).

  (2) *Radar.* Two copies of each print will be forwarded. Prints of radarscope photography will be titled in accordance with AFR 95-7 and forwarded in compliance with AFR 95-6.

 b. *Materiel.* Suspected or actual items of materiel which come into possession of any Air Force echelon will be safeguarded in such manner as to prevent any defacing or alteration which might reduce its value for intelligence examination and analysis.

9. **Release of Facts.** Headquarters USAF will release summaries of evaluated data which will inform the public on this subject.* In response to local inquiries, it is permissible to inform news media representatives on UFOB's when the object is positively identified as a familiar object (see paragraph 2b), except that the following type of data warrants protection and should not be revealed: Names of principles, intercept and investigation procedures, and classified radar data. For those objects which are not explainable, only the fact that ATIC will analyze the data is worthy of release, due to the many unknowns involved.

BY ORDER OF THE SECRETARY
OF THE AIR FORCE.

---

* From December, 1949, up to the time of this writing, no summaries have been released.